D0976158

CRITICAL DIALOGUES IN SOUTHEAST ASIAN STUDIES

Charles Keyes, Vicente Rafael, and Laurie J. Sears, Series Editors

CRITICAL DIALOGUES IN SOUTHEAST ASIAN STUDIES

This series offers perspectives in Southeast Asian Studies that stem from reconsideration of the relationships among scholars, texts, archives, field sites, and subject matter. Volumes in the series feature inquiries into historiography, critical ethnography, colonialism and postcolonialism, nationalism and ethnicity, gender and sexuality, science and technology, politics and society, and literature, drama, and film. A common vision of the series is a belief that area studies scholarship sheds light on shifting contexts and contests over forms of knowing and modes of action that inform cultural politics and shape histories of modernity.

DREAMING OF MONEY
IN HO CHI MINH CITY

Allison Truitt

UNIVERSITY OF WASHINGTON PRESS
Seattle and London

This book is published with the assistance of a grant from the Charles and Jane Keyes Endowment for Books on Southeast Asia, established through the generosity of Charles and Jane Keyes. This book is also supported by the Association for Asian Studies First Book Subvention Program and by the Dean's Office of the School of Liberal Arts at Tulane University.

© 2013 by the University of Washington Press
Printed and bound in the United States of America
Design by Thomas Eykemans
Composed in Minion, typeface designed by Robert Slimbach
17 16 15 14 13   5 4 3 2 1

All photographs are by the author.

Parts of chapter 5 were previously published as "Big Money, New Money, and ATMs: Valuing Vietnamese Currency in Ho Chi Minh City," in *Research in Economic Anthropology* 24 (2006): 283–308, and were later expanded upon and published as "Banking on the Middle Class," in *The Reinvention of Distinction*, ed. Van Nguyen-Marshall, Lisa B. Welch Drummond, and Daniele Belanger (New York: Springer, 2011), 129–41.

All rights reserved. No part of this publication may be reproduced or transmitted in any form or by any means, electronic or mechanical, including photocopy, recording, or any information storage or retrieval system, without permission in writing from the publisher.

UNIVERSITY OF WASHINGTON PRESS
PO Box 50096, Seattle, WA 98145, USA
www.washington.edu/uwpress

LIBRARY OF CONGRESS CATALOGING-IN-PUBLICATION DATA
Truitt, Allison, author.
    Dreaming of money in Ho Chi Minh City / Allison Truitt.
        pages cm. — (Critical dialogues in Southeast Asian studies)
    Includes bibliographical references and index.
    ISBN 978-0-295-99275-4 (hardcover : alk. paper) — ISBN 978-0-295-99274-7 (pbk. : alk. paper)
    1. Money—Social aspects—Vietnam.   2. Consumer behavior—Social aspects—Vietnam.
3. Monetary policy—Vietnam.   I. Title.
HG1250.5.T78 2013   306.3095977—dc23   2013005720

The paper used in this publication is acid-free and meets the minimum requirements of American National Standard for Information Sciences—Permanence of Paper for Printed Library Materials, ANSI Z39.48–1984.∞

For Quang, Kim Nhat, and Quang Minh.

Tiền!
Tiền là tiên là Phật,
Tiền là sức bật lò xo,
Tiền là thước đo lòng người,
Tiền lànụ cười tuổi trẻ,
Tiền là sức khỏe tuổi già.

—Thơ châm biếm

Money!
Money, a fairy, a god,
Money, the force of a coiled spring,
Money, the measure of a person's will,
Money, the smile of youth,
Money, the strength of old age.

—A satirical poem

CONTENTS

ACKNOWLEDGMENTS

Collecting material and writing this book has put me in the debt of numerous people, from Ho Chi Minh City to New York, New Orleans, and Houston. I would first like to thank those people who invited me into their homes, included me on their daily errands and trips outside the city, and taught me their streetwise ways. I am especially thankful for the goodwill and humor of Linh, Mai, Huyền, Chắc, Anh Minh, Anh Tường, and Anh Hải. I also benefited from the insights and expertise of others, including Howard Daniel, Mr. Tước, Mạc Đường, and Bùi Khánh Thế. And Luyến, Chị Hà, and Chị Lan, I thank you for your abiding interest in my well-being since I first arrived in Vietnam. All have been gracious with their time, their knowledge, and their experiences. I take full responsibility for the interpretations in this book.

The Social Science Research Council Predissertation Fellowship provided initial funding for training in Vietnamese and Southeast Asian studies. Cornell University's Southeast Asian Program offered comradeship and intellectual inspiration as well as funding through Foreign Area Studies fellowships to continue language training and ethnographic research. Nina Hien and I began our studies of Vietnamese together and have since crossed paths at Cornell and in Vietnam, New Orleans, and New York. She and Cabeiri Robinson have both been a constant source of support since our days as graduate students. I would also like to thank Erik Harms, Barbara Halpenny, Jonathan London, and Lynel Long, whose time overlapped extensively with mine. James Siegel and Keith Taylor were both inspirational teachers and mentors who helped shaped my way of seeing Vietnam. John Borneman provided sage advice and encouragement far beyond his duties as a member of my dissertation committee. The fieldwork in 2001–2 was carried out under the auspices of a Wenner-Gren Foundation for Anthropological Research Dissertation Improvement Fellowship. Finally, a postdoctoral fellowship at the Center for Advanced International Studies at New York University provided a stimulating forum for rethinking the status of economic expertise in the world today.

Writing this book has taken more than a decade. And during that time, I have been fortunate to have benefited from the work of other scholars. I am especially grateful to Hy Van Luong, who organized an important forum on anthropological perspectives that brought together a group of Vietnamese and international scholars in December 2007. He devoted considerable time to translating some of the ideas that appear in this book into Vietnamese, thus making them available to more scholars and students. I also benefited from Hue-Tam Ho Tai's generosity in extending an invitation to participate in a roundtable on urban studies in Vietnam. During my research trip in 2007, I was hosted by the Department of Anthropology at the Social Sciences and Humanities University in Ho Chi Minh City, where I had the opportunity to engage in conversations about economic anthropology with the faculty. I was able to present part of chapter 5 to the Council of Southeast Asian Studies at Yale University, courtesy of Erik Harms. I also benefited from Bill Maurer's comments on this material.

Scholarship involves fieldwork, but it also develops out of conversations and the inspiration of others working on similar questions and in similar fields. I would like to acknowledge the inspiration I gained from other scholars, some of whose paths I cross regularly, some who provided inspiration at particular moments, and others whose work has been indispensable to my own. These include Lisa Drummond, Diane Fox, Kate Jellema, Heonik Kwon, Ann Marie Leshkowich, Ken Maclean, Shawn McHale, Shaun Malarney, Lauren Meeker, Van Nguyen-Marshall, Melissa Pashigian, Harriet Phinney, Frank Proschan, Christina Schwenkel, Mark Sidel, Ivan Small, Nora Taylor, Philip Taylor, Libby Vann, and Peter Zinoman.

Since my first unsettling semester at Tulane University spent in Houston after Hurricane Katrina, I have enjoyed an ideal atmosphere cultivated by my colleagues in the Department of Anthropology at Tulane University. I especially want to thank Adeline Masquelier, Bob Hill, Bill Balee, and Shanshan Du for their support. Susie Chevalier, our department administrator, provided important logistical aspects when I most needed them. I was fortunate to have several colleagues at Tulane with long-standing connections to Vietnam and Vietnamese communities, especially Mark VanLandingham, Mai Do, Carl Bankston, and Kathy Carlin. Colleagues outside my department, including Michele White, Justin Wolfe, Vicki Mayer, and Edie Wolfe, provided a close reading of the introduction and helped me move my arguments beyond their place-based specificity. I would also like to acknowledge the generous institutional support from Tulane University's School of Liberal Arts, including travel funding to return to Ho Chi Minh City in 2007 and a book subvention grant.

Charles F. Keyes of the University of Washington offered enthusiastic support for this book project, and Lorri Hagman of the University of Washington Press saw it through several stages of revision. Kerrie Maynes straightened up my prose and prodded for clarification when necessary, and Nancy Grandjean provided a keen eye for the smallest of details. I would also like to extend my thanks to Mary Ribesky and Alice Herbig, who transformed this manuscript into an actual book.

While most of the work for this book was conducted in Vietnam, I received real-time lessons in how expressions of care within the Vietnamese community can trump money when my family and I evacuated from New Orleans in 2005. We gratefully accepted shelter with family friends in Houston, Texas, after Hurricane Katrina. Cô Hà and Chị Thủy and their families helped us find our footing after our abrupt departure from New Orleans.

Finally, this book could not have been completed without the support of my family. My mother read an earlier version of this manuscript in its entirety. My father provided a constant stream of relevant newspaper articles and blog postings. My two sisters offered encouragement and emotional support. My husband's parents, ông bà nội, provided loving care for our children in New York City, New Orleans, Ho Chi Minh City, and Hue. And to Quang, whose irreverence has raised my spirits since I first began this project, our son Quang Minh, whose arrival brought unexpected blessings, and especially our daughter Kim Nhat, who endured my preoccupations with this manuscript more than anyone else, thank you for your love and reminders to come home early.

A NOTE ON PLACE NAMES

A word on my choice of place names and how they are spelled is in order. People today often interchange Saigon and Ho Chi Minh City. The confusion over names is understandable. When I first purchased a ticket to Vietnam in 1996, the sales agent insisted that I couldn't fly to Ho Chi Minh City, only to Saigon. The miscommunication arose because the international code for Tan Son Nhat International Airport is still SGN, one of many remnants of the city's pre-1975 past. Throughout this book, I refer to the city as Ho Chi Minh City unless I refer to an event before 1975. It is the official name for the city and one that locates the metropolis within the administrative framework of the Socialist Republic of Vietnam. But the city's official name has not entirely displaced Saigon, nor has it erased the city's pre-1975 past. Saigon evokes for many residents reminders of the not-so-distant past associated with cosmopolitanism and commerce, while Ho Chi Minh City frames the city within the powerful narrative of national liberation. These visions of the city are incompatible and point to the city's peculiar place in the national imaginary. The reader may also wonder why I have chosen not to use Vietnamese diacritics, especially as they are far easier to use today than just a few years ago. I have used diacritics where possible in the book, but I refer to Ho Chi Minh City in order to distinguish the city from its namesake, Hồ Chí Minh.

Dreaming of Money in Ho Chi Minh City

INTRODUCTION

THIS book is about money. More specifically, it is about money in Ho Chi Minh City, Vietnam's largest and most populous city. The city's vibrant markets and alleyways teeming with homegrown businesses, its deepwater port and broad boulevards, and its ample restaurants and sidewalk vendors all signal the city's rightful place as the country's center of commerce and trade. But in this city so steeped in and structured by market transactions, money mediates more than exchange value. In its plural forms, money is a highly visible and material symbolic focus for commentary on national integrity, political authority, and membership in a globalizing world.

The arguments I present in this book are neither limited to money nor restricted to Ho Chi Minh City. They apply as well to other infrastructures of modernity, whether financial institutions or engineering projects. As with these other systems, we trust money precisely because of its impersonal qualities and abstract capacities.[1] But money can fail, sometimes spectacularly so. And money's failure is instructive insofar as it exposes "a series of conditions that [are] present but difficult to perceive."[2] Currency stability throughout the twentieth century has proved elusive for both socialist and capitalist societies. Instability has defined modern economic experience, increasing people's psychological investment in reliable money, a phenomenon that Karl Polanyi famously called "currency consciousness," in which "men and women everywhere appeared to regard stable money as the supreme need of society."[3]

This book takes people's experiences with state-issued currencies as an inquiry into the modern condition. Can people exert control over state-sponsored infrastructures such as territorial currencies? What happens when those infrastructures fail? How do we come to have faith in the currency we handle? How do people personalize money so that it becomes a vehicle for expressing qualities other than exchange value? And what happens when those efforts fail?

DREAMING OF MONEY IN HO CHI MINH CITY

In Vietnam, the official currency is the state-issued đồng. Hồ Chí Minh's official portrait is on nearly every denomination. In southern Vietnam, people would remark to me that "dreaming of Hồ Chí Minh" is to "dream of money." This inversion of value is not just a manifestation of the ascendance of the market; it arises out of the postwar experiences of defeat and dispossession. Inspiration for this claim is a well-known children's song, "Last Night I Dreamed I Met Uncle Ho" (Đêm qua em mơ gặp Bác Hồ), that was taught in schools after 1975. The lyrics describe Hồ Chí Minh as a kind old man with a long beard and white hair, who is kissed on the cheek by a young child. In postwar Saigon, people revised these lyrics as a commentary on how the new regime confiscated the wealth of the old regime.[4] Now Hồ Chí Minh, the icon of Vietnamese independence, has come to mean nothing but money.

Inverting the economic and the political resonates in an era identified with neoliberalism in which globalizing markets pose a formidable challenge to territorial states. And if territorial states are no longer the "exclusive, centralized referent of their citizens' idea of society," territorial currency is no longer the sole referent of money.[5] The sacred formula of one state, one currency, never quite characterizes a people's experience with money. People in Ho Chi Minh City handle multiple forms of currency, including the state-issued Vietnamese đồng, US dollars, and gold. By locating these practices of handling, saving, and spending money within broader political-cultural formations, I show how neoliberalism is but one regime of value animating the circulation of money. The influences of French colonialism, US imperialism, revolutionary aspirations, nationalist socialism, and market liberalization have all rendered money culturally visible in ways that have inhibited its transcendence into a "pure symbol."[6]

Despite such historical precedence, the circulation of multiple currencies is often explained in neoliberal terms, casting the Vietnamese đồng's devaluation as a problem of monetary and fiscal mismanagement. Inflation, already a problem in the late 1970s, reached more than 550 percent by 1986, although some estimates put it above 700 percent.[7] And while inflation subsided by the 1990s, the đồng has still been periodically devalued in relation to the US dollar. In February 1989, the exchange rate was 6,750 đồng to the US dollar. Ten years later, the đồng had dropped to fifteen thousand to the dollar. And the official rate at the time of this writing in 2012 was twenty thousand đồng to the dollar. The depreciation of the Vietnamese đồng has only rendered the consumption practices associated with the "West" ever more elusive.

Even in the face of their currency's unreliability, the Vietnamese attribute a spiritual power to *money*, summed up by the popular saying "Money is a fairy, a god" (Tiền là tiên là Phật).[8] And, indeed, money did seem endowed with an almost magical quality that would restore Ho Chi Minh City, formerly known as Saigon, to its pre-1975 eminence. This spiritualization of money cannot be wholly explained by Western scholarly understanding, which attributes money's spiritual qualities to the historical process of abstracting economic value from the material body, a process in which the commodity form has been gradually abstracted into a pure symbol of exchange: money.[9] In Vietnam's pervasive cash economy, money occupies a visible and tangible place: stacks of US dollars, piles of gold bars, and wads of Vietnamese notes figure as the excess of money, the physical substance that cannot be dematerialized, abstracted, or objectified as pure value. The fact that people readily buy and sell these currencies is ample proof of their status as commodities. But money's spiritualization cannot be attributed simply to the ascendance of the market. Money circulates as the universal equivalent in the marketplace, but many people in Vietnam appropriate money to express asymmetrical and even hierarchical relations.[10] Money is an infrastructure that expresses rank and status in the world at large, condensing the geopolitical dynamics of Vietnam's reintegration into global markets into intimate encounters.

This book situates global monetary politics alongside the revival of household economies, local interpretations of prosperity, and transnational kinship relations in Vietnam's largest city, Ho Chi Minh City. It offers an ethnographic study of how money has conspired with the cultural politics of identity to create new sources of status and prestige. *Dreaming of Money in Ho Chi Minh City* grounds the often elusive effects of the global monetary system in daily life by showing how different currency objects circulate as measures for making specific claims about personhood, moral values, and national integrity.

I first arrived in Ho Chi Minh City in 1996 after having lived in Hanoi for several months. People in Hanoi had warned me about the city. They cautioned me to hold my cash close to my body, leave my gold jewelry at home, and pay attention to my immediate surroundings. In spite of these warnings, I found it difficult to keep my eyes straight ahead. My gaze was drawn upward to the large billboards that towered over the crowded traffic roundabouts, projecting images of consumer lifestyles associated with the West. During the day, large department stores, gleaming office buildings, and oversize restaurants offered spectacles of technology and of newfound spending power. At night, the neon signs of transnational companies such as Hong Kong Shanghai Banking Corporation loomed large on the horizon. While these buildings pointed at the city's orientation toward global capitalism, they did not wholly define the city's economic culture. From counterfeit currencies to streetside lotteries, from gold shops to crowded temples, money's restructuring animated the cultural politics of identity, shaping ordinary people's sense of belonging and citizenship in the city.

I returned to Ho Chi Minh City in 2000, this time to look for money. "Looking for money" (*kiếm tiền*) was a common preoccupation of residents. Everyone in the city was in one way or another looking for income-generating activities. As inflation in the 1980s and devaluation in the 1990s eroded the purchasing power of many state employees, some workers sought to supplement their salaries. Others were recruited into new forms of wage-based labor by factories producing goods for the growing export markets. Still others sought to escape the countryside and find opportunities in the city's rapid urbanization. "Looking for money" defined people's orientation toward the city.

People's preference for cash provided a tangible object for my study. How people handled, stored, and used cash made visible their encounters with and understandings of money as well as a wide range of other institutions, including the family and the state. I was part of this economy as well. Anthropologists have demonstrated that ethnographic objects of study are constituted through encounters. This should not be read as a claim that my ethnographic findings are simply a study about the beliefs I held about money prior to arriving in Vietnam, as well as the beliefs of my interlocutors; rather, it is a recognition of my necessary involvement in my subjects' projects for locating money as a condition of entering into their lives. As an

American woman living in Ho Chi Minh City, I was identified with money. But I was also identified with the West, and the conflation of wealth and power shaped both how I was seen and what I was able to come to know about everyday life in the city.

Many southern Vietnamese were eager to demonstrate their connections to the United States. On numerous occasions, people pulled a small piece of paper out of a pocket to show me the addresses of their family and friends who lived in the United States. One man showed me a receipt for one thousand dollars that he had received from his daughter living in Michigan several months earlier. Another man, in his sixties, approached me with a certificate he had been given for learning how to repair aircraft in the United States. He had lost the original certificate after 1975 but requested that the university that had sponsored the class issue another one, and his request had been granted. These documents, in themselves, were not subversive. They were just small slips of paper, souvenirs of particular experiences or relationships. By showing them to me, people were expressing a form of social membership that defied bounded national identity. The meanings of money, as we will see, are situated within people's ongoing attempts to unbundle place, identity, and value.

My own daily transactions contributed to that unbundling. I relied on technologies that were not widely available to Vietnamese citizens at the time, particularly the ATMs affixed to the Hong Kong Shanghai Banking Corporation that I used to withdraw cash from an account at a credit union near my house in the United States. The arrangement was ideal because it reduced the amount of cash I had to keep on me. I was a visible target for purse snatching, even though early on I learned to carry my cash on my body rather than in my handbag. During a two-year period of fieldwork, I was stripped of three cell phones and two research notebooks. I didn't realize how vulnerable I had become until, on September 12, 2001, the digital networks on which I relied were in danger of being shut off. Flights to the United States were canceled. US citizens and residents clustered around the consulate to receive updates. A few people advised me to trade my dollars for gold bars, until it became clear to everyone involved how little worth I had; I did not have enough cash to purchase even a single tael, a unit of gold used for large economic transactions.

Anthropologists are often surprised to realize how they are seen by others is constructed within geopolitical structures of power and difference. Because these geopolitical structures are reinforced by international debt relations, interpersonal relations also are mediated by money.[11] The ethnographer is never fully prepared for requests for money, which are fraught with ethical questions of appropriate reciprocity and the discharge of debt, especially when they come from those people with whom the anthropologist cultivated relationships during fieldwork. Still, the persistence with which people approached me for money in Ho Chi Minh City startled me and raised a question: Why did I draw forth requests in southern Vietnam but not in northern Vietnam? And what were the consequences of these differences for understanding the promise of money?

Ho Chi Minh City is rapidly being integrated with global markets, but market transactions cannot fully account for how money mediates sociality. I do not mean to deny the long history of monetization in the region. Rather, I want to stress that the city's monetary culture, so readily described today in terms of underdevelopment, should instead be situated within specific formations of nationhood and modernity. What I learned was that people's quest for cash in the city needs to be situated within the economies of recognition and escape. Just as people solicit recognition in the form of monetary transfers, they also seek to evade state-based and other institutional controls over their transactions. Cash serves both purposes by granting intimacy as well as anonymity to exchange relations.

RICH PEOPLE, STRONG COUNTRY

The dominant narrative of economic reform in Vietnam emphasizes the Communist Party's leading role under the banner Đổi Mới, or "Renovation." Unlike in Eastern Europe, the Communist Party has neither relinquished control over political and administrative power nor refashioned its inventory of national symbols. Hồ Chí Minh, the first president of Vietnam and the icon of the Communist Party, is still the face of the national currency. Reforms, then, have not sparked a wholesale rejection of the past so much as a reordering of key concepts. The absence of such transformations does not, however, mean that the axes of economic activity and political control are stable.

The reordering of these concepts is evident in slogans displayed on streetside billboards. Placards posted around the city proclaim "rich people, strong country" (dân giàu nước mạnh). This slogan reinforces two key concepts: the people and the nation. It is not an explicit endorsement of market fundamentalism; after all, "country" is still a key term. Several people claimed that previous iterations of the slogan in the 1970s promoted "strong people, rich country" and resonated with the ideals of socialism premised on the unity of society and the state. In northern Vietnam, unity was manifested in people sacrificing self-interest for national liberation. These sacrifices engendered a concept of wealth conceptualized in collective, not individual, terms. Collective wealth, moreover, was to be achieved through the virtue of "economizing" or "thrift" (tiết kiệm), later enshrined as a national value by Hồ Chí Minh.[12] Thrift would bring about prosperity by economizing on its resources—labor, time, and money. Campaigns promoting thrift also discouraged monetary outlays for feasts and other rituals as part of a larger effort to create a revolutionary society.[13]

In the 1970s, the city of Saigon stood as a symbol of capitalism's excesses. After the United States withdrew its troops, the Army of the Republic of Vietnam tried in vain to hold back the communist forces but failed. Saigon fell on April 30, 1975, a date that is now commemorated as national unification. Under the new regime, the lifestyles of city residents were widely condemned in newspapers and in political indoctrination meetings.[14] Saigon's past was symbolically erased as the city was renamed to commemorate the country's first president, Hồ Chí Minh. The city underwent deurbanization as residents were moved to new economic zones to reduce the city's swollen population. Reunification did not bring about regional stability. Vietnamese troops occupied Cambodia, followed by an invasion of Chinese troops into northern Vietnam in 1979, which then triggered a crackdown on ethnically Chinese residents as far south as the Mekong Delta. By the early 1980s, the socialist model was discredited by widespread shortages of everyday goods and a failed currency reform, which galvanized a group of leaders to pass a series of reforms in 1986 known as Đổi Mới or "Renovation."

Today Ho Chi Minh City is the commercial center of Vietnam, but it is still enmeshed within the institutional apparatus of the territorial state.[15] Not only does the city attract massive flows of foreign direct investment, but it is a major contributor to national gross domestic product and the government's fiscal base. The sheer economic importance of Ho Chi Minh City to Vietnam as a whole means that the city has not been granted the autonomy that has characterized the rapid growth of the special economic zones in Guangdong Province, China.[16] Yet many southerners still envisaged northerners enjoying greater access to state-based resources. Those resources—employment opportunities, access to state financing, and even visas to study abroad—were critical to financial success. These understandings circulated as a counterdiscourse to the widespread claim that southern Vietnam was an entrepreneurial culture with a more liberal attitude toward government legislation.

When I carried out this research in 2000–2002, people in Ho Chi Minh City framed their experiences not in terms of Đổi Mới but rather of "open doors." The phrase refers concretely to the Vietnamese government's decision to recruit foreign investment, ending the isolation that many people experienced in Saigon after 1975. But residents in the city also attributed the social transformations to the reordering of the foreign and the domestic, the public and the private, marked by the end of postwar social isolation and a return to the consumer-oriented environment that had defined the city still known as "Saigon." Herein lay a problem for how economic reforms were constructed in relation to Vietnam's south. Money in its different guises, as I demonstrate in this book, mediates the tension between the political and the foreign.

VIETNAM'S SOUTH AS THE FRONTIER OF CAPITALISM

Ho Chi Minh City lies just north of the Mekong Delta. The delta environment provides residents with a potent treasury of metaphors for everyday life, including money. People assured me that in southern Vietnam, money was easy to earn and easier to spend, while in northern Vietnam, people had to scrimp and save what little money they had. The city's prosperity was seen as a natural endowment of the region. Scholars have likewise attributed the fluidity of the region's frontiers to its long-standing links to regional trade routes and market exchanges.[17] The early twentieth-century Vietnamese scholar Phan Bội Châu described the region in much the same way: "Southerners have the will to prosper in a hurry, but they also have deeply materialistic tendencies."[18]

Foreign observers, by contrast, see state-led economic reforms as evidence of the triumph of capitalism. A *New York Times* reporter who visited Vietnam in the early 1990s declared the "freewheeling Southern spirit—one that is pro-Western and avidly capitalistic" to be taking hold even in northern Vietnam, the symbolic seat of communism.[19]

Both Phan Bội Châu and the *New York Times* reporter's claims position Ho Chi Minh City as a frontier of capitalism, one that is naturally materialistic and pro-Western.[20] And while they remind us that the nation-state is composed of heterogeneous elements and marked by a succession of strategic claims, they play other roles as well. They obscure both the influences of the region's incorporation into the Socialist Republic of Vietnam and the epochal transformations in global monetary politics since the 1970s. This book, by contrast, addresses how these two transformations—the defeat of Saigon and the loosening of money from territorial states—have amplified the power of money in Ho Chi Minh City. The expanded use of money was a global phenomenon, propelled by the opening of new markets, the spread of digital telecommunications, and the ideological emphasis on the market's autonomy from the state. How this expansion was localized in Vietnam's south makes evident the role of money in creating new hierarchies of privilege and inequality, demonstrating how both domestic and global monetary politics have conspired to shape the cultural politics of identity in Ho Chi Minh City.

MONEY AND THE CULTURAL POLITICS OF IDENTITY

Stories of modernity are often stories about money. Despite money's privileged role in the modernity project, it is an elusive concept. Money all too often disappears from analytical scrutiny because it is regarded as a "veil," a medium of exchange, that must be pulled aside to reveal what supposedly matters more: the economy.[21] The emphasis on money's functionality arises from the widespread belief that its origins lie in the marketplace, a belief that in turn naturalizes property relations and obscures the role of money's institutional backers.[22] By locating money in the marketplace, we see its role primarily in mediating exchange rather than an instrument of debt and sociality.[23]

Recent historical studies have focused instead on the cultural visibility of monetary instruments. In England, the creation of monetary forms and instruments of credit spawned public debate over what lent those forms their credibility.[24] Even in the United States, while the federal government consolidated currency into a single form, the US dollar, individuals challenged the singularity of money by dedicating cash to particular public and private uses.[25] These dynamics are even more visible in postcolonial societies where territorial currencies were issued as symbols of independence and sovereignty but designed on the model developed for European and North American economic cultures. In reform-era Indonesia, citizens defaced currency as a visible act of critique of the moral authority of the Indonesian state.[26] Elsewhere ordinary people subverted the political project of the state to standardize values and constitute citizen-subjects by drawing on "traditionalist" objects for exchange. In Melanesia, for example, state-issued currencies have not wholly replaced other currencies, such as shells. Valued by their possessors as signaling a (perceived) older, and thus more authentic, cultural order, these currencies also mediate a "bargain with modernity," in which people attempt to reconcile notions of personhood within increasingly disconnected relations of production and consumption.[27]

In postsocialist Europe, paper money—its scarcity, its withdrawal, and its refashioning—has been a powerful mediator of new conceptions of sociality. For many Russians, US dollars triggered concerns over the moral worth of who held what currency. Even though most Russians were eager to hold hard currency, they still regarded those dollars held by the Roma or gypsies as socially illicit.[28] In rural Russia, money was made liquid as people used moonshine in place of cash that was all too scarce.[29] Ukrainians greeted the introduction of a national currency with ambivalence, particularly in remote areas of the country where citizens transacted with multiple currencies.[30] In Romania, by contrast, people rationalized the otherwise inexplicable yields from a pyramid scheme in the 1990s as redemption for the suffering they endured under socialism.[31] Even in Western Europe, the euro—a "currency without a state"—tested European competence.[32] Greeks, for example, initially regarded their competency in handling euros as a measure of their worthiness as Europeans.[33] Today, however, the euro has become an instrument for disciplining Greek citizens.

I follow these lines of inquiry throughout the book by examining how monetary politics have both underwritten and subverted claims of sovereignty and belonging in postwar Ho Chi Minh City. By highlighting the cultural visibility and performative dimensions of money in daily life, we see how the properties of money are not universal but are historically constituted, socially mediated, and politically regulated. These performances counter a widespread idea of money as a transhistorical and transcultural value form by highlighting how specific currencies conjure different horizons of exchange and mediate different transactional pathways.[34]

REFRAMING GLOBAL MONEY

We now know that the global reordering of money and commerce has significantly altered transactional orders that had been assumed to be stable, having uneven effects on differently situated populations. But we do not know what these alterations entailed in specific places and what this has meant for individual experiences of self-actualization. How then can global discourses of money be reconciled with the ethnographic project that locates money within a specific cultural matrix?[35]

Daily life and ritual practices, as I show in this book, are neither immune to nor isolated from broader transformations in the international political economy and global finance. People's understandings of and experiences with money reflect their inclusion in or exclusion from global markets. Vietnam, however, provides a political context for these questions. The Vietnam War, also known as the Second Indochina War, has been an important political and cultural frame for understanding the restructuring of the international monetary system. The United States' massive military expenditures in Southeast Asia led to the collapse of its ability to maintain the dollar's fixed value relative to gold. When the US government put an end to the dollar's convertibility in 1971, it ushered in a new era of more flexible and more volatile exchange rates.

Subsequent macroeconomic policies succeeded insofar as capitalism "present[ed] itself as a gospel of salvation."[36] Policymakers emphasized the market as a self-organizing and self-regulating system, displaying "religious-like certitude of those who believe in the moral superiority of organizing all dimensions of social life according to market principles."[37] Multilateral financial institutions, including the World Bank and the International Monetary Fund, promised prosperity to those governments that adhered to proper rituals, such as granting autonomy to central banks and maintaining a public commitment to low-inflationary policies. These monetary therapies appeared designed for an increasingly connected world in which money was becoming deterritorialized and digitized, a world in which markets, not nations, facilitated the creation of wealth by accelerating the dynamics of conversion and exchange.[38] Market fundamentalism made socialist alternatives almost unthinkable in the "post-Vietnam" world[39]—nearly everywhere except in Vietnam.

In the 1980s the circulation of multiple currencies in Vietnam was attributed to the state's mismanagement of monetary policies. The Vietnamese đồng has in fact long circulated alongside other currencies, blurring the categories of "domestic" and "foreign." As in the Philippines, overseas remittances in Vietnam provide one of the largest sources of foreign currency, an "infrastructure with which to extend one's reach while simultaneously bringing distant others up close."[40] Vietnamese diasporic communities, especially in the United States, contribute to new social imaginaries of prosperity framed by familial forms of belonging. Yet even as financial institutions vastly increased the money supply through new digital networks, these developments spurred movements to create alternative currencies,[41] thereby challenging a key ethnographic insight that the morality of money would be contained within "long-term transactional orders" that sustained the reproduction of specific communities.[42]

Does people's allegiance to reliable money in Ho Chi Minh City then simply confirm one of the principal axioms of neoliberalism, namely that price stability matters above all other qualities? People's experiences with economic liberalization have been mediated through the international circulation of global images and goods, improvements in telecommunications, and the expansion of Internet services. Vietnamese newspapers regularly interview both domestic and foreign economists for advice about which currency people should hold and where they should invest. US-trained economists are actively involved in representing the economy, a process that sociologists have called the "dollarization of knowledge" in which "the values of expertise in the south depend on their market value in the United States."[43] The rapid translations of textbooks and trade books about the stock market, banking, and other financial institutions draw on US institutions as models of financial development. While Vietnam's reintegration into global markets increases money's power, people still refer to existing cultural frameworks, social relations, and even state-based institutions to control its circulation.

Ho Chi Minh City's rapid integration with global financial markets has animated alternative standards of value that are often culturally specific. People turn toward ancestors, temple deities, and even hungry ghosts as sources of profit and prosperity. Like elsewhere in Southeast Asia, state officials have generally relied on cultural constructions of inheritance for political legitimation, drawing, for example, on discourses of "ancestor consciousness" that posit value as a manifestation of proper moral comportment.[44] "Prosperity religions," by contrast, have been interpreted as reactive configurations of power congruent with globalization.[45] In Thailand, for instance, government officials made efforts to demonstrate their fidelity to spiritual practices by reworking national identity in relation to Buddhism and the Thai monarchy.[46] By endowing money with spiritual potency, these movements fostered a sense of social membership that transcended the nation-state and provided individuals with new techniques of selfhood. Even practices invoking the spirit world are indicators of how prosperity is always inflected and interpreted locally.

Anthropologists conducting research in cities have found innovative methods for circumscribing their studies, especially in terms of a designated locale. A neighborhood or marketplace usually provides the situated context for ethnographic research. Money as an ethnographic object, however, is not so easily confined. So I instead cultivated relationships with people who gave me access to their lives in order to understand the dynamics of the money economy in their particular location. I accompanied these people during activities, some of which took me far from the city proper, including to a factory in Japan where one woman worked as an overseas laborer for two years. I also witnessed exchanges that ended in failure. I accompanied one man who offered the director of a government institute a gift in the hope of securing a job, and a woman in her forties who unsuccessfully tried to sell a plot of land.

Most of the fieldwork was carried out between the 1997 Asian financial crisis and before Vietnam joined the World Trade Organization in 2007. I conducted the study between October 2000 and July 2002, with follow-up trips in 2003, 2007, and 2008. I refer to the period I conducted this research as "postreform" for several reasons. First, after the Asian financial crisis, the pace of economic growth in Vietnam slowed considerably after its peak in the mid-1990s, but the đồng was not devalued as much or as fast as in neighboring countries. Some economists attributed Vietnam's relative stability during the Asian financial crisis to the country's shallow integration with global financial institutions and to the benefits of pegging the value of the Vietnamese đồng to the US dollar. Still, the crisis was visible as foreign investors pulled out of projects, leaving empty or half-built lots. The crisis presented a paradox for economists: is shallow, partial, or even uneven integration preferable to deep financial integration?

Representatives with the IMF and the World Bank nevertheless urged the Vietnamese government to pursue a reform-oriented agenda, which gained traction during the period in which I conducted the bulk of this research, in the early 2000s, when Vietnam had the second-fastest growing economy after China. The country was poised to benefit even more from its bilateral trade agreement signed with the United States and its anticipated membership in the World Trade Organization.

When I returned to Vietnam in 2007, the country seemed poised to enjoy the profits that economic globalization had promised. The VN-Index, Ho Chi

Minh City's securities exchange, edged toward a new benchmark of 1,000. New apartment cities were being built with astonishing speed on the outskirts. Even as people expressed awe over prices in the *billions* of đồng, they also voiced concern over the sharp jump in the prices of everyday commodities. Newspapers that year reported what people already knew: Inflation was on the rise. Vietnam's month-by-month consumer price index (CPI) was the highest in the region, hitting a peak of more than 28 percent by August 2008.

What lessons this might show about the global financial crisis are not addressed head-on. This book instead offers a history of the present, describing conditions that reflected the almost dreamlike quality of the global economy but that were always realized within localized systems of meaning.

THE SCOPE OF THIS BOOK

In order to document how Vietnam's integration with the global monetary system influences daily life, *Dreaming of Money in Ho Chi Minh City* examines daily lotteries, the arrival of US dollars, and the installation of ATM machines and other phenomena that have come to shape economic culture. Through interviews with shopkeepers, bankers, vendors, and foreign investors, it highlights the diverse and uneven distinctions that money creates in everyday life. From counterfeit currencies to streetside lotteries, from gold shops to crowded temples, this book provides a detailed portrait of how money's restructuring intersects with performances of identity. By locating money in domains often relegated to the margins of the economy—households, religion, and gender—it makes visible how money is shaping ordinary people's sense of belonging and citizenship in Vietnam today.

As money is an unconventional subject for ethnography, a few words are in order about what this study is not. It is not organized around categories of savings, expenditures, income, and investment.[47] It resists the logic of quantification by instead emphasizing particular events and encounters in which people describe, handle, and respond to the emergence of money. It does not systematically address questions of corruption, one of the dominant frames for interpreting the monetization of Vietnamese society. It instead emphasizes the performance of street-level transactions, moments in which people refuse the leveling processes associated with the marketplace even as they draw on the power of money in ritual and ceremonial exchanges.

The creation of territorial currencies has largely been framed within a distinctly European experience. How then was experience, at least in the form of monetary organization, translated into other territories via colonial expansion? Chapter 1 examines the fraught social history of making the Vietnamese đồng in the twentieth century. Based on an encounter with a woman who donated a stash of old notes to the national museum in Saigon, as well as interviews with currency collectors, memoirs, and newspaper articles, this chapter traces how the making and unmaking of a Vietnamese *national* currency contributed to its excessive visibility. Far from signaling the mutual constitution of the state and markets, the currency's cultural visibility exposes that relationship as fraught, partial, and contested. The chapter examines as well how the unification of national currency in 1978 precipitated the disunification of money, a process institutionalized as a two-price policy but eventually dismantled by economic renovation policies.

In postwar southern Vietnam, many residents were not recognized as full citizens of the Socialist Republic of Vietnam. The state allocation system reinforced the classification of citizens, while outside markets offered an escape from the rigid limits on consumption imposed by the state. Economic renovation policies, however, helped to dismantle the two-price policy as a means of stabilizing the value of Vietnamese currency, and in so doing reordered the relationship between national identity and money. Chapter 2 explores the role of money in both remaking and unmaking households in Ho Chi Minh City, challenging two popular assumptions: first, that prosperity in southern Vietnam reflects long-standing cultural familiarity with capitalism, and second, that households are immune from economic transformations. Subsequent economic reforms repositioned households as key economic units but also stimulated migration and mobility, which in turn altered people's experiences of both family and the household.

The force of money in altering notions of identity is evident in people's efforts to "keep" dollars. Chapter 3 examines why Vietnam's integration into the global monetary system was expressed so forcefully as dollarization. Some economists consider southern Vietnam to have been dollarized with the arrival of US soldiers, but that claim ignores transformations in global monetary politics, specifically the US dollar's transformation from the convertible dollar of the Bretton Woods era to the global dollar associated with dollarization. Dollars have reinforced conceptions of both privacy and integration with the global economy.

The US dollar was domesticated by both spirit money and overseas remittances. Chapter 4 explores the structural similarities between these two economies by demonstrating how people seek to personalize dollars and how such efforts have increased money's power in Vietnamese society. But even as people use money as an object for conveying intimacy and relatedness, their attempts expose the calculations that underlie human relations.

In the face of these transformations, how do people judge the "qualities" of money? On the streets of Ho Chi Minh City, people evaluate cash in terms of "new money" and "big money," assessments that also index new forms of subjectivity within wider global markets. The State Bank of Vietnam participates in this economy of qualities by targeting cash as an object of regulation. Chapter 5 demonstrates how people's evaluations of the qualities of money, paradoxically, inhibited its circulation. Did these judgments signify a counter-discourse to commodification or simply reinforce the idea of "good" and "bad" money? This chapter examines how people look for qualities in money that cannot be reduced to its role in pricing. It also details how the State Bank of Vietnam has participated in this economy of qualities by targeting cash as an object of regulation.

Chapter 6 emphasizes how people elude the state-based controls imposed by the new financial landscape in Ho Chi Minh City. I examine these attempts by showing how *số đề*, the privatized version of the state-run lottery in Ho Chi Minh City, provides a model for how people realize personal gains in the real estate and securities markets. These gains or new sources of wealth are situated within a broader global economy that links Asia's emerging economies to the fallout from the 2008 global financial crisis.

The epilogue revisits the main ethnographic findings of the book to demonstrate how monetary pluralism has structured people's experiences. Money—whether embodied by specific currencies, circulated within institutionalized networks, or conjured by social imaginaries—is never singular. As anthropologists, we must reckon with how money is becoming increasingly institutionalized, its power expanding, not contracting. At the same time, these findings also challenge a key call by economists and policy makers to rebalance the world's economy. Such efforts to regulate the flow of money, as this book demonstrates, will also generate alternative mechanisms, although in ways that are not necessarily coherent. Money—what it means and how it means—is a field for understanding sociality in the world today.

ONE

THE MAKING OF
VIETNAMESE MONEY

ATIONAL currencies have been described as signaling the mutual constitution of the state and its markets as a single moving whole.[1] These currencies have standardized economic value in a geopolitical space, reinforced the borders of national markets, and legitimated the role of their issuer, the territorial state. Still, we must be cautious when situating these currencies within a teleological narrative that culminates in a coherent concept of money. Such caution is especially warranted in a place where the legitimacy of political authority and the morality of market economies have been as contested as in Vietnam. The state-issued currency in the Socialist Republic of Vietnam is the đồng. But the đồng mediates more than exchangeability; it is also a screen for assessing more difficult topics, such as the legacies of revolution and socialism, especially in Vietnam's south.

A STASH OF NOTES

In 2002, *Tuổi Trẻ* newspaper published a feature about a woman outside of Ho Chi Minh City who had preserved a stash of old paper notes known as Venerable Ho's money (Đồng Tiền Cụ Hồ). Printed in various places throughout Vietnam in the 1940s and early 1950s, these notes circulated primarily in regions with strong support for national independence. Varying wildly in both physical appearance and value depending on the place and even the circumstances of their exchange, the notes were identifiable as a single currency by the image of Hồ Chí Minh. Venerable Ho's money has subsequently been commemorated as Vietnam's first *national* currency, a symbol of value intended to convey a territorial sense of peoplehood.

What made the story so remarkable was not the stash itself. By the 1990s old paper notes and coins were resurfacing as souvenirs and collectibles.[2] Itinerant traders in the city would walk through narrow alleyways, selling coins and metal for recycling and calling out to people, "old coins, silver pieces, anything to sell, gold teeth, silver filings, anything to sell." Paper notes turned up accidentally as well when construction workers dug up strings of dynastic coins and stacks of old notes while demolishing buildings. Those finds rarely merited mention in a newspaper.

This particular story of Venerable Ho's money generated interest because the stash had been printed after 1945 in southern Vietnam, where their circulation was even more restricted than in northern Vietnam. After 1946 multiple currencies circulated, and French troops confiscated those notes with images of anticolonial resistance. By 1952, the Institut d'Emission of Cambodia, Laos, and Vietnam issued three currencies—the Vietnamese đồng, the Cambodian riel, and the Laotian kip. Residents of southern Vietnam were required to swap notes with the portrait of Hồ Chí Minh for the new series. After the partitioning of Vietnam into two zones, a new national currency was issued by the National Bank of Vietnam in Saigon. That bank also carried out a campaign to replace notes with the portrait of Hồ Chí Minh with the newly issued currency of the Republic of Vietnam. The campaign, however, collected only 80 percent of the outstanding stock of currency, a fact that one government official attributed to "belief in President Hồ Chí Minh and belief in the unification of the country."[3] Venerable Ho's money has been commemorated as artifacts that signaled support for the revolution. That Mrs. Tính, an ordinary woman in southern Vietnam, had preserved these notes for so long reaffirmed the symbolic value of the notes as support for the revolution and national unification. Mrs. Tính eventually donated the notes to the National Museum in Ho Chi Minh City, where they were to be displayed with other artifacts of the revolution.

In southern Vietnam, Venerable Ho's money was not the first state-issued currency. Dynastic coins stamped with Chinese characters to proclaim the king's reign circulated well into the twentieth century. Cast with square holes in their center, people carried them on strings of as many as several hundred, depending on their metallic content. The coins symbolized the king's divine power, the inscriptions announced his reign, and their circulation constituted his realm. Venerable Ho's money was also not the last state-issued currency. When we turn our attention to the history of currency, the popular teleological narrative that orders commodity money and representative money is upended. How and why people's confidence in territorial currency falters is a story of the contentious relationship of states and markets that contributed to their dissociation rather than their mutual constitution. The introduction of paper currency in Asia *preceded* the rise of modern nationalism but also *followed* in the wake of European imperialism.

SILVER COINS

The arrival of national currencies in Asia should not be told exclusively in European terms.[4] In Western Europe, philosophers described money as a gift of nature rather than of the sovereign, although the powers to coin and validate money with a specifically defined territory eventually came to be regarded as a prerogative of sovereignty.[5] Europeans in the sixteenth century valued money in terms of material reality. Chinese philosophers, by contrast, emphasized the moral obligation of the ruler to overcome fluctuations in resources, an obligation that extended to coinage: "Money [was] an artifact of the supreme ruling authority. It is the ruler's stamp, not the intrinsic value of the monetary medium that confers value."[6] It was not uncommon for dynastic coins in China and Vietnam to be made from a variety of metals, including base metals such as zinc and bronze, as strategies to ensure adequate coinage.

It was this moral obligation and the need to extend credit over vast distances that led to the invention of paper currency in Asia. During the Song dynasty (960–1279), a shortage of coins threatened the supply lines that provisioned the military garrisons on the frontiers. As a strategy to encourage merchants to supply the garrisons, the Chinese state restricted the export of copper coins and also issued paper currency or "exchange bills." The production of these bills was made possible by technological innovations in papermaking and printing, but they eventually fell into disuse in the face of popular demand for silver.[7]

In Asia silver eventually emerged as one of the predominant mediums for organizing trade routes on a global scale, as it moved from the mines of the Americas to the markets of Asia, where it was exchanged for silk, ceramics, and other goods. For almost three hundred years, the most widely traded currency was the Mexican silver dollar. These coins maintained a standard weight and fineness, which ensured their reliability. Growing demand for silver in China and Vietnam in the seventeenth century metabolized these economic cultures; new deposits from Japan, and later from Mexico, monetized social relations and challenged the existing political order. In southern Vietnam, folksongs referred to "Con Ó" (the eagle), the symbol of the

Mexican silver dollar. Although most people in Vietnam's largely agrarian economy may not have actually handled silver coins, the popularity of these songs emphasized the increasingly competitive world of merchant capitalism in the face of Confucian bureaucracy.

With the influx of silver, imperial rulers in both China and Vietnam could no longer control supply and demand, the basis for their moral legitimacy. The "ruler's stamp" on exchange bills did not eliminate the hierarchy of status conferred by different metals, even in Asia. Access to different metals signified differences in status. Copper coins were used in China for military wages and local retail trade, while silver was used to pay officials and for long-distance transactions.[8] Given popular demand for foreign silver, Confucian officials in both countries devised alternative explanations for the moral order of rule. The challenge for Vietnamese officials was especially stark.[9] How could the economically poorer political center in the north govern the more prosperous southern frontier regions?

Monetary pluralism, read from a different perspective, contributed to the region's entanglements in wider, globalizing trade routes and galvanized imperial desires. Gold flowed to Europe, and silver to Asia, generating the conditions of price arbitrage or "marginal gains" that linked once geographically disparate places.[10] These competing models of value organized around precious and base metals stimulated global trade through their disjunctures of value, not a universal one. For Europeans in the nineteenth century, the plural coinage in Asia signaled a monetary system in disarray, "a hodgepodge of coins of different weights, metals and standards, all in use at the same time," defying the expectations of those used to a system organized around a single standard of value, a universal signature of money.[11] The French conquest of Indochina would create a new model for territorial currency based not on the dynastic coin but rather on the Mexican silver dollar.

THE CURRENCY PROBLEM IN FRENCH INDOCHINA

The colonial currency of Indochina—what is today Vietnam, Cambodia, and Laos—was the piastre. The Bank of Indochina was established as a private bank in 1875. It also regulated local monetary policies through its privilege of issuing the Indochinese piastre to French colonies, a currency that resembled the Mexican silver dollar, both in name and in substance.[12] By grounding the value of the colonial currency in silver, the Bank of Indochina acknowledged regional preferences. But it also ensured that the value of the

Indochinese piastre relative to the gold-backed French franc could not be fixed. The problem of valuation came to be known as the "currency problem," a problem ostensibly about stabilizing prices but one that exposed the unstable foundations of colonial categories of value.[13]

Fluctuations in the relative prices of gold and silver undermined the French franc's role of "master currency."[14] In French Africa, the French franc signaled the political domination of the metropole. But in Indochina, the value of the piastre was tethered to world prices for silver. Colonial policies focused on the role of the Mexican silver dollar as a competitive currency and did not eliminate dynastic coins from circulation. Many indigenous residents relied on locally produced coins, thereby signaling the incomplete incorporation of colonial subjects into the fiscal regime of the state as well as the preservation of an alternative regime of value. When silver depreciated in the 1890s, the value of the dynastic coins increased relative to both the Indochinese and the Mexican piastre. In 1893 a Mexican piastre was equivalent to eight strings of dynastic coins, but to only six strings in 1898, a drop in value that led to disputes over salaries that were denominated in piastres but paid in the local denomination, strings of dynastic coins.[15] In response to these fluctuations, the French colonial regime banned the import and export of silver to ensure that only currency issued by the Bank of Indochina would be accepted as legal tender. The divergent grounding of the piastre and the franc threatened the hierarchical ordering of the French franc as the origin of value and the Indochina piastre as its derivative, thus signaling the limits of another colonial project, the use of economic value to ensure French citizens were superior to indigenous residents.

Imperial ambitions were evident in the early designs of colonial currencies. Allegorical figures on currencies invoked the aesthetics of Western mythology and a romantic view of Western imperialism. The first Indochinese coin carried an allegorical female figure in Greek dress, a common feature first seen on the currency of the Bank of England.[16] Paper notes later elaborated on the theme, with images of a European colonial ruler (fig. 1.1). The colonial administration reinforced this "distant view" by instituting pricing policies to safeguard European privilege and power. Indigenous railroad workers, for example, could not earn more than their European counterparts.[17] Wealth could not secure colonial categories of identity any more than one's shade of skin or education.[18] Fluctuations in the value of the Indochinese piastre relative to the French franc only magnified the instability of colonial categories.

1.1   The front side of a twenty-piastre note issued by the Bank of Indochina, 1936–39.

In the 1920s French Indochina enjoyed an almost decade-long round of "currency prosperity." Both small French investors and metropolitan banks invested capital to profit from the colony's perceived riches and its reputation as a "secure, although temporary investment risk,"[19] and vastly expanded the stock of paper currency as the price of silver declined. Metropolitan banks in particular expanded their operations in southern Vietnam, feeding the currency prosperity with speculative money.

During this period, residents in Saigon invoked new forms of signifiers to define personhood. One of the signifiers was *tôi*, a referent for "I" or the first-person singular. The self-referential term had been used to address superiors, but in the early twentieth century it became associated with "nascent individuality."[20] While European scholars such as Georg Simmel credited money with detaching individuals from kin-based relations, the self-referential term *tôi* also offered a mode of subjectivity that reordered notions of selfhood relative to others. The term never became fully commensurate with *moi* or *je* in French, in large part because of the hierarchical etiquette that defined Vietnamese intersubjectivity. Nevertheless, the widening circulation of both paper currency and *tôi* as a signifier of selfhood offered colonial subjects new terms of self-reference that overturned traditional orders of status and privilege defined by the imperial bureaucracy and village hierarchies.

The power of money to commodify status and prestige was a recurrent theme in Vietnamese-language novels and newspapers. Debates over moral authority focused on the formation of new class divisions, fiscal policies such as taxation and tariffs, and poverty relief.[21] These debates took on greater urgency with the collapse in the world price of rice and the imposition of taxes that stripped away some security for peasants in the Mekong region.[22] Private investment in the 1930s fell to one-fifth of its level in the previous decade, and the Bank of Indochina rapidly printed paper currency to contend with rising prices, far outstripping the mandatory reserve requirements of its charter.[23]

The global depression in the 1930s amplified debates among colonial administrators about which economic policies could stem the growing discontent among their subjects but not threaten France's economic interests. In 1930 the French government moved the piastre to a gold standard and fixed its nominal value at ten francs. Paul Bernard, an architect of colonial economic policy, advocated for structural reforms, particularly policies to encourage industrialization and the creation of domestic markets.[24] Despite this support, economic development continued to be comprehended within the paradigm of a security strategy, hindering reform and strengthening the moral basis of anticolonial movements.[25]

During World War II, the Japanese army's occupation of Vietnam further depreciated the Indochinese piastre. Japanese promises of Asian racial solidarity under the slogan "Co-prosperity Sphere" were undermined by extracting resources from Indochina. The Japanese army transferred the gold reserve of the Bank of Indochina to Japan and then confiscated printing presses in Hanoi in order to print money to meet its fiscal obligations. The banknotes increased from 494 million piastres in December 1942 to 1.344 billion in 1944, fueling inflation.[26] Even the images on the newly printed currency reflected the changing politics of value. Those notes printed during the Japanese occupation no longer depicted images of European grandeur but instead displayed images of an Asian population tethered to an agrarian economy.

After the Japanese withdrawal from Vietnam in 1945, rumors spread that the Bank of Indochina would demonetize the notes printed during the Japanese occupation. Newspapers such as *Cứu Quốc* described how some merchants refused to accept the five-hundred-piastre note altogether, or accepted it only at steep discounts. In one widely publicized event, French troops shot into a crowd of people gathered in front of banks to exchange such notes and killed several people. A journalist for *Cứu Quốc*, however, dismissed the demonetization of the five-hundred-piastre note, claiming that French colonialists and their printing presses were irrelevant to Vietnam as a nation:

> Actually, with regard to the piastre, the printing press, just like French colonialism, has little importance. It could also be said no importance at all. The piastre only has value among the Vietnamese themselves. That gang of colonizers won't use the five-hundred-piastre note because we won't trade with them anymore. When the government and the Vietnamese people regard something still has value, then it still has value.[27]

In this statement, the journalist proclaimed that the Vietnamese people themselves could nationalize the five-hundred-piastre currency, thus wresting power from the French colonizers to determine what counted as money.

CURRENCY OF THE REVOLUTION

When Hồ Chí Minh declared Vietnam's national independence on September 2, 1945, people still transacted with the Indochinese piastre. In France, the de Gaulle government envisioned a future for an Indochinese federation within the French Union in which power would ultimately reside in Paris. By October 1945, General Philippe Leclerc reached Saigon to reassert French control. In Hanoi, the treasury of the colonial government was empty save for a pile of well-worn piastre notes that had been withdrawn from circulation. The currency problem would soon demonstrate how limited was the provisional government's authority in terms of both territorial sovereignty and fiscal power.

The provisional government led by Hồ Chí Minh initially appealed to citizens to sacrifice their personal wealth to the nation. From cities to villages, people were asked to donate gold jewelry and gold bars to support national independence:

> The GOLD campaign will express to the whole country and the entire world that just as the Viet Minh warriors in the front are sacrificing their final drops of blood to preserve independence and freedom of the country, their compatriots in the back arena, especially the wealthy ones, can also sacrifice a bit of gold in order to defend the fatherland.[28]

Through his appeal, Hồ Chí Minh constructed a moral equivalence between people who sacrificed their personal wealth and those who sacrificed their lives. Casting these sacrifices as commensurate inscribed both revolutionary warriors and their wealthy compatriots as members of the newly independent nation. This vision would later be dismantled in the 1950s when campaigns such as land reform sought to level social status and eliminate private wealth. By early 1946, it was evident that the provisional government could not rely on donations to finance its operations indefinitely. While Hồ Chí Minh initially agreed to join the Indochina Federation, which would create an Indochinese currency within the "franc zone," the discussions faltered when French representatives insisted on maintaining metropolitan control over the design of notes and coins. The diplomatic truce ended with the bombing of Hải Phòng in November 1946.

In January 1946, the government authorized the treasury to issue notes on par with the Indochinese piastre. One story describes the appearance of the first note in Quảng Ngãi, a province in central Vietnam. On February 3, 1946, the president of the provincial administrative committee held up a hundred-piastre note in front of a crowd and burned it to symbolize the destruction of imperialist money.[29] He then displayed a paper note that carried the portrait of Hồ Chí Minh. Citizens were asked to exchange their piastre holdings for these notes, in so doing providing the government with the means to purchase weapons and other needed supplies. Some historians have observed that these notes were "financial notes" rather than money. By 1947 the government declared the notes legal tender throughout Vietnam. They were propelled into circulation by slogans such as "Vietnamese people spend Vietnamese money" and "Vietnamese people use Vietnamese products."[30] Vietnamese historians have since called these notes and coins Venerable Ho's money (Đồng Tiền Cụ Hồ).

Given the emphasis of the Vietnamese Community Party on solidarity and unity, the portrait of Hồ Chí Minh was an obvious choice. According to one curator, the appeal of faces and figures on money should "hold our attention, [and] also provoke an emotional response" even as people use currency "with scarcely a glance."[31] In the 1940s, however, possessing particular currencies indicated membership in competing political and moral communities. Venerable Ho's money circulated in those regions controlled by the Việt Minh. In some places the notes traded above par with the Indochinese piastre, signaling strong support for the anticolonial government. In southern Vietnam, the circulation of these notes was far more contested and fractured. The varied appearance and denominations of the notes were unified only by the image of Hồ Chí Minh. Some provincial administrative committees just stamped piastre notes with a special chop mark. In areas controlled by French troops, however, the currency was confiscated. People who traversed these two regions—one controlled by the Viet Minh and the other by French soldiers—had to handle both currencies in order to demonstrate their proper allegiance. And because their exchange value was so limited and the conditions for their survival so tenuous, any extant notes have come to be highly valued in present-day Vietnam.

Venerable Ho's money served as vehicle for displaying support for the revolutionary regime. Songs proclaimed, "Vietnamese people spend Vietnamese money, and even when it's tattered they use it provided it has the image of Uncle Ho."[32] Indeed, the notes themselves were not industrial products as were the standardized, mass-produced piastres. Industrial technologies such as intaglio printing, in which finely etched plates made possible detailed features that were difficult to counterfeit, produced banknotes that appeared secure and reliable. Venerable Ho's money was visibly different. It was not printed with finely etched plates but often from woodblocks, a process that made visible the labor of their production (figs. 1.2 and 1.3). Printed on rough paper made from mulberry trees, the notes resembled votive offers or spirit money. Grainy, slightly off-center images depicting the struggle for liberation, with crowds rising up and male bodies hardened from physical labor, promoted a regime of value that challenged the colonial vision. Even today, people who see the notes in an exhibit or for sale as souvenirs often marvel that they ever circulated as money.

Let us now return to the stash of Venerable Ho's money I introduced at the beginning of this chapter. Mrs. Tính's mother acquired the notes in exchange for food. But once in possession of the notes, she could not find anyone else willing to accept them as money. Every time the family moved to escape the upheaval, Mrs. Tính's mother concealed the notes by wrapping them on her body and then burying the stash in the ground near the area she used for cooking. Only when her mother was close to death did Mrs. Tính learn of the stash.

Upon reading the story in *Tuổi Trẻ*, I set out to find Mrs. Tính. When I finally located her house, she was gone for the day. Neighbors gathered, curious as to why an American should be trying to locate Mrs. Tính. I told them of my interest in the stash of notes, and they explained that Mrs. Tính and her mother never threw anything away. The next day Mrs. Tính called

1.2 The front side of a hundred-đồng note, one of "Venerable Ho's notes," 1948.

1.3 The back side of the hundred-đồng note, 1948.

me, and I returned to her small two-room house on the outskirts of Ho Chi Minh City. She showed me what she and her mother had hoarded—labor contracts from the 1970s, receipts from the 1980s, even old currency from the 1940s.

The article in *Tuổi Trẻ* had framed the value of the notes in terms of national allegiance and support for the revolution. Mrs. Tính cast their value in terms of a scarce cash economy where people hold on to objects of uncertain value. Mrs. Tính realized that the notes had more than sentimental value. After her mother's death, she took them to a police officer, hoping that she might be rewarded for having preserved them for so long. A short time later, her house was inexplicably burned down and the stash of notes went missing. She eventually recovered the notes after a protracted legal struggle that led to the dismissal of the officer.

The afterlife of these notes, unearthed after fifty years, shows how even revolutionary debris can open up questions about the "material and social afterlife of structures, sensibilities, and things."[33] Venerable Ho's money is not inert; the notes carry stories of reconfiguring political subjectivity in post-revolution Vietnam, stories that were nevertheless contested in the meaning of the notes' symbolic power. For Mrs. Tính's mother, the notes were simply too valuable to throw away.

Venerable Ho's money was merely one episode in the making of Vietnamese national currency. The Institut d'Emission eventually issued notes whose design evoked the cultural imagery of the three newly formed states of Laos, Cambodia, and (southern) Vietnam. Much like euro coins today, the currency designs carried different visual icons for each country, including political figureheads different visual icons for each country, including political figures on one side and images of nationhood, ancient relics, and women in national costume on the other (fig. 1.4). The French vision of creating an Indochina Federation was finally dismantled with their defeat at Dien Bien Phu in 1954. The fate of Indochina was later decided at the Geneva Convention when Vietnam was partitioned into two zones, north and south, at the

1.4   A 100-piastre note issued by the Indochinese Currency Commission. The three women represent Cambodia, Laos, and Vietnam. The currency circulated briefly before 1954.

seventeenth parallel. The partition was proposed as temporary until nation-wide elections were held, but it was then institutionalized with the formation of two different state governments, each issuing a separate currency. Thus the Vietnamese đồng was divided into two visions of Vietnamese nationhood, each allied with the aesthetics and institutions of socialism and capitalism.

DIVIDED CURRENCIES

Scholars remain divided on the usefulness of designating currencies as "socialist" or "capitalist." Socialist money may not have deviated significantly from capitalist money in that citizens living in such regimes often handled cash in similar ways and imagined similar cashless utopias.[34] But these imaginaries also need to be measured against the techniques in which socialist regimes sought to tame currency by transforming it from an object of desire into a purely notational device for the purposes of reallocating wealth.[35] Socialist money thus "circulate[d] as the official embodiment of an egalitarian consumerism and a ceremonial reminder of socialist legitimacy."[36]

In two national socialist countries, the German Democratic Republic and the Democratic Republic of Vietnam, the primacy of socialist money over capitalist money was never established. Price controls failed to eliminate spaces in which mechanisms of supply and demand prevailed, a failure that in the German Democratic Republic underscored its competition with the West for legitimacy.[37] While the dynamics structuring the politics of value in divided Germany cannot be mapped onto divided Vietnam, the competition over moral legitimacy played out in how the national currency was valued.

After the 1945 Revolution, Venerable Ho's money signaled a new version of national currency, one that promoted popular sovereignty and national independence over dynastic privilege and colonial rule. By 1951, the Democratic Republic of Vietnam had solidified its currency by establishing a central bank that issued money with a standardized portrait of Hồ Chí Minh. The designs on the front and back highlighted a militarized society: workers manufacturing bombs and soldiers pushing cannons and aiming antiaircraft at the sky (fig. 1.5). In 1958, a new series of notes and coins was introduced at an exchange rate of one thousand old đồng for one new đồng. A new inventory of images adorned the series in which images of the revolution were replaced by those of industrialization and technological progress. A train was featured rushing toward the viewer on the one-hào note (one-tenth of a đồng), while a hydroelectric dam was featured on the two-hào note.

1.5   A hundred-đồng note, issued by the national bank of the Democratic Republic of
       (North) Vietnam in 1951.

Vietnamese currency expert Howard Daniel speculated that the currency
may have been printed by a factory in China, while others suggest that the
site of production was in Eastern Europe.[38]

The National Bank in Saigon reportedly maintained bullion reserves
equal to one-third of the value of the currency in circulation. This regulation followed the institutional requirements of the Bank of Indochina, which
continued to conduct business, as did branches of more than thirty other
international banks, including Chase Manhattan and Bank of America.[39]
Despite such institutional continuities, Ngô Đình Diệm, the first president
of the Republic of Vietnam, reportedly declared currency the "real independence of the country"[40] and enrolled the country as the sixtieth member of
the International Monetary Fund, one of the two multinational organizations established by the Bretton Woods Agreement. The currency issued in
southern Vietnam by the National Bank of Vietnam in Saigon, by contrast,
was first pegged to the value of the French franc and later of the US dollar.
These exchange-rate subsidies for Vietnamese đồng by the US dollar would
later undermine the status of national currency as a conveyer of territorial
sovereignty.

While socialist regimes carried out periodic currency reforms to level
personal wealth by eliminating hoarding, capitalist regimes attempted to pre-

serve the economic value symbolized by the physical currency. The National Bank in Saigon periodically replenished the money supply by withdrawing notes deemed unfit for circulation and replacing them with newly issued notes. According to one former bank official, those notes were burned in a large incinerator on the banks of the Saigon River. This procedure destroyed the material body in order to preserve the symbolic value of the đồng as an adequate representation of money. By monitoring the quality of money, the national bank demonstrated its guardianship over the money supply and, by extension, over the banking system as a whole, thereby ensuring the currency's credibility.

In spite of these procedures, the currency in Vietnam's south was refashioned between 1956 and 1975 more often than the currency in the north. The design of the first series invoked a narrative of cultural evolution in which an agrarian-based economy gradually matured into a modern state. One of the lower denominations carried an image of an idyllic house on a riverbank flanked by a banana tree laden with fruit. The higher denominations carried images of monumental architecture, including the national bank building that had once housed the Hong Kong Shanghai Banking Corporation. Security techniques to ensure the currency's reliability led to its hasty recall. In the early 1960s, paper currency carried watermarks of president Ngô Đình Diệm, but the notes were pulled from circulation after his assassination in 1963. The next series issued in 1966 did not include portraiture of current leaders but invoked the mythic origins of the Vietnamese nation by using the portraits of national heroes. One of these heroes, Lê Văn Duyệt, an early nineteenth-century government official who supported Catholics, was later banished from state hagiographies after 1975.[41] On the other side was a depiction of the national bank. The next series carried swirling graphics on the front side, a striking visual depiction of the rampant inflation. The final series featured Independence Palace, where the country's president resided, on the front and images of animals, both wild and domesticated, on the back (fig. 1.6). The serial refashioning of the currency in the Republic of Vietnam replicated the politics of value in which political leadership was unstable but subsidized by its relationship to the United States.

Throughout the 1960s, the value of the Vietnamese đồng was propped up by the United States through currency swaps. Licensed importers purchased US dollars at a fixed rate of exchange. They then bought goods abroad in dollars and sold them for the local currency to raise funds to finance government activities. These currency swaps contributed to raising the stan-

1.6   A five-hundred-đồng note, issued by the national bank of the Republic of (South) Vietnam, 1972.

dard of living for urban residents, but they also created new structures of dependency. Even domestically grown rice was replaced by surplus American exports.[42] The United States even used local currency as a weapon in its attempts to discredit North Vietnam. One of its campaigns involved printing notes that resembled five-đồng notes. In all, the US Information Agency produced sixty million "propaganda banknotes" between 1965 and 1972.[43] US officials defended the strategy by arguing that the notes were never intended to be used as currency: they had been printed with noticeable differences, including the color and the quality of the paper, and even included statements that the notes could be exchanged for "safe passage." Despite such claims, people incorporated these notes into their transactions much as they did the currency issued by the national bank.

The problem of counterfeits was not just a matter of currency. It was also a question of which government would represent the Vietnamese nation. By March 1975, the viability of the Republic of Vietnam was in doubt. Troops with the Army of the Republic of Vietnam were in retreat. Residents in central Vietnam fled to ports in the south. International banks closed their doors. On April 30, 1975, Saigon finally fell.

Reunifying the northern and southern zones after 1975 required dismantling the infrastructure of the defeated regime. Currency was one such infrastructure. The process of creating a single territorial currency for the Socialist Republic of Vietnam must also be understood as the disunification of money.

In the months after April 1975, the banks in southern Vietnam remained shuttered. The staff at the national bank provided a full accounting "to the penny" to representatives of the new regime, including gold bullion, Mexican silver dollars, and a fleet of American-made cars, as well as the accounting records for deposits and loans. But residents who held bank accounts or safety deposits waited in vain to hear an announcement about when the banks would reopen their doors. When they did repoen in November 1975, their coffers were empty.

Residents in the city continued to transact with the currency they held. In September a surprise announcement was broadcast throughout the city. Residents learned that a new currency would be issued. Over the following two days, households in southern Vietnam had to declare their cash holdings; only afterward were they able to exchange their old currency for a fixed amount of new currency at a rate of five hundred old đồng to one new đồng. Strict limits were placed on how much cash each household could exchange. Not all notes issued by the national bank were removed from circulation. The fifty-đồng notes, valued at ten xu or one-tenth of a đồng, continued to circulate, a visual remainder and reminder of the old regime and its price structures.

Historians refer to the currency issued in September 1975 as the "transitional series," but exactly when the currency was first printed remains the subject of speculation. Several dealers point out that the date printed on the notes was 1966 and speculate that the currency was printed in anticipation of a victory following the Tet Offensive in 1968. They suggest that the notes were kept in storage in Hanoi after the uprising failed. The imagery of the transitional series was not a tribute to Hồ Chí Minh; instead it was replete with symbols of southern Vietnam, including the flag of the Southern Liberation Front (fig. 1.7). The notes also carried images of military power: workers with weapons strapped to their shoulders and camouflaged troops attacking a tank sanctioned the violence that led to a reunified Vietnam.[44] The transitional currency and its iconography of a distinctly southern variant of the revolution circulated for fewer than three years before it was absorbed into

1.7   A transitional series two-đồng note (back side), circulated in southern Vietnam
       from 1975 to 1978.

a new regime—the Socialist Republic of Vietnam. On May 3, 1978, the State
Bank of Vietnam once again recalled the entire inventory and issued a new
series, one that would circulate throughout the entire country.

Currency reforms in 1975 and 1978 involved more than refashioning
money with images more aligned with the current regime. These reforms were
techniques designed to remake former subjects of the Republic of Vietnam
into socialist men and women, techniques that involved constructing new
models of value. As in other national socialist regimes, the reforms included
fixing prices within a specific social space of state-based production, distri-
bution, and consumption. Official salaries were based on social payments
that included allocations of everyday items such as food and cloth.

In market-based societies, one of the primary roles of money is to convey information through pricing. Prices in the marketplace are ideologically
justified as a natural point of rest between supply and demand, a construction of value that naturalizes economic principles by drawing on the laws
of physics.[45] Notions of "equivalence" thus operate as a powerful moral discourse, but they do not exhaust how price is constructed across societies. In
some places, goods are priced relative to the buyer's moral or social standing
within the community.[46]

Such was the case in socialist regimes where the state-allocation system
was premised on fixed prices and limited allocations based on how citi-

zens were classified with regard to their moral worthiness. Goods outside the state-allocation system were priced higher, but there were not the same restrictions. Differences in price thus marked two separate spheres—a command economy where prices were low but goods were scarce, and a free-market economy where prices were higher but goods were available. The dual-price policy ultimately enhanced rather than diminished the power of money precisely through its disunification: "Money had at the same time two values and two effects in two different arenas."[47] Even though the national currency was unified, money itself was disunified through the pricing policies of the socialist state. And this disunification led to the rapid devaluation of Vietnamese currency.

The State Bank responded to rising prices by issuing ever-higher-denominated notes. In 1981 the hundred-đồng note, the largest note in circulation, appeared, sparking anxieties over higher prices and the demonetization of low-denominated notes. The state-run newspaper *Sài Gòn Giải Phóng* sought to reassure the anxious public by claiming, "Our government has calculated when to issue new money in every respect."[48] The declarations only underscored that Vietnamese currency was not an objectification of "real" value but an artifact of the state. And if the state's planning apparatus was ineffectual at legislating prices, it could also not stop goods from flowing out of the state-controlled economy to outside markets.

By the mid-1980s, even state-run companies and official work units had to reckon with rising prices in outside markets. Work units, for example, had to purchase meat in outside markets, where prices were one hundred đồng a kilo; they then resold the meat to workers for a mere 1.5 đồng a kilo. The cost of covering these payments produced its own price structure in which state employees received extra payments to cover their in-kind payments (*phát tiền bù giá*). By 1985, these additional payments accounted for over one-third of the state budget as reported by the newspaper *Tuổi Trẻ* on July 20. Officials called for an end to subsidies by monetizing salaries as a solution to relieve work-units from their obligation to compensate workers for the basic provisions to which they were entitled. Consumer goods that had once been distributed through the state's rationing system would no longer be included in salaries; state workers would instead receive small amounts of cash.

In Ho Chi Minh City, rising prices emphasized the đồng's unreliability in outside markets. How did people handle an official currency that "lost value" but stayed in use? In colonial contexts anthropologists attributed the devaluation of local currencies to modernization, but such explanations seem weak when explaining the failure of a national currency. Anthropologist Virginia Dominguez has instead emphasized monetary disunification, a condition in which "much of what people took for granted about money lost its stability and with it the certainty of what money represented."[49]

On September 11, 1985, *Sài Gòn Giải Phóng* warned its readers that speculators were spreading rumors of an imminent currency reform. People rushed to buy goods—rice, fabric, and electric fans. These goods represented "value" in the face of the unstable and unreliable national currency. Meanwhile, vendors raised their prices as people began to purchase anything in order to use up the currency they held. One man recalled the thrill he felt when his grandmother handed him a large note and told him to buy whatever he wanted. By the time he arrived at the market, all he could afford was a mango. Three days later, the headlines of *Sài Gòn Giải Phóng* solemnly declared, "Issuing New Money, Exchanging Old Money."

Residents had several hours to declare their cash holdings at over nine hundred booths set up around the city. Each family would be eligible to exchange twenty thousand old đồng for two thousand new đồng. Individuals could exchange up to fifteen hundred đồng. Any additional cash had to be surrendered at the cashier's desk, and a receipt would be provided. Citizens were allowed to keep old ten-đồng notes, revalued at one đồng.

The newly issued notes were initially too large for everyday expenses. Vendors quickly raised prices. A cup of black coffee priced at ten đồng before the reform rose to two new đồng. Sidewalk traders who had previously sold cigarettes at seven đồng rounded the price to one new đồng. By the end of the year, prices for food had risen 50 percent. People devised informal credit schemes in order to reconcile the relatively large notes in circulation with the prices for everyday goods. A shopkeeper in his twenties invited his friends to eat noodle soup as a strategy to preserve value. By incurring their debt, he hoped they would reciprocate by purchasing food for him in the coming days. As the newly issued currency that initially provided citizens with too much value triggered rising prices, the State Bank responded by printing higher-denominated notes, but consumers and state-owned enterprises still suffered from a shortage of money. Inflation reached as high as 700 percent in 1986.[50]

The failure of the price-wage-money reform opened the way for an overall change in policy in 1986.[51] These reforms eliminated credit subsidies for state-owned enterprises and consumer goods. Nevertheless, people's experiences with monetary disunification influenced their perceptions of the

Vietnamese đồng as unstable and unreliable even as money assumed an increasingly important role in people's everyday transactions and exchanges.

THE FACE OF MONEY

During one of my first trips to Ho Chi Minh City in 1997, I asked a group of men in their twenties about the Vietnamese đồng. One man declared that he always "followed Uncle Ho's lead." At the time, I assumed that this man followed Hồ Chí Minh as a moral exemplar. Such an interpretation seemed reasonable given the ubiquity of quotations attributed to Hồ Chí Minh on billboards and in school textbooks. These quotations are so pervasive that they authorize a national discourse on morality and citizenship. When I asked the man to give me an example, he instead pulled out a fifty-thousand-đồng note and pointed to Hồ Chí Minh's portrait on the note. "This is what it meant to follow Uncle Ho's lead," he said as he held up the note.

Not everyone uses Hồ Chí Minh's name to refer to money. For many people, his image still conjures up powerful feelings of national independence and popular sovereignty. The cultivation of the image of Uncle Ho as a benevolent leader who stood in a familial relationship with all Vietnamese citizens began in the late 1940s. It was only after his death that the Communist Party propagated his official portrait. Vietnamese currency today still carries the portrait of Hồ Chí Minh, the first president of an independent Vietnam. An almost identical portrait of Hồ Chí Minh is displayed in spaces associated with state power, including post offices and schools. This portrait obscures alternative versions of modern Vietnamese history, versions that nevertheless still define people's family biographies and notions of selfhood in southern Vietnam. Historian Hue-Tam Ho Tai has observed that, while "the cult of Ho is the result of local initiatives rather than state policy in the defeated South, there is sometimes an element of coercion in his cult."[52] In southern Vietnam, Ho's portrait conjures up memories of defeat, devaluation, and displacement. Vietnamese currency may indeed be realized as a "single moving whole," but it is interpreted and encountered in different ways. The inversion of "Uncle Ho" from a symbol of national independence to one of money points toward a peculiar orientation in Vietnam's south—the role of the market in reassembling national identity.

The ironic substitution of Hồ Chí Minh for money suggests an uneasy alliance between economic and political power in everyday life. The gesture foregrounds the icon of the communist party, even as it overturns that icon to reveal nothing more than money. "Following Uncle Ho's lead" could be read as an indictment of the monetization of Vietnamese society, the ascent of money over politics. But it could also suggest how market power must be cloaked in the guise of political symbolism. Thus, in Vietnam's largest city, Hồ Chí Minh has been transformed into a code word for money.

This problematic of representation that haunts Vietnamese national currency helps us to decode the meaning of Mrs. Tính's stash of old notes. Had her mother kept the notes as a souvenir of the revolutionary moment? Museum officials think so. Mrs. Tính, however, claimed that her mother would never throw anything away, especially money. In her own desperation to find something to sell, she had dug up the notes that her mother had kept hidden. Here we can see how even defunct Vietnamese currency straddles two different models of value—one being the object's ceremonial value in representing the nation and the other the object's promise of future value.

In southern Vietnam the arrival of a national currency with the revolution involved highly specific historical and cultural circumstances—the elimination of the South Vietnamese currency and the forced exchange of the new currency. Pricing mechanisms were a device for classifying people in postwar Vietnam. Subsidies, in-kind payments, and even job security were intended to classify citizens in terms of their contributions to the revolution. Monetary reforms in the 1980s overturned these classifications, liberating both citizens and households but also leaving both more vulnerable to the dictates of the marketplace.

TWO

RENOVATING HOUSEHOLDS

CAPITALIST ideologies cast the household as a threshold separating the realm of the public from that of the domestic or the family.[1] Money crosses this threshold, providing a bridge that integrates this institutional dualism into a coherent and stable whole.[2] Renovation policies in the 1980s emphasized "household economies" (*kinh tế gia đình*) as a way of containing the alienating and impersonal forces attributed to capitalism. The revival of household economies in Vietnam exposes some of the presumptions within the dominant ideologies of capitalism. Households in Ho Chi Minh City were elevated as the "locus of economic, social, and cultural reproduction and transformation" and continue to be a key arena for understanding money's widening role.[3] How money both remade and unmade household economies illuminates the paradoxical qualities of its mediating role in Vietnamese society.

CONTRIBUTIONS TO THE REVOLUTION

The word for "household" in Vietnam invokes a moral economy characterized by unity and solidarity.[4] Both a physical dwelling and a social structure, the household defines the roles and obligations of its members. Its ideological importance in Vietnamese society is rooted in Confucian doctrine. The household was one of three foundational concepts of community: household (*nhà*), country or realm (*nước*), and people (*thiên hạ*) were the basis for a stable and harmonious social order. Today households are metaphorically linked with order and governance, most explicitly in the Vietnamese term for "government," *nhà nước*. But to assume that households have always been the ethical basis for the modern nation-state is to overlook how they were targeted for reform in Ho Chi Minh City after 1975.

In postwar Vietnam, citizenship was framed by the struggle for national liberation. The word for "citizen," *công dân,* conveyed an abstract notion of personhood, one stripped of personal obligations and social ties. But in Vietnamese the word also conveyed the word for "contribution" (*công*), which designated virtue and moral worth. Citizens were recognized for their contributions to the revolution. Citizenship in postwar Vietnam was not reduced to a formal relationship between the individual and the nation-state. It was also regulated through membership in a specific household, an understanding of membership that contrasted sharply with citizenship in liberal democratic societies where an ideology of equality and universal citizenship prevailed, an ideology that in turn sustained the institutional dualism of the public and private spheres.[5]

In postwar Vietnam, the household and family were still key elements in how the rights of citizenship were distributed in society. An individual's contribution to the revolution was not simply a historical act; rather, it signified a moral quality that was extended to all members of an individual's family. And because citizenship was defined in terms of allegiance to the new regime, many southern Vietnamese families were regarded with suspicion.[6] Households were thus defined within a geopolitical vision of the Cold War in spite of the official reunification of northern and southern Vietnam into the Socialist Republic of Vietnam.

Constructing a socialist society in postwar Ho Chi Minh City required remaking citizens, and the household was a target of reform. As in other national socialist regimes, state policies aimed to eliminate the "private" through the extension of state control over economic activities, public spaces, and personal relations.[7] Residents in southern Vietnam, as we saw in chapter 1, were forced to turn in their old currency for a new currency of uncertain value as a technique for eliminating private wealth. Pricing mechanisms were later instituted to fix prices and subsidize consumption. These mechanisms were not incidental to defining personhood; they were central to classifying citizens.

Full membership was not extended to all residents in the Socialist Republic of Vietnam. Many people in southern Vietnam were cast as outsiders and denied access to state-based employment and its accompanying allocation system. Men who had served in the Army of the Republic of Vietnam or government were accused of betraying the nation and sent to reeducation camps. Women and men who earned their livelihoods through commerce and trade were accused of profiteering and were often required to leave the city for new economic zones. After 1975 men who had once taught French in the university earned a living as cyclo drivers or sold petrol on the sidewalk, while lawyers tutored school children. A former automobile dealer walked the streets selling noodles.

By the late 1970s, the state's ability to provision its workers was strained by rising prices. Even state workers engaged in outside market activities to earn scarce cash to provision their households. In 1986, the National Assembly approved a series of reforms under the slogan of Đổi Mới (Renovation) to dismantle the state allocation system, a key mechanism for ranking and classifying Vietnamese citizens. What emerged in place of this revolutionary regime of value was an emphasis on purchasing power signified above all by money. While philosophers of money tend to emphasize money's relation to individual freedom, the household in Ho Chi Minh City was a primary site for expressing and embodying this transformation in value from one structured by contributions to the revolution to one organized around the expanding market. The centrality of the household in reforming the Vietnamese economy offers an alternative narrative to the dominant capitalist ideology in which the household is the threshold that divides the realm of the market from that of the family. But if the renewed emphasis on household economies helped legitimate and even propel the expansion of money, it also unleashed money's power to dismantle households.

GOVERNING HOUSEHOLDS

The Vietnamese state administered the population through two documents—the household registration (hộ khẩu) and the individual's personal background (lý lịch). Like national currency, these documents were modes through which people encountered the state, reminders both of the state's domination and "its penetration into the life of the everyday."[8] Like currency, these documents could be counterfeited or altered, demonstrating that personal biographies and family histories were subject to revision and erasure.

As in China, household registration was intended to reinforce central planning, public security, and the state allocation of basic goods. In practice, household registrations were the basis for creating and sustaining a "hierarchy of citizenship with different entitlements to property, work, social mobility, and political and cultural advancement."[9] In China, the household registration system created a hierarchy of citizens that privileged urban residents.[10] Market reforms in China have not entirely eliminated the two-tier system in urban environments in which urban residents are entitled to state benefits such as health care and education, but migrant workers are not. Likewise, in Ho Chi Minh City, the tiered household registration system has erected barriers to education and increased poverty rates.[11] The household registration in Vietnam has its roots in the French colonial regime's method for controlling population movement and assessing taxes. Registration was implemented in northern Vietnam in the 1950s and then extended to southern Vietnam after 1975.[12] Every individual at birth was assigned to a particular household in a specific locale, which would later have consequences for education and employment opportunities.

Unlike in China, it was the official "personal background" (*lý lịch*) that structured people's opportunities in postwar Ho Chi Minh City. Personal background records reinscribed the state's version of national history and maintained a divided population by identifying the occupations of a person's parents and even grandparents before 1975. Through such designations, personal background records distinguished those who had morally appropriate family backgrounds from those who did not. Household membership was thus a political condition that served to reproduce the social order of the revolutionary state. Even in northern Vietnam, problematic personal backgrounds could result in a denial of state employment, education, or access to state allocated resources, all necessary for survival.[13]

People associated with commerce were condemned for having exploited the workers and enriched themselves through speculation, hoarding, and profiteering. Individuals could be redeemed by purging themselves of their former class background through physical labor. University professors and business owners in Saigon were sent to desolate areas called "new economic zones," where they were expected to transform largely uncultivated land into fields for agriculture. These forced population movements were intended to reverse the overpopulation of Saigon, increase food production, and convert the bourgeois class into the proletariat. More than 750,000 residents were relocated to these zones, but, when they returned to the city, many were still excluded from state-based employment.[14]

The possibility of redeeming one's family biography was a tenuous proposition. *Tuổi Trẻ* newspaper published a letter titled "My personal background" in April 1978. A young woman named Nguyễn Thị Thủy in District Three described her anguish at her personal history record being recorded as "bourgeois" (*tư sản*) even though she had undergone reeducation in her trade (*cải tạo thương nghiệp*). How then, she wondered, should she identify herself? The reply printed in the paper emphasized how Thủy's record was a reflection on her parents as well:

> No one chooses beforehand the family they are born into; your personal record is because of the old society and your parents' way of earning a living. That way is altogether unsuitable with our new society. You must hold fast and convince your parents to abandon their old exploitative ways and find new occupations appropriate with the changing economic conditions in order to enjoy the honest life of a worker. That is also what the government and the people hope for in the waves of re-educating traders. When your parents have participated in this process, of course your old personal history record will disappear and you will be happy and proud about your legitimate family life. You will no longer be miserable as today. Wishing you much resolve and success.[15]

The official reply explained that it was not simply Thủy's own actions that would redeem her background record; it was her parents' actions as well. Thus her redemption depended on recruiting her parents to join the revolution.

Not all family backgrounds could be redeemed. Military officers in South Vietnam were cast as still *possessed* by the Saigon-led regime and its sponsor, the United States. The officers' affiliation with the Republic of Vietnam or the United States served as an alternative source of identity and was thought to give them access to material and symbolic resources that would undermine the revolution and national liberation. Many officers were confined to reeducation camps. Some observers estimated that as many as one-third of all families in southern Vietnam had at least one member in prison or in reeducation camps.[16] Even being released did not necessarily mean that one was a full member of society. Many men found it impossible to secure employment after returning from these camps.

The household registration and personal background documents identified worthy "households" for the purpose of allocating state resources. During the time I conducted research, people in Ho Chi Minh City invoked the euphemism "my personal background has a problem" (*lý lịch có vấn đề*) to explain why they had been prevented from enrolling in universities or obtaining state-based employment. The subsidized economy thus generated a regime of citizenship in which rights and benefits were not equally distributed to all residents. This economy was eerily congruent with a Vietnamese model of kinship based on a bounded genealogy. Those individuals who were not recognized by the state embodied the nameless spirits who stood outside the cultural model of patrilineal relations.[17] Excluded from the subsidized economy, these residents relied instead on the city's outside markets for their livelihoods.

PETITIONING FOR RECOGNITION

People's biographies with regard to the revolution are subject to revision and reinterpretation. Possessing artifacts such as Venerable Ho's notes, as we saw in chapter 1, was an important symbol of allegiance to the revolutionary regime after 1945. But what about those people who sacrificed their wealth without material return? How were the contributions of those individuals in Ho Chi Minh City recognized?

On one occasion, I was introduced to a man who had been described to me as having successfully petitioned to have his contributions to the revolution recognized. The proof of his success, I was told, was his house. During our conversation, he recounted how in the 1940s he had followed the "communists," along with his parents and siblings. He later ended his affiliation, but before he did so, he presented the provisional government of his province in central Vietnam with a large house and twenty taels of gold.

In our conversation, this man described his contribution with the phrase cúng nhà cúng vàng. The word cúng, or "offering," is generally used in relation to ritual offerings to one's ancestors or to temple spirits. But in this case the man used the term offering to allude to a sacrifice in which his gift was not reciprocated by an adequate return. Still, he declared with pride that he had been the first person to offer his house and gold to the revolutionary government in 1947. When I asked him what had happened to the house, he shrugged. The building had eventually been destroyed by the Việt Minh, who feared it would be used to lodge French troops. The man eventually moved south to Saigon, where he found a job as a French instructor. In the years after 1975, he filed a petition with the government in order to receive acknowledgment of his contribution.

The man's wife, who had been listening to his account, interrupted. She gave a different story. She had been the daughter of a wealthy landowner in the Mekong Delta. Her brother had been affiliated with the Japanese army, which occupied Vietnam during World War II. He later recanted and joined the Vietnamese Communist Party. When he died, he was recognized as a national hero who had sacrificed his life for the party. The house, the woman claimed, had been awarded for her older brother's contribution to the "revolution."

I was confused. What happened to her husband's petition? I asked.

Nothing, she replied, because he didn't have papers to prove that he had given his house and gold to the Viet Minh. They eventually lost their apartment, which had been torn down in the city's relentless drive to modernize. And because their household registration did not list the apartment as their official residence, they were evicted without compensation. They had then rented another apartment until they received the house in which they now lived as compensation for her elder brother's sacrifice. As the man listened to his wife's version of the story, he slumped in his chair. His version was unacknowledged by both the Vietnamese state and his own wife.

In these two personal biographical accounts, the house signified a return gift in recognition of an individual's sacrifice or "contribution" to the nation. While the husband insisted that the house was a return gift for his sacrifice of gold and property, his wife considered the house acknowledgment of her brother's role as a national hero. In these divergent narratives, the house stood as a return gift, but whose contribution counted and whose did not underscored the challenges of classifying citizens in postwar Ho Chi Minh City, even between spouses.

While the allocation of state-subsidized housing has almost disappeared in Ho Chi Minh City, the construction of "houses of compassion" has emerged as an important publicity campaign for both municipal authorities and multinational corporations. Once awarded in recognition of a family's contribution to the revolution, the houses are now given to families identified as poor who are thus excluded from the new modalities of citizenship organized around purchasing power. Rapid economic growth has not resolved the problems of exclusion, but it has transformed the bases of inequality.

OUTSIDE MARKETS

During the revolution, the symbolic power of national currency was summed up by the phrase "Vietnamese people use Vietnamese money." And, as we have seen, the campaign to unify currency after 1975 led to the disunification of money. In an effort to resolve the fiscal crisis, the Vietnamese state monetized wages in 1985, replacing guaranteed levels of state-allocated goods with cash. By the end of the 1980s, subsidies for many goods and services, including health care and education, had been substantially reduced. By eliminating the subsidized system, however, the state effectively dismantled the mechanisms that maintained its postrevolutionary classification of citizens.

The disunification of money described in chapter 1 was compounded by people's income-generating activities.[18] These activities were condemned in state-run newspapers and by officials because they were not within the state's sphere of sanctioned activities. But they could just as well be seen as responses to exclusion, a dilemma observed not only in revolutionary societies such as that in Vietnam but also in societies in places such as Nigeria, where the oil industry hardly affects the livelihoods of the majority of people.[19] In socialist regimes, the nonstate sector has often been identified as the "black market," a modifier that is aligned with the state without attending to the exclusionary mechanisms that define what counts as "illegal" and "legal." By designating such activities as "informal," "black," "popular," or even "second," scholars have sought to demarcate those activities that are "unmeasured, unrecorded, and in varying degrees, outside or on the margins of the law."[20] These designations presume that the state is not already implicated or complicit in these activities.[21]

In Ho Chi Minh City, as we have seen, the rights and benefits of citizenship were not distributed equally. The state allocation system and its pricing mechanisms classified citizens in terms of their contribution to the revolution, reinforcing the power of the Vietnamese state over household provisioning. Most people recollected the system not in personal terms but as an abstract alphabetized system that designated an individual's consumption level. "A" was reserved for the leaders, who were entitled to greater levels of state-subsidized consumption. A level "C" teacher might be entitled to purchase one hundred grams of meat, while a high-ranking government cadre was entitled to purchase half a kilo. Coupons were distributed based on household registration cards and on employment at state work units, but they were also bought and sold in the "outside markets." Those individuals who were denied state-sponsored employment and access to the state allocation system turned to outside markets where access was not determined by one's moral standing in the postwar state. In this regard, these markets should not be understood as an already constituted zone of activity in southern Vietnam; rather, these markets were formed out of the exclusionary mechanisms of the socialist state.

By the early 1980s, the Vietnamese state could no longer finance its own domestic obligations. Burdened by a war-ravaged infrastructure, the costs of integrating communication and transportation systems, and foreign debt repayment, the Socialist Republic of Vietnam already faced difficult conditions. The state allocation system obligated work units to purchase goods at the higher "free market" prices in order to pass goods onto workers at the "official price," as we saw in chapter 1. As prices were increasingly determined by outside markets, the government launched a reform to monetize salaries, thus relieving work units of their obligations to provide basic provisions at the prevailing prices. The government then issued a new currency in a move designed to rationalize the pricing structure at a ratio of ten to one by monetizing salaries and introducing a new currency.

As the locus of control shifted from the state to the household, newspapers exhorted people to become "masters of money" (*làm chủ đồng tiền*). Unmarried women, in particular, were cast as being at risk.[22] One survey reported that less than a third of the young women interviewed intended to give their entire salaries to their families, although no data was reported for young men. Almost half of those interviewed intended to use one-fifth of their salary for personal expenses such as shopping, entertainment, eating, and drinking, and then give the rest to their families, while the remaining respondents said that they would keep the entire amount for their own personal use.[23]

The wage reform and the subsequent currency reform did not resolve the problem of pricing. The following year, the Sixth Party Congress adopted a set of policies known as Đổi Mới (Renovation) to unify official and market prices and encourage economic production. By dismantling price subsidies, the Vietnamese state also dismantled the system for classifying citizens by their contribution to the revolution. The locus of value orientation thus shifted from the revolution to income-generating activities. Migrants flocked to cities, especially Ho Chi Minh City, but even in rural areas the power of commodification could be felt as household registrations (*hộ khẩu*) were transformed into documents that could be bought or sold.[24] Households were now defined not by their contributions to the revolution but by their pursuit of money.

ON THE THRESHOLD OF A NEW ECONOMIC ORDER

By the early 1990s, commerce overwhelmed public spaces in Ho Chi Minh City. Street traders occupied sidewalks by laying out their wares for passing motorists, and drivers parked their motorbikes in front of stores, while pedestrians were pushed into the streets. The streets were jammed with vehicles. Even small alleyways became clogged with people buying and selling ordinary goods. The expanding marketplace blurred the boundaries between "private" and "public," and households were the threshold of this new economic order.[25]

The reordering of households in Ho Chi Minh City was visible in the enhanced value of "street-front property" (*mặt tiền*), or buildings that faced the street. People converted the bottom floors of buildings into small storefronts, rented the sidewalk areas in front of their houses, and turned entryways into small eateries, thereby blurring the line between commercial activities and interior family life. Front rooms were used to store spare bicycle parts or burlap bags of coffee, signaling that households were increasingly defined not by the revolution but by market prices. Even areas reserved for entertaining guests were occupied by motorbikes, visible symbols of mobility and status in the city.

At the threshold of this new economic order, residents depended on visibility. Yet this very visibility also rendered them vulnerable to state-led plans to rationalize economic activities.[26] One such resident was Mrs. Chín, a woman in her late forties who had a second husband and four children. She and her husband became my informal guides to the city's pork market in 2001, allowing me to accompany them on their early morning trips, as they prepared the meat for their regular customers, and then rested through the afternoon until they collected the day's proceeds. Mrs. Chín depended on her proximity to the marketplace even though her activities were on the threshold of the street and her house. Vendors such as Mrs. Chín thereby avoided the costs associated with selling in officially designated marketplaces, but their location rendered them vulnerable to the modernization plans of municipal authorities.

Mrs. Chín lived down the street from a central market. The street itself was not much wider than an alleyway, but she and other residents earned their living selling food and clothes there in the morning. She referred to herself as "wholesale dealer of pork." Every morning she and her husband drove their motorbikes to a large pig market in District Six. Vans and trucks brought in the already slaughtered pigs, usually cut into three parts—the head and the two sides. The pieces were casually tossed into wheelbarrows, which three or four men pushed up ramps and into various stalls. The stalls consisted of long tables covered with ceramic tiles that could easily be washed down. While the market was populated by both men and women, it was primarily the women who were the traders. The majority of men acted as butchers, carving the meat into pieces that could be easily transported on their customers' motorbikes, the most popular form of personal transportation. The butchers' bare chests and tattooed arms, together with the blue numbers inked on the pigs' thighs, created a scene of flesh, both human and pig.

Mrs. Chín usually sold two hundred to three hundred kilograms a day, and as many as five hundred kilos in the weeks leading up to Tết, the celebration of the lunar New Year. Many of her customers were vendors themselves who sold *hủ tiếu*, a popular noodle soup usually offered in the mornings. Mrs. Chín's daughters prepared customized bags for her customers. As each customer passed by on a cyclo, Mrs. Chín handed her a bag of meat. Mrs. Chín was the first one on the street to open her doors in the morning, but within an hour or two, more people began to open their own doors and display meat in their doorways. By 8:00, Mrs. Chín had sold almost all of that day's supply of pork, just before the entire block became clogged with people laying out their wares on tarps.

Like the women she supplied, Mrs. Chín relied on the cash she received to pay for what she had purchased the day before. Her trade required multiple calculations based on weight, cut, and price. Money was exchanged quickly. A few women threw down their money on the ground, reminding me of the way people played the card game *tiến lên*. At the end of the day, flush with the cash they had received from their morning customers, the women returned to pay for the pork, and Mrs. Chín and her two daughters sat on the floor to count up the money. The wholesale trade was an all-consuming lifestyle, which her husband described succinctly: "If you sell pork, you will return [to the market]."

Before 1975, the main distributor of pork was a company named Vissan, and while prices were controlled, profits were low. In 2001, the Vissan sign still hung above the stalls of vendors who worked in the official marketplace, but most of the people in Mrs. Chín's neighborhood purchased their meat from private houses that lined the perimeter of the market. Ho Chi Minh City's wholesale pork market had not yet been defined by the tastes of foreign consumers.[27]

Mrs. Chín was still vulnerable to municipal campaigns to "modernize" marketplaces. Like countless other small vendors, she was located outside the formal network of licensed traders, but her livelihood still depended on her proximity to the marketplace. During the early morning hours, the entire alleyway was transformed into a bazaar that competed with formal market stands by offering similar goods at lower prices. By seven in the morning, the alley was virtually impassable. Yet Ms. Chín's visibility also meant that she was vulnerable to municipal plans to rationalize commercial transactions by razing houses, widening roads, and outlawing unlicensed merchants. She anticipated the city government's attempt to regulate trade and space by purchasing another house down a narrow alleyway, one that remained untouched by the bustling buying and selling. This house was newly tiled, its walls freshly painted. For the moment, the new house served as a showcase of the family's purchasing power. Her children and husband used the space for entertaining guests and as a parking area for their motorbikes.

When I returned to visit Mrs. Chín in 2003, I learned that she had separated from her husband. She still lived in the house facing the street, but her husband occupied the house down the alley. Because she could no longer depend on her husband to accompany her to the market or to prepare the meat, she hired a man and several women. While hiring these people reduced her earnings, she seemed optimistic about her prospects. She had just raised the floor of her house to protect it from street flooding, and the floor sparkled with its new tile.

Her husband relied on the seclusion provided by the back-alley location of the new house. It was in that house that he made "hot loans," unsanctioned loans that accrued high rates of interest by the day or the week. There he made deals, drawing prospective clients into a ritualized exchange over beer and roasted meat. Mrs. Chín depended on visibility, but her husband required the seclusion provided by the house tucked down an alleyway as a cover for his role in making covert loans. Ironically, it was that house he now occupied that served as a showcase of middle-class aspirations—with its painted walls and tiled floors and new motorbikes—rather than the labor of Mrs. Chín.

THE MAKING OF CONSUMERS

Household formation in Vietnam, even in Ho Chi Minh City, is organized around extended family networks. Yet money splinters even those families that live together. Hà, a young woman who worked in Bến Tre Market, rented a house with her husband, her older sister, her sister's husband and child, and Hà's two younger brothers. The ground floor was used for making nails, and the ground was scattered with the steel remnants. It first appeared to me as though Hà and her siblings had recreated an extended family through migration. Migrants negotiated the highly monetized urban landscape in ways that often reinstated the importance of kin-based networks even as they sought opportunities to demonstrate their identities as consumers. Money had the power to remake families through new strategies of householding.

Hà's household in 2002 was symbolically divided into small cells based on the nuclear family, with each cell closely monitoring and guarding their scarce cash resources. The physical structure of the house reinforced this arrangement, as Hà and her husband slept and cooked in a separate room from the others. Their arrangements were sparse. A portable fan on the floor whirred away. Their clothes were hung on a wire strung across the room. Their single possession was a small CD player and a stack of CDs. While Hà and her siblings lived as an extended family, they ate separately, which increased their costs, as each unit purchased their own separate condiments—fish sauce, MSG, and sugar. Hà and her siblings did not pool their resources for everyday expenses, only for those occasions intended to express the solidarity of the family over time.

The spatial division within the household was overcome through different strategies. Hà received significant resources from her extended family, including employment. And the dynamics I observed that appeared to favor nuclear family arrangements were countered through ritual expenditures that emphasized extended family ties. Weddings and death-day anniversaries were important occasions for the exchange of labor, money, and goods, which emphasized the collective importance of kinship ties. On these occasions, family members combined their resources in order to display the strength of the extended family, ties that were reinforced in daily life through strategies such as child-care arrangements, tutoring, and even running daily errands. Such arrangements defined membership and belonging in the face of the commodification of services in the city.

Yet people still drew on the marketplace as a model of value, even for life-cycle rituals. In the 1950s, government officials in northern Vietnam had targeted the ritual elaboration of kinship relations and life-cycle rituals, including weddings and celebrations of death anniversaries, as unsuitable for a revolutionary society.[28] By the 1990s, however, the growing size of weddings throughout the country was fueled by the willingness of guests to offer gifts of cash as the means of acknowledging social affiliations. In Ho Chi Minh City, weddings were an important marker of belonging, drawing on two competing regimes—one in which people defined themselves through consumption practices, another that emphasized family relations by borrowing money from kin and near-kin. Weddings served as a stage on which to display the strength of the extended family in relation to the marketplace.

Hà depended on her extended family even as she sought to identify herself as an urban citizen through her consumption practices. She first found employment through a cousin who owned a retail stall in one of the city's largest wholesale markets. Her first romance in the city ended badly, and she returned to her village in central Vietnam. She then got engaged to one of her childhood acquaintances, and the wedding became a subject of intense debate for both families—including where the wedding would be held and where the newly married couple should reside. Hà worked in one of Ho Chi Minh City's bustling markets, while her fiancé, Đài, was an unemployed goldsmith in central Vietnam. Hà wanted her wedding to be held in Ho Chi Minh City. She spoke at length about how many people she wanted to invite and what venue the wedding party would be held. Her plans took shape within Ho Chi Minh City's consumer culture.

City weddings were costly, not least because of the large cash outlays that the feasts and associated activities required. Public discussion in newspapers and television then and now focused on the wedding couple dressed in "envelopes," symbols of the gifts of money they would receive from the invited guests. By holding the wedding in the city, Hà symbolically declared that she was a full if not legally registered citizen of the city. Her household registration still listed her residence in central Vietnam.

In the days leading up to the wedding, Hà and her fiancé carried out the consumer rites that marked marriage in the city—a trip to Đầm Sen Park for photo opportunities, a large reception at Sinh Đôi Restaurant, and a wedding album filled with photos of the new couple in several outfits, both modern and traditional. On the morning of the wedding, the two families engaged in an exchange of gifts, a ritual that honored both. Đài's family presented the couple with a gift of one million đồng. Other family members presented Hà with a gold necklace and a bracelet. The friends who attended offered the couple small orange boxes with either a gold chain or a ring. Hà glittered with wealth.

The gift exchange was soon eclipsed by the wedding feast, a large boisterous event. Bottles of Coke and beer were set up on each table. Before the meal was served, representatives from both families were asked to walk to the front of the stage. They stood awkwardly under the bright lights as they waited for the two masters of ceremonies to make the announcements. A bubble machine began to churn as glitter fell to the ground. The masters of ceremony then popped open a bottle of champagne so that Hà and Đài could pour a bottle over the mountain of champagne cups. Only the wedding cake was left untouched.

The luster of Hà's city wedding was soon overshadowed by the expenses for the feast that quickly accumulated. Newly married couples use the monetary gifts they collect to pay off the wedding expenses, but these expenses—rented vans, photographers, musicians—often exceed what the couple collects from their guests. After the wedding, Đài did not find employment in the city. Hà was briefly unemployed as well. She reluctantly sold some of the jewelry to pay part of the expenses. Weddings in Ho Chi Minh City make visible the paradoxical role of money in the making and unmaking of households. Hà drew on her family's and guests' resources for financing the wedding, but these resources did not provide enough for the new couple to cover the cost of the wedding in the city and provide them with savings for their new household. Hà used the gold jewelry, a popular present symbolizing intergenerational inheritance, to make up the difference between the money she could muster and her aspirations for a city wedding.

THRESHOLDS TO THE GLOBAL ECONOMY

Many people in southern Vietnam had friends and family who lived in the West and enjoyed standards of living that were beyond the reach of even most city residents, at least in 2002. While capitalist discourses located households at the threshold of the market and the family, in postreform Vietnam, households were also at the theshold of the global. And households were important sites for both inciting and domesticating desires that were channeled through these intimate relationships.

Phương's family was based in central Vietnam. When we first met in 2001, all but three of her eleven brothers and sisters had migrated to Ho Chi Minh City. Phương's eldest sister had been the first to arrive in the city and had found work as a seamstress, eventually leasing two stalls in Bến Tre Market. Phương followed her sister to Ho Chi Minh City, where she worked at first as a seamstress, and later moved in with her sister, who needed help raising her children and preparing meals. Since she was at the house most of the day, she set up a small stand to sell packets of shampoo, containers of crackers and candy, bottles of cooking oil, and other foodstuffs. Because she was not paid for her domestic duties, she relied on selling everyday items to her neighbors to earn cash.

One evening, Phương's sister asked me to translate a letter she had just received from the US consulate. The letter she showed me briefly stated that her father had been found to be ineligible to immigrate to the United States through the Orderly Departure Program. He was among the 20 percent of applicants who were eventually denied. Even though he had been confined to a reeducation camp, the US government had determined that he did not qualify for immigration status because he had been confined for fewer than three years.

The Orderly Departure Program served two constituents—Amerasians, or people believed to be the children of US servicemen, and former veterans of the Army of the Republic of Vietnam who had been imprisoned in reeducation camps for more than three years. Those who qualified were entitled to immigrate with their immediate families under the support and sponsorship of the US government. In providing this service, these programs redefined households and family relations. Unmarried daughters, for example, were allowed to emigrate, but married daughters were not. Thus many women postponed marriage as a strategy of immigration. Phương, along with a younger sister, had anticipated that their father would be allowed to seek asylum in the United States and that they would join him.

While the letter effectively ended the long-standing petition by Phương's family, it did not end Phương's personal quest to leave Vietnam. Since the 1990s, ties between family members in Vietnam and those abroad had been revived by increased opportunities for family visits. Many of Phương's own hopes of emigrating were pinned on the vague promise of a cousin in New York who owned a nail salon, and a childhood friend who lived in Los Angeles and periodically returned to visit his brother's family in Ho Chi Minh City.

Once Phương had exhausted these alternate routes, she applied for a position to work overseas in Japan through a Vietnamese state-owned company. In our conversations, she alternately stressed her independence, particularly her desire to purchase a house for herself, and her ability to help her family, especially her parents. She needed to use her family's resources in order to be eligible as an overseas worker. Not only did she have to make a substantial cash deposit, she also had to give the company the title to the house her sister owned in order to ensure that she would return to Ho Chi Minh City at the end of her contract. Like the city wedding that I described above,

Phương relied on her extended family's financial resources to participate in a capitalist mode of production, a Japanese factory that produced cushions for automobiles.

Household economies, new labor markets, and the state conspired to create new opportunities for young women such as Phương. Yet the scarce cash economy that defined the lives of many migrants also threatened to dash them. Phương needed to raise ten million đồng (approximately US$670) as a recruitment fee. A few days before her departure, she had not yet scraped together enough. Her family expected to receive twenty million đồng from the government in compensation for demolishing their home in order to widen the road, but this money was in limbo, and the house could not be sold because the street was slated to be widened. In order to discourage speculation, the government required residents to prove that they had occupied the building prior to the proposed site clearance in order to receive compensation.

In the days leading up to her departure, Phương showed signs of stress from what she described as "chasing money." She had visited close friends and distant acquaintances to raise money for the deposit. People who could not give her money offered her clothes. Those who couldn't provide clothes let her borrow a motorbike. On the last day, one of her sister's customers paid a long-standing debt, so Phương was able to meet the required deposit, and she departed on time with the other women bound for Nagoya, Japan.

In 2003, I visited her in Japan for a brief afternoon, with an American friend who spoke fluent Vietnamese. Our visit was curtailed in part because Phương's Japanese employers worried that, as Americans, we were inspecting the labor conditions of the workers rather than making a personal visit. Phương showed us the dorm rooms and the common areas and then took us to a nearby supermarket. Phương and the other women from Vietnam insisted that they wanted to earn as much as possible during their two-year contracts. They worked eleven to fourteen hours a day in order to earn overtime so they could better their lives once they returned to Ho Chi Minh City. Their Japanese boss did not distribute their overtime wages to the young women. He instead delivered the cash to their families as a way of ensuring that they saved that money rather than spend it.

When I returned to Ho Chi Minh City in 2007, Phương invited me to her new house, located on the outskirts of the city along one of the expanded provincial highways. She had purchased a house alongside one belonging to her older brother, his wife, and their two sons. The two houses were connected by a balcony on the second floor, allowing for easy movement between the two residences. Phương had used most of her savings from her time in Japan to buy the house and its furnishings. Her employment at the factory had given her an escape, one in which she had realized an economic potential that was not possible in the streets of Ho Chi Minh City. I watched as she resumed many of her old duties, providing meals and domestic work for her extended family. Her aspirations, however, were not as global as they had been before she left for Japan. She instead wondered aloud about opening up a small café serving a specialty dish from central Vietnam. Her brother drove a truck between central Vietnam and Ho Chi Minh City and, she mused, would provide her with the chickens she would need.

Households in Ho Chi Minh City are enmeshed in broader processes of economic change. We have seen how they are important locations from which people engage in broader market-based activities that have come to define Ho Chi Minh City. Yet insofar as households define an individual's proper role and moral obligations, they can be especially difficult to escape for women. While women are recruited as workers in global production, their value remains shaped by their participation in household economies, a dilemma observed by anthropologists in other export-oriented economies, such as in Thailand and Indonesia.[29] Phương used her finances not to launch a small business but rather to set up a household where she was financially independent but still socially tethered to her extended family. For many women, their role in trade and commerce is entwined with their obligation to ensure the financial stability of their household through wage-based labor.[30] The market, as we have seen, is redefining how residents in the city fulfill their family obligations and their proper gender roles, but in ways that have not necessarily liberated women from the strictures of gendered ideologies.[31] Women who consent to this gendered ideology as the source of subjectivity find, like Phương, that it is difficult to escape. Yet for middle-aged men in Ho Chi Minh City, the dilemma of negotiating the role of the household within an economy increasingly organized by money was even more challenging.

RETURNING HOME

The emphasis on income-generating activities has led to new forms of classifying citizens in Ho Chi Minh City. Value is no longer defined by the revolution but in terms of purchasing power. Government-sponsored programs for poverty reduction make evident this shift. While poverty was valorized during the revolution, the government has sought to target poor households for the purpose of poverty reduction. Income rather than contributions to the revolution now define a household's standing in the city. Mr. Huy, an engineer, worked for a state-owned rubber enterprise before he was summarily dismissed in the early 1990s. When I met him, he lived in the very center of the city, in an apartment building subsidized by the Vietnamese state. The apartment had first housed four single men. One by one, the other men had married and then moved elsewhere. By 2002, only Mr. Huy remained in the room. The building, despite its prime location in the city center, resisted efforts to be converted into something else. With its caved-in ceiling tiles and exposed wires and the rubble filling the stairways, the building was dingy and dilapidated. The surrounding buildings gleamed as centerpieces of the city's newfound orientation toward global markets. Only this building, and in particular one of its lone residents who still occupied a subsidized apartment, seemed from another time.

Mr. Huy did not receive a pension from his state employer, a fact that he attributed to his whistle-blowing about corruption but that I could never verify. He moved around the city on his bicycle and traded on his network of relationships cultivated during his years working as a state-employed engineer. His relationship to the city demonstrated the uneven relationship between the market and the state. By inhabiting both the geographical center and the economic margins of Ho Chi Minh City, he described his conditions as poor; he still received state-subsidized housing and, on every lunar New Year, a basket of fruit. He also benefited from his wide range of acquaintances, many of whom he had known from his university days in Hanoi and were now well-placed managers in state-owned enterprises.

Mr. Huy's position contrasted with that of another man who was his cohort in terms of age but who had been raised in Saigon rather than northern Vietnam. Like Mr. Huy, Mr. Thắng also struggled to earn a living. Mr. Thắng had many stories to tell me of his friends and distant relatives who had immigrated to other countries. Like many of them, Mr. Thắng had been drafted to serve in the Army of the Republic of Vietnam. When I first met him, his wife had just divorced him, a fact he attributed to his inability to earn cash in Ho Chi Minh City's rapidly changing economy. No longer able to rely on his wife, he turned to the sympathy of friends to advance him money, sometimes as loans, at other times as outright gifts. As the forgotten veteran whose body reminded people of the sacrifices some men had made for the southern Vietnamese regime, Mr. Thắng was the perfect figure for seeking cash assistance that would be forgiven, if not entirely forgotten. As an American in southern Vietnam, I was a player in this economy of storytelling as well. Mr. Thắng tried to leverage his relationship with me, an American, to repay a poor investment, by promising the lender that I would guarantee his loan and that my motorbike would be the collateral.[32]

Mr. Thắng showed no remorse over how he had converted his friendship with me into ten million dong. It was a strategy of getting by in the city's scarce cash economy. Yet he seemed resistant to declare himself "poor," refusing to apply for a state-issued certificate attesting to his poverty. Even when his second wife was expecting a child after a previous miscarriage, he still refused to apply for a certificate that would reduce his medical payments. When I asked him why, he explained that he and his wife had never officially registered, and without the state-issued license, the evidence of their marriage would be the child, proof of an "actually existing marriage" (*hôn nhân thực tế*). But such proof, he pointed out with irony, would not occur in time to pay the hospital bill. And without proof of an actually existing marriage, the police would not issue him the certificate.

On December 31, 2003, Mr. Thắng called to inform me that his wife had delivered the baby. I drove to District Four and bought a twenty-five-kilo bag of rice and some powdered milk and filled an envelope with several hundred thousand đồng, or roughly twenty US dollars. I followed him to a medical center located on the bank of a river. The center was rustic. Beds had been laid out with small mats; most were unoccupied. In the family planning section, three women had just delivered babies. The building was cool. A veranda overlooked the river and passing boats. He later surprised me with a story of how a relative of his landlady who lived in the United States had proposed to sponsor him to immigrate. In anticipation of this opportunity, he quietly completed documents with the Vietnamese state to legalize his marriage to ensure that his wife and newborn daughter could immigrate with him.

In 2007, I returned to the small room where Mr. Thắng had rented space for a workshop to fix small household appliances; it was closed up tight. I asked the men in neighboring houses where Mr. Thắng had gone. They claimed that he had "returned home" (*về quê*). Their response left me puzzled, for Mr. Thắng, unlike many people who lived in the city, had been born and raised in Saigon. I then went to the evangelical church he had attended, just a few blocks away. A man who worked in the church remembered who Mr. Thắng was but offered the same explanation: Mr. Thắng had "returned home."

Mr. Thắng's disappearance from the city in which he struggled to make a living and Mr. Huy's insistent claim of belonging even though he lost his official position both speak to the fractured terrain of postwar, postreform Ho Chi Minh City. In both cases, each man's relationship to the city was defined in terms of the revolution. Mr. Huy still resided in the housing he had been granted upon first moving to the city. Mr. Thắng, by contrast, had moved several times following his divorce, often speculating on where and how he might be able to earn a livelihood.

Households are not sentimental vestiges of a premarket economy in Ho Chi Minh City. Rather, households have been on the threshold of changing regimes of value, made and remade and unmade by both the institutions of the territorial state and the power of money, demonstrating the limits of scholarly understandings that emphasize money's role in fostering individual freedom and neglect its place in defining households.[33]

THREE

DOLLARS ARE FOR KEEPING

ONE evening in Ho Chi Minh City, I showed Mr. Xuân a đồng note issued by the State Bank of the Democratic Republic of Vietnam in 1958. Mr. Xuân had grown up in Hanoi, and I wondered if he remembered the ten-đồng note, the largest note in circulation in northern Vietnam until 1978, when the unified currency was introduced. At the time I was conducting my research, the hundred-đồng note was the lowest denomination. Mr. Xuân held the note fondly. "Ah, the red note." He recalled that young men in the city would wear white dress shirts with one of these notes folded in their front pocket, a badge announcing that they had money. "Now people just value 'green notes,'" he said. "You mean the fifty-thousand-đồng note?" I asked, referring to the then highest denomination in circulation. He laughed, "No, a hundred-*dollar* bill; we're not talking about Vietnamese money anymore!"

After 1945, the symbolic value of Vietnamese currency was framed in terms of national allegiance: "Vietnamese people use Vietnamese money." What now frames the value of the US dollar for Mr. Xuân? If the Vietnamese đồng reinforced a territorial identity that came into being with the revolution, then the US dollar expressed membership in a globalizing economy. And, like the young men who tucked the red ten-đồng note in their front pockets, young people now displayed dollar bills in the plastic ID cases worn around their necks, a social skin that marked their membership in a global economy. Single dollar bills were taped onto glass display counters or framed on the wall behind cashiers. Of course, not everyone displayed their dollars. Some people tucked them into their wallets, stored them in iron safes, or locked them in wardrobe closets as a private reserve that would be difficult to spend.

These everyday acts of displaying and concealing dollars exposed the centrality of money in defining selfhood in reform-era Ho Chi Minh City.

People expressed this centrality by claiming, "Dollars are for keeping, not for spending." "Keeping" should not be reduced to hoarding, although people clearly held dollars as an asset to protect their purchasing power. Rather, US dollars signaled a social power that eluded the Vietnamese đồng, and it was this social power that people claimed when they insisted, "Dollars are for keeping." By highlighting the manifold ways in which people kept dollars in Vietnam, we see how the currency expressed new forms of selfhood, providing an alternative account to the usual story about why economic liberalization in Vietnam has been expressed so forcefully by dollarization.

DOLLARIZATION

Dollarization is conventionally defined as currency substitution. In economies beset by high inflation and low confidence in domestic financial institutions, people seek out alternative currencies. Most economists regard these substitutions as rational. Driven partly by monetary geography, these substitutions can confer advantages: prices are stabilized, transaction costs are reduced, and economic productivity increases.[1] But substitution can also be determined by forces that are not spatialized, including structural transformations in the technology of money or financial institutions.[2] Such arguments, however, help to reinforce the paradigm of market fundamentalism in which markets serve as a model of society. And no currency sums up market value better than the US dollar.

Dollarization is a twentieth-century version of monetary pluralism. As we saw in chapter 1, people in Vietnam had long transacted with plural currencies, including Mexican silver dollars, dynastic coins, Indochinese piastres, revolutionary currencies, and later the state-issued Vietnamese đồng. And, while by the twentieth century the institutions that issued and validated money were increasingly centralized, they could not eliminate currencies that invoiced and settled international transactions and served as foreign currency reserves. In the mid-twentieth century, newly independent territorial states such as Vietnam issued distinctive currencies to announce their independence and proclaim their sovereignty. But imports and exports were increasingly denominated in US dollars, a role that was enshrined by the Bretton Woods system following World War II. That system established the thirty-five US dollar price for one ounce of gold. During the subsequent two decades, the US dollar served as a global reserve currency, a unit of account in global trade, and the dominant means of settling international payments, a lingua franca of global trade.[3]

The "exhorbitant privilege" of the US dollar eventually collapsed because of the military and domestic commitments of the United States.[4] US military expenditures in Southeast Asia, combined with an ambitious domestic agenda, proved fiscally unsustainable. While other countries had to "earn" their dollars by running a trade surplus, the US government financed its operations simply by printing more dollars. National governments, especially in France, lost confidence in the United States' commitment to maintain the value of dollars at a fixed rate of thirty-five dollars per ounce of gold. Central banks that had stockpiled US dollars as an international reserve currency demanded those dollars be converted into bullion. By 1971, foreign countries held three times as much in dollars as the US government had in gold.[5] On August 15, 1971, President Richard Nixon suspended the conversion of US dollars into gold, which led to an immediate devaluation of the US dollar. Over the next few years the value of the US dollar plummeted, while the price of gold and oil skyrocketed.

In the 1980s the US dollar regained its status as a reliable currency, its reputation restored by the Federal Reserve's anti-inflationary monetary policies. The dollar's role as a substitute currency was promoted by the World Bank and the International Monetary Fund as a technique to discipline other national currencies by enforcing fiscal and banking reforms in developing economies. These policies coincided with the demands of ordinary people, especially in socialist regimes. With the end of the Cold War, people in the former Soviet bloc also clamored for dollars, "as if [the currency] were a passport to the capitalist world they were all free to enter."[6] People's confidence in US dollars converged with the goals of bankers and technocratic experts to transform the US dollar into the global dollar, signaling a new economic paradigm that emphasized the power of the marketplace over political sovereignty. How, then, was this biography of the US dollar shaped in southern Vietnam?

Dollarization, as we will see, is not just a matter of concern to Vietnamese bankers and Western-trained development experts. It is also the concern of ordinary Vietnamese citizens. The place of US dollars in the Vietnamese domestic economy demonstrates that money cannot be defined wholly within Vietnamese terms. By holding, handling, and even hiding dollars, people challenged the boundaries between the national and the global that state-issued currency was intended to secure. Dollarization was not just a rational strategy to preserve value but a powerful form of self-making and a claim of global membership that eluded the territorial state. It is this form of self-making that people evoke when they claim, "Dollars are for keeping, not for spending."

RED DOLLARS

One often hears in Ho Chi Minh City that southern Vietnam was dollarized with the arrival of US troops in the 1960s. Indeed US military troops were accompanied by considerable US financing, the installation of American Post Exchange (PX) stores, and American aid programs. Arguing that dollarization is simply a return to the city's prewar economy overlooks the US dollar's particular biography in Vietnam, and conflates the US dollar in Saigon with the global dollar of Ho Chi Minh City. This claim also asserts that money is a coherent, transcultural value that is immune to local regimes of value.[7]

Most people in Ho Chi Minh City were keenly aware of the US dollar's status relative to the Vietnamese đồng. Yet I was initially surprised when most people in southern Vietnam dated their first experiences of handling dollars to the mid-1980s, well after the last US troops and diplomats had fled Saigon. The only two people who recalled handling dollars in the early 1970s had lived in northern Vietnam. One man told a story that verged on the apocryphal—the first dollar bill he had held was on a battlefield in Laos. He recalled how he and other soldiers often searched bodies for valuables, and it was on the body of one corpse that he found his first hundred-dollar bill, along with one hundred Thai baht and some Chinese currency. At the time, people in the north were not allowed to hold US dollars, but this man kept the bill as a souvenir, turning it over in his hands to look at the front and back, and showing it to his close friends. He kept it between the pages of an old book, one of many stacked up in his house. After 1975, he needed some money and decided to trade the bill for Vietnamese đồng. He and his wife spent two days looking for the bill but did not find it. Presumably the book it had been hidden in had accidentally been sold.

The second person I spoke with who recalled handling dollars in the early 1970s emphasized how dollars flowed along trade routes that crossed national borders. This woman described handling dollars "well before the country was liberated." She described how people who bought and sold dollars recorded the serial number of each note as a strategy to deter counterfeiters. She emphasized that, at that time, people used US dollars not for spending but for trading (*không ăn xài nhưng buôn bán*). Dollars eliminated the problem of measuring the purity and weight of gold and so were especially in demand by people traveling to the Soviet Union or Eastern Europe as students or through labor-exchange programs.

In southern Vietnam, those people who handled dollars before 1975 emphasized a particular quality of those dollars. They were red, not green. Red dollars (*đô-la đỏ*) was a term used by people to describe two different kinds of currency objects. The first were specially marked dollar bills printed for circulation overseas. Unlike notes intended for domestic circulation, the symbol of the US Federal Reserve on these notes was printed in red ink, not the familiar green. The second and more widespread kind of red dollar was the military payment certificate. Although they circulated in a limited transactional sphere, these dollars were hardly "primitive money."[8] Primitive money provided anthropologists a means of attributing objects with some but not all of the functions of modern state-issued currency. Unlike the objects that conventionally serve as the traditional precursors of modern state-issued currencies, such as shells, brass rods, or cattle, red dollars were still a state project designed to shore up the value of "real" money.

During the 1960s and early 1970s, US military personnel and American civilians who worked on military installations were all paid in red dollars, also known as military payment certificates. Their importance was noted by Tim O'Brien in his description of the things American soldiers in Vietnam carried in their packs: "Among the necessities or near-necessities were P-38 can openers, pocket knives, heat tabs, wristwatches, dog tags, mosquito repellent, chewing gum, candy, cigarettes, salt tablets, packets of Kool-Aid, lighters, matches, sewing kits, Military Payment Certificates, C rations, and two or three canteens of water."[9] Red dollars were issued to segregate US and Vietnamese currency, deter the black market use of dollars, and prevent Communist sympathizers from obtaining an international currency that could be used to purchase weapons and other scarce supplies. Red dollars were the instruments of the military, but in design they promoted American popular culture. Like early twentieth-century branding, which employed tokens of an imperial visual culture, these certificates carried images of Indian chiefs, astronauts, beauty queens, and grizzly bears.[10]

Red dollars could not officially be converted into "greenbacks," but they could be transferred through postal orders. American soldiers and others were able to profit by converting red dollars into green ones just before military payment certificate conversion dates, when a series of certificates would be officially withdrawn from circulation and replaced by a new series.[11] On "C-Day," only soldiers were allowed on the bases and were required to exchange their entire stock of certificates for the new issue. The old certificates were declared worthless, and all the notes were burned.[12] American soldiers sometimes conspired with Vietnamese residents to generate profit from these exchanges, causing more certificates to be in the hands of traders than of American military personnel.

The circulation of red dollars in southern Vietnam, the frontier of capitalism, secured the value of real dollars. By referring to these notes as "red," people emphasized their specificity in relation to the Cold War. Sudden conversions from one series to another, the restrictions on conversion, and the black market activities that were spawned on the fringes of the PX stores aligned red dollars more with socialist than capitalist money. How then did the circulation of red dollars in southern Vietnam provide an alternative social biography of the US dollar?

Greenbacks were "kept out of sight" by two mechanisms: red dollars and subsidized exchange rates. According to a former employee of the National Bank of Vietnam in Saigon, ordinary Vietnamese who traveled abroad—including army officers, technicians, and students—purchased dollars at a preferential exchange rate. Upon returning to Saigon, most converted their dollars back into Vietnamese currency. Former officers who traveled to the United States might keep few dollar bills as a souvenir of their trip. One man recalled receiving dollars for work he had done as a photographer's assistant in Saigon in the early 1970s. He described having to exchange those dollars for the local currency, which required an extra step before he could spend the money, as "a waste of effort," he recalled. He then paused. "It's not like today," he mused. "Anyone in a café will take dollars."

A second strategy for keeping dollars out of sight involved technocratic forms of currency swaps, also called the Commercial Import Program (CIP), which started in 1955. Through the CIP, licensed importers purchased consumer goods with subsidized dollars, which were then resold in South Vietnam, as we saw in chapter 1. The profits from the sale of these goods financed the government in Saigon. Unrealistic exchange rates and a high demand for consumer goods triggered inflation and devalued the South Vietnamese currency. In 1961, the official rate was 72 đồng to the dollar. In 1966, the currency was devalued to 118 to the US dollar, and by 1970, the black market premium was almost 400 percent (or 423 đồng to the dollar). American officials called for a devaluation of the currency, arguing that it would help to "dampen inflation, curb corruption and protect morale and morals of Americans fighting and working in that country."[13] The General Accounting Office estimated that selling discounted dollars provided at least 80 percent of South Vietnam's domestic revenue. By heavily discounting the US dollar, the General Accounting Office warned that the credibility of the United States and the integrity of the US dollar were at risk.

The US dollar's biography in southern Vietnam runs counter to the popular descriptions of the Bretton Woods era as "embedded liberalism" that promoted the proper management of domestic economies as the key to a sound international monetary system.[14] National governments were charged with maintaining domestic monetary policies that would, in turn, preserve the system of fixed exchanges. The Bretton Woods system of fixed exchange rates hinged on a paradox: the world's reserve currency was also the United States' domestic currency. As the United States increased its expenditures in Vietnam, in terms of both troops and budget appropriations, its gold reserves plummeted, raising doubts as to the US government's ability to protect the US dollar's value.[15] In 1971, President Nixon closed the gold window, and the US dollar ceased to anchor the fixed exchange-rate system of the Bretton Woods system.

The biography of the US dollar in southern Vietnam raises a question: Why did people regard the dollar as a reliable currency, given its rapid devaluation after 1971? Its credibility, after all, was jeopardized by the withdrawal of US troops. After 1975, symbols of the American presence in Saigon were transformed from objects of prestige into political liabilities. As we saw in chapter 2, people affiliated with the South Vietnamese regime or with the US military had to flee the country or risk incarceration by the socialist government for their association with the United States.

The cause for the revival of the US dollar lies in its transformation from the convertible dollar of the Bretton Woods era into the global dollar of neoliberalism.[16] Despite the dollar's devaluation, the qualities of hardness and softness eventually realigned along the lines of the Cold War's geopolitical order.[17] "Hard currencies" (for example, the US dollar, Hong Kong dollars, and German marks) were associated with the First World, whereas "soft currencies" referred to money issued by the Second and Third Worlds. But for many people in southern Vietnam, the luster of dollars pales in comparison with gold.

In Ho Chi Minh City, gold shops are open long after other shops and market stalls close their doors. During the day, gold shops appear luminous, their radiance enhanced by hanging lights and mirrors. Their glass counters are filled with jewelry, and the walls are covered with embossed figures that symbolize wealth and success, such as galloping horses, believed to ward off bad luck. Gold, while treasured for its perceived "hardness" or immunity from political manipulation, is also soft and pliable, making it an ideal metal for jewelry work. Yet despite its pliability, the jewelry on display tends to be unadorned, for one simple reason. The price of a ring or bracelet is calculated on its market value as measured by the purity and weight of the gold. Only a nominal sum is added for craftsmanship; when the jewelry is sold, the value of the craftsmanship vanishes with the gold's recommodification.

Before 1975, Saigon was a thriving regional center for the gold trade, with more than two hundred tons of gold said be in circulation. Gold shops such as Kim Thanh produced bars that were traded as far away as Hong Kong.[18] After 1975, government officials referred to gold as simply a "yellow metal," in an attempt to strip it of its fetishistic qualities of wealth. But officials also conducted household raids to confiscate it, thus reinforcing its status as something to be withheld from the government. Gold's role as private wealth was reinforced after 1975, when people used it as an instrument of payment for passage out of Vietnam. People recalled the price of escape not in US dollars but by a number of gold rings or bars. Many people also traveled with gold, usually paper-thin gold leaves or gold bars that could easily be rolled up and concealed in clothing. And it was the promise of gold on the bodies of these evacuees that turned sea journeys into such dangerous crossings.

The ordinary southern Vietnamese people I spoke with recalled their strategies for hiding gold in the postwar city. One woman waved her hand around the room as she exclaimed, "Gold was everywhere!" She described how she hid gold bars behind the toilet, a place people regarded as filthy and impure. While stories of buried gold in Saigon are often evoked to explain the region's wealth, some people pointed out that buried gold was often unrecoverable. The earthen layers of the delta were constantly shifting, changing the position of jars of gold buried beneath the surface. People recounted stories of relatives (never themselves) having buried a jar of gold, only to dig in the same spot later and find that the jar was gone. These stories functioned as myths underscoring the fleeting qualities of wealth; even gold could not be trusted as a store of value. For people who arrived from northern Vietnam, the postwar city sparkled with gold. One man who arrived from Hanoi in 1977 described his surprise at the sight of women wearing gold bangles, gold rings, and gold earrings.

People in Hanoi still remark on the habit of southerners to wear gold, which they attribute to a regional tendency to display rather than conceal personal wealth. For women in southern Vietnam, however, gold is a valuable that is most protected when it is worn on the body. A popular style worn by vendors in Ho Chi Minh City is a set of seven gold bangles called *xi-men*, after the French *la semaine*, meaning "week."[19] Today, however, most people firmly associate the bangles with market women in southern Vietnam. The bangles are worn tightly so that they don't interfere with the woman's daily tasks. When purchasing a set, women pull a nylon stocking over their hand before putting on the bangles to ensure that they are as tight as possible. This means that removing the bangles requires them to be physically cut, destroying their attributes as adornment in order to realize their market value.

Although the value of gold is derived from its status as a commodity, it also conveys the values of inheritance and intergenerational continuity. This contradiction is not specific to Vietnam and has also been described in Indonesia and Palestine.[20] Weddings reinforce gold's significance as a symbolic value, as family and close friends present gold to a newly married couple. On several occasions, I attended the gifting ceremony, where, in the presence of the bride's family, both living and dead, the family offered gifts of gold to the bride in front of her ancestral altar. On one occasion, the representative of the bride's family announced the weight and purity of the gift. By doing so, he also announced the market value of the gift, should anyone have wanted to do the calculations. After the ritual exchange of gifts, brides wear the jewelry during the wedding feast, which is attended by distant relatives and friends of the family. Guests also present the newly married couple with gifts, but rather than gold, they tuck cash into the envelope that had contained the invitation. Once the wedding is over, the jewelry is kept at home, its value no longer invested in its display but in its immanent value in the city's markets.

Gold circulates not only in the form of rings and bangles but also bars that have a specific weight and purity. These bars are small enough to fit comfortably in the palm of one's hand and are measured in taels (*cây*, *lạng*, or *lượng* in Vietnamese), a unit of measurement equivalent to 37.5 grams. Because gold's value ultimately resides in its potential recommodification, most people prefer gold in its purest form, designated as "999.9." The price of gold varies with its place of origin, too. Gold from Italy, for example, is more highly valued than gold from Russia, which is mixed with bronze and so has a reddish tint, whereas Italian gold is an amalgam made with silver.

In Ho Chi Minh City, people regard the taels of gold produced by the Saigon Jewelry Company as the standard.[21] Established in 1988, the company is state-owned but has gained a reputation for producing reliable taels, each stamped with the company name and its logo, "Saigon Jewelry Company," followed by "999.9" and a serial number to attest to the bar's singularity, a form of accountability used as well for state-issued paper currency. Most of the bars are sealed in a plastic casing. While people cannot be certain about a bar's purity, they do not dare open the case. Doing so would reduce the bar's exchange value by two thousand Vietnamese đồng (around thirteen cents), because the bar would then be classified as "unclean."

The gold trade provided a legitimate cover for the exchange of US dollars. By the early 1990s, the Vietnamese State Bank designated licensed gold shops as authorized venues for currency exchange (fig. 3.1). Shops posted large boards with the price of gold in Vietnamese đồng and the selling price of US dollars. The ubiquity of gold shops ensured that the market price of gold and dollars was always on display. Gold shops also functioned as guarantors

3.1   A gold shop advertising itself as an authorized exchange bureau (a sheet of US dollar bills lines the back wall).

for the notes. In District Five, gold shops still stamp US dollar bills; these marks attest not to the bill's authenticity but rather to the shop's willingness to exchange that particular bill for another should the customer encounter problems using the bill.

The biography of the US dollar in Vietnam has thus been animated in part by the cultural economy around gold—but in ways that cannot be explained by the Bretton Woods system. Like gold, US dollars also mediate a form of private wealth that eludes the territorial state. And, more significantly, both gold and US dollars conveyed value within moral economies. While gold provides an intergenerational vehicle for transferring money signified by bridal wealth, US dollars provide a transnational vehicle in the form of remittances. While both dollars and gold are readily bought and sold in the city's ubiquitous gold shops, people tend to view these value-forms as something that should be kept, not spent. Spending dollars requires sacrificing their symbolic value, a ritual act of conversion to realize their market price, much like the women who cut off their bangles to sell them.

DOLLARS AT THE DOORSTEP

Remittances refer broadly to sending money over a geographical distance. In Vietnam, overseas remittance is a catchphrase for the huge flow of money— largely dollar denominated—sent by people who reside outside Vietnam to people who never left the country. Remittances ascribe dollars as conveyers of relatedness and belonging within a moral economy that cannot be reduced to the market.[22] Culturally constructed as gifts in opposition to other monetary flows, specifically foreign investment, remittances have reordered the place of money, especially US dollars, in postwar Ho Chi Minh City.

Remittances are one of the largest sources of US dollars in Vietnam. Banking officials estimate that more than US$2.6 billion is remitted every year to Vietnam through banks and other agents.[23] Some estimates run as high as eight billion dollars because so much money flows outside institutional payment networks. Because remittances are classified as interhousehold transfers and not payments, they do not create *economic* value even though they exert force as a vehicle for expressing Vietnamese personhood in transnational terms.

The bank officials I interviewed drew parallels between the remittance economy and US military aid in the 1960s and 1970s. Two Vietnamese bankers pointed out that the annual level of remittances to Vietnam was roughly equivalent to the amount of average annual foreign aid and military assistance provided by the United States between 1955 and 1975. Yet unlike that assistance, one banker explained, the vast remittance sums only stimulated consumption. While this critique appeared to place a Keynesian emphasis on national wealth, rather than a neoliberal emphasis on individual freedom, it also recalled the Commercial Import Program, which built up an urban middle class but neglected the domestic manufacturing base.

The emphasis on the US dollar stimulating personal consumption is part of its subversive quality. Insofar as the dollar is a political symbol of the United States, access to dollars in both Cuba and Vietnam has been attributed with eroding revolutionary precepts by emphasizing consumerism and acquisitiveness and resurrecting prerevolutionary social divisions.[24] In Cuba, the remittance economy has contributed to processes of racialization that privilege white residents.[25] In Vietnam, by contrast, dollars have reinstated the politico-cultural categories of the Cold War. While both "northerners" and "southerners" had access to US dollars, they transacted with the currency via different networks. In northern Vietnam, workers and students returned from eastern Europe and the Soviet Union with scarce consumer goods and dollars earned from these elaborate trading networks.[26] In southern Vietnam, dollars were channeled via the diaspora as gifts. But in both cases, dollars signaled value in the marketplace.

During the US-led embargo of 1975–94, people could send medical and other essential supplies to family members still in Vietnam. These packages were valued not by their contents but by the exchange value of those contents. A package of medicine valued at two hundred US dollars in the United States or Canada might have a street value of three hundred US dollars in Ho Chi Minh City. Later people sent anything that could be resold—blue jeans, T-shirts, old electronic items such as television sets and radios, and even dollar bills and gold jewelry. These packages were not delivered directly to residences. People had to pick up their packages at Tan Son Nhut Airport, where customs officers inspected the packages, sometimes even slashing cardboard boxes with knives to search for contraband.

During the 1970s and 1980s, gold and dollar bills that circulated outside of state-approved channels were classified as contraband (hàng lậu) and subject to confiscation. People who sent packages often devised elaborate codes to tell the recipients where currency and gold were hidden. These codes were sometimes so encrypted that the actual value of the gift was never realized. Occasionally the package would contain a hundred-dollar or fifty-dollar bill, sometimes tightly rolled up and concealed in a ballpoint pen or placed around a medicine bottle and covered over by the label. On one occasion, a note indicated that a package contained two pairs of jeans to little "Luong" (*gửi bé Lượng hai cái quần*). The words Lượng (a proper name, also a unit of gold) and *hai* (two) were underlined, but the family who received the package did not understand the message. The woman who opened the letter recalled shaking her head because there was no one named Lượng in the family. Years later, when the relatives who had sent the package returned to visit Vietnam, they explained that the underlined words were to be reversed (two bars of gold), a hint that gold had been concealed in the jeans, which had long since been sold in the outside markets of Ho Chi Minh City.

By the 1990s, the flow of gifts sent to Vietnam—clothes, electronics, medicine, and toys—increasingly became simply money. This transformation coincided with both economic reforms in Vietnam and new global forms of telecommunication that facilitated monetary transfers. One man described the change this way: "They know their relatives have a need, but they do not know what that need is." Companies such as VinaUSA encouraged their customers to write to relatives in other countries by sending letters free of charge. These letters coded the customer's financial needs for meeting expenses for an upcoming wedding or engagement, or for schooling or an unexpected illness.

Efforts of the Vietnamese State to harness the vast sums of remittances by requiring that recipients receive money in the national currency met with failure. A decree that all remittances be paid in Vietnamese đồng led to a steep drop in the level of official remittances. The Vietnamese government has subsequently authorized remittance companies—including Western Union, VinaUSA, and MoneyGram—to offer customers the option of receiving their funds in gold, US dollars, or Vietnamese đồng.

These licensed companies, however, still faced steep competition from unregulated businesses. Businesses would pop up right before the lunar New Year, when the annual demand for money peaked, and then disappear. These private companies delivered money to people's doorsteps, a trend that emphasized the private power of money during the time I conducted this research. It was difficult in Ho Chi Minh City to know where these companies were located, as people organized remittances from their homes or in small, unmarked offices. One office was located in a small room behind a storefront in which expensive perfumes and jewelry were on display. The woman who ran the company relied on a machine to count the dollars, a computer, and a vast network of family and close acquaintances in the United States. She conducted business on the basis of her reputation and a network of people who knew and trusted her to deliver the dollars to their destination. And while her operation was small, she provided competition for official means of controlling the vast flows of dollars in and out of Vietnam.

By keeping remittances in the form of US dollars, Vietnamese citizens engage in a process of self-making not wholly defined by the state, a strategy resembling "keeping-while-giving"[27] by which people withhold particular valuables from exchange. The inalienability of these valuables then serves to symbolize individual or collective identities. Dollars, however, are valued precisely because of their alienable, even foreign, quality. Keeping dollars as a symbolic act must contend with the fact that their value is only realized in exchange.

Mr. Huy, an unmarried man in his early sixties, described the first time he received dollars. A few days before Tết, he came home to find a letter stuck on his door. It was an invitation to go to an overseas remittance company in the center of Ho Chi Minh City and bring his household registration and identification card with him. When he arrived, he showed his documents and was told that two cousins had sent him three hundred dollars. He described his thrill in holding the bills. He held them up to the light to inspect them, although he admitted he didn't know what to look for to ensure that the bills were legitimate. He was given a little card to write a few lines back to his relatives. It was their first correspondence in ten years. He then began planning how he would spend the money (*kế hoạch xài tiền*), using the very language of the command economy invoked by Vietnamese state-enterprises to determine the horizon of production and consumption. While he wanted to keep the bills, he could not afford to do so. He went to a gold shop to exchange the bills into Vietnamese đồng so that he could meet his everyday expenses.

While the dollarization of the Vietnamese economy has been accomplished via transnational kinship networks, overseas remittances alone cannot account for the privileged place of dollars in Ho Chi Minh City. The US dollar as a privileged value form is situated within the broader reordering of the global monetary order. As we will see, the vexing problem was not just the flow of US dollars but also the way dollars were absorbed into the Vietnamese domestic economy.

Dollarization is usually explained as a strategy by ordinary citizens to preserve value in a country experiencing staggering rates of inflation. Outside markets in Ho Chi Minh City generated a demand for money that could not be met by state-issued currency. Despite restrictions on foreign currency ownership, dollars circulated as a second currency trading for a premium as high as 1,600 percent in 1983, the third-highest premium in the world.[28] Dollars in the domestic economy thus signaled the limits of sovereign authority.

The State Bank of Vietnam also required dollars to meet international debt repayments and to purchase Western consumer goods. As in other socialist economies, hard currency shops in Ho Chi Minh City displayed the purchasing power of the West: Johnny Walker liquor, electronic goods, perfume, and branded cigarettes beckoned would-be consumers in the 1980s. Women lingered outside the shops, offering to buy or sell dollars at a premium. Even as inflation subsided in the 1990s, people's preference for dollars did not decline.

US dollars were "big money" in Ho Chi Minh City's markets. Their high value made them ideal money objects to transport and conceal. A stack of Vietnamese notes could be condensed into one hundred-dollar bill, which was easy to conceal in a pocket, at the bottom of a shoe, or in an envelope. People affectionately referred to hundred-dollar bills as "tickets" because they condensed value into a portable, concealable form and could immediately be converted back into Vietnamese đồng. Yet many people attributed the power of dollars to their image and their materiality, rather than the power of circulation. Like Russians in postsocialist Moscow who expected to find a key to the reliability of the US dollar in the physical properties of the note itself, people in Ho Chi Minh City likewise delighted in the dollar's sensuous qualities.[29] One man demonstrated how, after he scrunched up a one-dollar bill, it sprang back into shape, unlike Vietnamese money, which he described as "torn and wrinkled like an unironed shirt." After the redesigned hundred-dollar bill began to circulate in Vietnam, people insisted on receiving bills with "big men," referring to the enlarged the portrait of Benjamin Franklin. People's preference for "big men" was symptomatic of their prior experiences with currency reforms in which old series were demonetized.

People attributed to dollars a feeling of security, a sense of enrichment and blessing. One afternoon, on the outskirts of the city, a vendor carrying a large board laden with trinkets such as cigarette lighters, sunglasses, and costume jewelry handed me some currency written in script and bearing the portrait of a male dignitary I didn't recognize. "It's a fake dollar bill," she whispered to me and a Vietnamese companion. She claimed that she had been tricked into accepting the bill and then begged my companion to take pity on her by giving her Vietnamese money in exchange. He refused and instead pulled out of his wallet a colorful Dutch guilder with a brilliant sunflower that he had kept as a souvenir from a trip to Europe. When he pointed out the beauty of the note, the woman claimed that she didn't have any "feeling" toward the bill. Dollar bills generated a feeling of confidence and security, qualities that both the Vietnamese đồng and the guilder lacked. The vendor attributed this feeling to the greenness of the currency, the spring in its paper, and the size of the portraits. While economists might dismiss an interest in the appearance of the dollar as irrational or uninformed, the credibility of currency was invested in an economy in which these contingent evaluations mattered.

In southern Vietnam, people's faith in the US dollar verged on redemption. Holding dollars, for some people, represented a source of salvation. Mr. Thắng, a man in his fifties, proclaimed, "If someone offered me fifteen thousand đồng or a dollar, I'd take the dollar," tucking the imaginary dollar bill into the front pocket of his shirt. A single dollar bill was nothing but pocket money, but by holding dollars, the man redeemed his personal history. A soldier for South Vietnam, Mr. Thắng earned his living on the streets of Ho Chi Minh City. As diplomatic relations between the United States and Vietnam thawed, the flow of dollars increased with the arrival of tourists and returning friends and family. Handling dollars signaled this man's inclusion in a global economy. Yet this redemptive quality also conveyed the growing economic inequality in the city. One woman gasped at my suggestion that she keep a dollar bill rather than convert it into Vietnamese đồng. She quickly converted the dollar into Vietnamese đồng (15,000 VND to one USD at the time) and pointed out that amount was what she needed to buy groceries at the market to feed her children. In her accounting, keeping a dollar was commensurate with withholding food from her children. For both people, the value of the dollar was only realized upon its conversion back into Vietnamese đồng.

US dollars did not, however, circulate often as ones or fives. People preferred to keep the hundred or fifty dollar bill. But the two-dollar bill had a special place as a talisman of the luck needed to survive in Ho Chi Minh City's globalizing economy. In the United States, gamblers hold two-dollar bills as symbols of the elusive quality one needs to win at the racetracks. In Ho Chi Minh City, most two-dollar bills entered into circulation as gifts from people from the United States. Their value was heightened in northern Vietnam, where they were commodities to be bought and sold. Along the road leading to Phủ Tây Hồ, a popular shrine in Hanoi, vendors asked for as much as 100,000 VND for a two-dollar bill printed in 1976, the equivalent of four dollars. When I tried to bargain for a two-dollar bill at the shrine at the request of a friend in Ho Chi Minh City, the vendors insisted that those bills were "for keeping, not for spending." In Ho Chi Minh City, however, one currency dealer remarked that he sold two-dollar bills to vendors in Hanoi because there was no longer a market for them in southern Vietnam. The regular visits of family members and friends from the United States ensured a steady supply of the bills.

Not everyone I interviewed in southern Vietnam agreed with the privileged place of the US dollar. Mr. Lịch, a former army officer and member of the Communist Party, dismissed the dollar as a legitimate means of transaction. He had migrated south after 1975 and now owned a small shop where he sold animal feed and fertilizer. When I asked him about his experience handling US dollars, he quickly replied that dollars were "nothing special." He then pulled out a one-dollar bill from his wallet to prove his point. He had acquired the bill when a Vietnamese customer had approached him to buy animal feed. Although he refused to sell his feed for dollars, he did accept a single dollar bill that he had kept in his wallet until the day I met him. If he was not willing to accept payment in dollars, I asked, why did he keep the note? "For fun," he replied. Mr. Lịch rejected the purchasing power of dollars by turning a single dollar bill into a souvenir.

People's preference for keeping dollars showed how money was underwriting new economic subjectivities. The reasons people attributed to withholding money from circulation—a feeling of security, a sense of good luck, or just for fun—contributed to the widespread belief that the US dollar embodied "real" value. By keeping dollars rather than converting them into the domestic currency, even if only "for fun," Vietnamese citizens actively created a monetary system in which the US dollar circulated as quasilegal currency in Vietnam. More importantly, people used the currency to redefine selfhood in reform-era Vietnam. The US dollar embodied a form of value that drew its power from a global marketplace, universal and unrestricted. While the circulation of US dollars signaled the country's integration with the global monetary system, it also provided citizens with a currency that eluded state control. The parallel circulation of đồng and dollars in Vietnam thus marked a confrontation between two competing regimes of value in Vietnam, and two constructions of citizenship.

PEGGED TO THE DOLLAR

During the time I conducted my research (2000–2007), most people in Ho Chi Minh City, even boys and girls, knew just about how many Vietnamese đồng a single dollar could "eat," a colloquial expression for the exchange rate.[30] The official exchange rate for dollars and đồng was printed in newspapers, announced on the evening news, and posted in front of gold shops. Restaurants catering to foreigners in Ho Chi Minh City listed their prices in US dollars. Dealers selling imported household appliances and motorbikes posted prices in dollars. Even taxi drivers and petty vendors accepted dollars but provided change in đồng.

Since the early 1990s, the State Bank of Vietnam has followed a managed peg exchange policy. This policy stopped short of "denationalizing" money, a proposal associated with Friedrich A. Hayek, a proponent of individual freedom.[31] Denationalizing money, he argued, would allow individuals the freedom to decide in what currency debts would be paid and permit financial institutions to decide their own currencies. And, through choice and competition, an optimal level of the money supply would be generated. Dollarization, by contrast, imposes institutional discipline by reducing the flexibility of political authorities over monetary policies.

The International Monetary Fund (IMF) never officially endorsed dollarization in Vietnam. It was Vietnamese officials in southern Vietnam who advocated for greater transparency in the foreign exchange position of the Vietnamese government and for structural reforms in the banking and financial sectors. Nguyễn Xuân Oánh, for example, served as a senior official with the IMF from 1959 to 1963 before returning to act as the governor of the National Bank of Vietnam in Saigon. As an advisor to the new postwar government, his advice was still in line with the IMF's agenda of promoting currency convertibility. A "viable" and "relatively free" exchange rate, Nguyễn advised, would enable the government to cut subsidies and its budget deficit. These policies were supported by other Western-trained economists within Vietnam, who began publishing articles in the state-based press in the early 1980s, allowing a "different voice" to be heard that also helped to domesticate reforms.[32]

Monetary policies in Vietnam transformed the US dollar from "contraband" after 1975 into quasilegal currency by the late 1980s, one of the most significant—yet easily overlooked—consequences of reforming the Vietnamese economy.[33] By 1991, almost 40 percent of all bank deposits in Vietnam were denominated in dollars, prompting the World Bank and the International Monetary Fund to classify Vietnam as an "informally dollarized economy."[34] While the level of foreign-currency-denominated bank accounts in Vietnam had shrunk to 28 percent by 2001, the US dollar continues to circulate as a quasilegal currency.[35]

Today the Vietnamese đồng is valued in relation to the US dollar, stabilizing the rates of exchange between these two currencies but creating new structures of dependency that rise and fall with the US dollar's fortune in world markets. Pegging the value of the Vietnamese đồng to the US dollar has been a source of official disagreement within Vietnam. Some Vietnamese government officials have attributed the widespread use of dollars in the domestic economy to speculation in the real estate market and the corruption of public officials. Foreign currencies, officials warn, should be kept in the state banking system, not in the wallets, cash drawers, or iron safes of ordinary citizens. But policies restricting the domestic circulation of dollars have been ineffective. A 1994 decree requiring domestic and foreign companies to sell a fixed percentage of their foreign currency to the State Bank was widely ignored. Even the 1999 mandate to list all prices in Vietnamese đồng did not eliminate dollar signs from posted price lists. Even international economists have raised concerns about dollarization.[36] While praising monetary reforms that ended inflation, they cautioned that dollarization still poses a risk to the stability of the domestic financial market and of the banking sector. The risk may even increase with rapid financial deepening, a measure of the expansion of the money supply relative to the gross national product. The dollar's potential effect on creating a bubble in asset prices, especially in the real estate and securities markets, has only increased as Vietnam's financial deepening has skyrocketed, from below 30 percent in the early 1990s to almost 70 percent in 2003. Given the high rate of cash transactions, the full extent of dollarization is impossible to measure—actual figures vary from six hundred million to two billion US dollars—but most experts suggest that almost one-third of cash is denominated in dollars.

Insofar as US currency represents global purchasing power, it is a power that people want to keep rather than spend. US dollars signal the possibility of communication beyond Vietnam's territorial borders, a monetary passport that allows one to escape state-imposed restrictions that govern domestic economy. The arrival of dollars in postwar Vietnam confound the political and social boundaries that mediated the national and the global, the domestic and the foreign, and thus complicate the cultural politics of identity that are based on distinguishing "us or the West" (*ta hay Tây*). Through the sometimes covert, sometimes highly visible deployment of dollars, people challenge the Vietnamese state's classification system and, in so doing, demonstrate how ordinary citizens are agents of economic reform through their allegiance to reliable money.

Dollarization in Vietnam is not just a project of reordering money. It is also a project of redefining selfhood. In the streets, homes, offices, and alleyways of Ho Chi Minh City, dollars do not circulate as taken-for-granted representations of money; they are also potent objects for expressing selfhood. Keeping dollars in southern Vietnam, as I have described, should not be seen as hoarding. It is a social practice situated within the global and local logics that animate the circulation of money. It is this potentiality in redefining Vietnamese selfhood that the government has attempted to ward off, not by reducing the supply of dollars in circulation but by enhancing the value of the Vietnamese đồng. Pegging the value of the Vietnamese đồng to the US dollar has until recently stabilized the đồng's value. Yet the currency's devaluation relative to the dollar also demonstrates how Asia's condition of rapid economic development—especially its exposure to global capital flows—is also a condition of perpetual crisis.[37]

When I was in Saigon in 2007, people did not shun US dollars, but most were reluctant to accept them. I was turned away even by bank tellers, who claimed the quality of my dollars was unacceptable. Their refusal anticipated the dollar's loss of value in world markets. Although the USD-VND exchange rate held steady, the price of gold had more than doubled. Monetary instability was no longer caused solely by the fiscal policies of the Vietnamese state of the 1980s; the country's rapid integration into the global monetary system was pushing prices higher. By the end of 2007, the Ministry of Planning and Investment estimated that more than twenty billion dollars in foreign investment had been approved, a year-by-year increase of almost 70 percent. The influx of dollars helped to fuel the domestic finance market as people used new credit instruments to invest in the securities and real estate markets. The specter of inflation in Vietnam had returned, and people again turned to the US dollar. Banks found that even when they offered attractive interest rates for đồng deposits, many people preferred to sell their excess đồng for dollars, thus thwarting the State Bank's attempt to de-dollarize the Vietnamese economy.

The State Bank of Vietnam attempted to control the power of US dollars, first by controlling the supply of dollars in circulation, and later by hitching the value of the Vietnamese đồng to the value of the US dollar. This latter technique helped stabilize the value of the Vietnamese đồng. As the Vietnamese government has pursued a program of aggressive growth organized around export-oriented production and foreign direct and indirect investment, it has attempted to infuse the Vietnamese đồng with the qualities of the US dollar. And while it may still be too soon to know how long global confidence in the US dollar will last, it is through this refashioning of Vietnam's national currency that the US dollar may exert its most lasting influence.

FOUR

SUMMONING SPIRITS

REMITTANCES denominated in US dollars in southern Vietnam created a social infrastructure for families that were stretched out across vast geographical distances. These gifts in the guise of US dollar bills were also valued as signs of membership in a globalizing economy. Are there parallels that can then be drawn between the economies of remittances and spirit money, paper replicas of money offered to the world of spirits? Although capitalist theories of value marginalized both practices and Vietnamese bankers and officials disapproved of them, they have been crucial domains in the production of Vietnamese personhood and in negotiating the complex meanings of sociality within a newly liberalized but not yet neoliberalized economy. Yet there is a danger with these economies as well. Money once stripped of its guise of sentimentality and relatedness can make even ghosts become real.

BÙI GIÁNG'S MONEY

Just off Highway 13, a dusty road lined on both sides by stands offering yellow mums, bundles of incense, and assorted paper offerings led to the entrance of a cemetery. People arrived in vans and on motorbikes to pay respect to deceased family members and friends. On this particular morning in 2002, I was with Mr. Thiệu, a man in his sixties, who had been invited to accompany a friend, Mrs. Nhung, whom he affectionately referred to as his "sister." They had grown up together in central Vietnam, and, even decades later, she relied on his wide range of contacts, often to great profit. But she rarely compensated him for his efforts, or so he claimed. His complaint made visible a paradox of kinship, namely that as people express their relatedness to others through gifts of money, they expose those relations to the hazards of commoditization as affective labor becomes measured in terms of market activity.[1] The paradox of economic calculation, as we will see, extends as well to relations with the dead.

On that day Mrs. Nhung intended to make offerings to her deceased parents. She had a reputation for lending money at high interest rates and for organizing rotating savings associations. Still, I was surprised to see how simple her offerings were. She laid a bouquet of flowers, a bundle of incense, a special rice dish, and a small set of spirit money on the gravesite. Behind her, other groups were preparing far more elaborate offerings: trays laden with cans of Heineken beer, boiled chickens, tins of fancy butter cookies, fresh fruit, and piles of spirit money. Mrs. Nhung was discreet; she was also thorough. After lighting a bundle of incense, she passed out a few sticks to everyone in the group, to offer at the neighboring gravesites. The adjacent spirits might be accidentally summoned by the offerings, and could be vengeful if they were not also acknowledged. Finally, Mrs. Nhung slipped one of the attendants a fifty-thousand-đồng note to motivate him to keep the area clean and well tended in her absence. Her attentiveness in acknowledging both the attendants and the neighboring gravesites made me skeptical of Mr. Thiệu's claim of being overlooked by his "sister." I soon realized that Mr. Thiệu had plans of his own.

Mr. Thiệu's interest in the trip was not in carrying out ancestral rituals for his sister's parents. He had joined the entourage as an excuse to visit the gravesite of an old friend, a poet. While he never described the man as his brother, they had had an especially close relationship. The poet, Bùi Giáng, was still well known in Ho Chi Minh City, famous as much for the brilliance of his poetry and translations of modernist philosophy as for his descent into poverty and madness after 1975. Mr. Thiệu urged me to come with him to the gravesite.

When we found the gravesite, I was startled by its elegant but serene design. Lines of Bùi Giáng's poetry were carved in marble, and vines with blooming tendrils trailed down the wall. In front of the wall were a bronze bust of the poet and some benches for visitors to rest on. Someone had left a large bouquet of dried flowers next to the bust. Mr. Thiệu lovingly touched the bust with his hand, as he might his old friend. He then picked up the vase of flowers and tossed them aside, explaining, "Bùi Giáng hated flowers."

As we stood in front of the gravesite, two people approached to pay their respects as well. The man introduced himself only as a writer and the young woman as his daughter. He took out three small, red cups and a miniature tin teapot wrapped in a plastic bag and sealed tight with rubber bands. He placed three duck eggs and some sprigs of fresh herbs on a plate and then tossed rice wine over the gravesite. "That's for Bùi Giáng," he said. "He wouldn't be happy if we didn't drink to the bottom." He then placed a stack of hell dollars, simulated hundred-dollar bills, on the grave.

Mr. Thiệu picked up the hundred-dollar bills and counted them as he laughingly observed that Bùi Giáng never enjoyed so much money while he lived. He asked where the man had found such beautiful dollar bills—the notes were so green, the printing so clear. In District Five, the main commercial district of the city, the man replied. Mr. Thiệu then took several notes and tucked them into his pocket, calling them "Bùi Giáng's money." When we returned to Mrs. Nhung, she asked Mr. Thiệu to burn the paper offerings she had prepared for her deceased parents, the final step in the ritual process, and he did so without taking a single note from the plate.

The story of Bùi Giáng did not end that day. Several days later, Mr. Thiệu received visitors who had just arrived from California. One of the men presented him with a hundred-dollar bill, a gift from Mr. Thiệu's older brother, who had been a high-ranking government official in one of the city's outer districts before 1975. To Mr. Thiệu, the money was not from his brother but was a return gift from Bùi Giáng. The hundred-dollar bill he had taken at the gravesite had miraculously turned into the hundred-dollar bill he now held in his hand.

DEBT AND THE PRODUCTION OF MORALITY

The Vietnamese distinguish between two categories of debt: contractual and socially sanctioned relations. Objective debts (*nợ*) are contractual, and, because they can be repaid, are generally regarded as amoral. Subjective debts such as gratitude (*ơn*), on the other hand, require continual affirmation of the primary social relationship. Through acts of remitting and burning money, people acknowledge these socially sanctioned forms of debt. But money blurs the distinction between these two categories of debt—*ơn*, which is intersubjective or intrinsic to claims of sociality, and *nợ*, which is not.

The model of intersubjective debt is expressed in the parent-child relationship. Children are bound to their parents by a debt that can never be repaid except through the continual performance of filial piety (*hiếu*) that reinforces the social relation. This debt grounds a moral economy insofar as it is a bond that cannot be negotiated and so stands outside market transactions.[2] People perform their social roles within this economy through concrete displays of indulgence and deference. Parents indulge very young children with small treats and refusals to discipline them. But they expect deference from their older children, even into adulthood. Children enter into this symbolic exchange by demonstrating respect through their bodily comportment and speech. As they learn how to talk, they are taught to fold their arms across their chest, bend down, and utter "*a*," to demonstrate respect. They later use terms of address in which they acknowledge who they are in relation to the addressee.

Children learn how to relate to the invisible world of spirits through similar practices of deference and deferral. Even adults refer to themselves as "child" (*con*) or "grandchild" (*cháu*) when addressing spirits, structuring their claims for recognition in terms of genealogical descent. Families often prepare dishes to offer to the spirits of ancestors, a practice they describe as *cúng trước, ăn sau*, or "offer first, eat after." This deferral of consumption or enjoyment makes visible the place of spirits in everyday life. Children are sometimes tempted by the plates of cookies, fruit, and sweets left on the altars of the god of wealth and the god of land. These altars are often on the floor and well within reach of their little hands. If a child reaches out to grab something off the plate, a nearby adult will sweep up the child and gently remind her that the plate is reserved for someone else. Once the plates are taken away from the altar, children are instructed to "come eat with grandpa," thus encouraging a sense of family that includes the presence of ancestors. By calling upon the spirits of deceased relatives to bless the world of the living and by providing those spirits with displays of ritualized care, people actively construct genealogical continuity.

These debt structures are transnational in that they bind Vietnamese Americans to their homelands. Andrew Lam, who writes about the Vietnamese diaspora, describes how his mother would insist that he read the letters from his relatives still in Vietnam. In those letters his relatives described their hardships and then "timidly asked for money, for antibiotics, for a bicycle, and, if possible, for sponsorship to America."[3] The social relations organized around indebtedness reinforce a geopolitical relationship in which Vietnam symbolizes poverty and deprivation and the West indicates wealth and plentitude. But even when families reconstruct social relations in the United States, children are not free of their debt-bond. These debt structures are used by parents to extract filial obedience from their (often) American-born and raised children: "Having *sacrificed* to *come to this country* for the *sake of their children*: a martyrdom for which they are entitled to repayment."[4]

In this economy of relatedness, money circulates as a privileged sign. People draw upon its mediating powers to express indulgence, deference, and gratitude, a symbol that materializes socially sanctioned debts. But these culturally specific forms of indebtedness cannot fully domesticate money or control its association with market activity. What is sanctioned as a debt external to the marketplace is in fact represented by the very form that signals calculation and self-interest. This dilemma of negotiating sociality in a period of market expansion has only been partially resolved through remitting and burning money.

"REAL" MONEY

Where does "real" money reside? People in Ho Chi Minh City distinguish "real money" (*tiền thật*) from "spirit money" (*tiền mã*), the easily disposed replicas of both past and present currencies. Even the Vietnamese term for spirit money, *tiền mã*, conveys the paradoxical sense of something of little value. The word *mã* means "ghost," but it is also used to describe an object that is disposable or not worth keeping.[5]

Both remittances and spirit money are discursively framed as spectacles of consumption that discourage productive investment. Spirit money is portrayed as squandering resources. State-run newspapers estimated that by the late 1990s the production of votive offerings consumed 15 percent of paper production in Vietnam (fig. 4.1).[6] This criticism parallels the concerns raised by bankers and economists that overseas remittances encourage consumption rather than investment in the national economy. These portrayals should be read as cultural work to designate some exchanges as productive and others as wasteful in an effort to fix the national economy as an object of representation. Yet the emphasis on state-led development and modernization has overlooked how both remitting and burning money have contributed to economic growth. Just as overseas remittances supplement the otherwise scarce income-generating activities of city residents, the actual production of votive offerings has led to new avenues of employment and compelled people to accumulate more wealth to distribute and thereby to garner social status and prestige.[7]

Overseas remittances and spirit money both make foreignness visible within the domestic economy. Remittances are associated with "overseas Vietnamese" (Việt Kiều). Because they are so readily associated with the West, those Vietnamese nationals who live outside the territorial state

4.1   Burning a fistful of dollars for the spirits.

have come to be seen as wealthy, worldly subjects whose power cannot be domesticated. The term Việt Kiều itself is contested. For some people, it suggests a temporary state of displacement, disregarding the fact that many overseas Vietnamese are citizens of other countries, both by birth and through naturalization. The term also collapses intergenerational differences that are reordering individuals' commitments to Vietnam as a homeland. Just as the term Việt Kiều makes visible dilemmas of identification, particularly the conflation of geopolitics and the origins of wealth, money in the guise of remittances likewise confounds efforts to fix the national economy. Remittances circulate as privatized and deregulated transfers that cannot be harnessed by state officials for purposes of national development.

With the opening of the country's borders to tourism and foreign investment, ritual life has become a contested arena for the cultural politics of identity. Spirit money has been partially rehabilitated as part of a wider inventory of cultural practices that signify national character, an inventory "to reinforce Vietnam's sovereignty as a counterweight to the seductions of the West."[8] State officials who once shunned prerevolutionary sources of authority now visited temples and offered incense as a means of legitimating their own claims of sovereignty in a transnational world.[9] The state's increasing involvement in ritual life, however, underscores a basic contradiction: How can Vietnam's sovereignty be reinforced when such practices are mediated by the currency of the West?

Spirit money, in all its fantasy presentation, establishes distance between this world and the other. Communicating with the "other world" (*thế giới bên kia*), a world inhabited by ancestors, gods, and ghosts, requires symbolic mediation. Spirits are summoned by incense, the fragrance of freshly cut flowers, the taste of specially prepared dishes, and objects of wealth. By offering replicas of currencies, people attempt to domesticate the foreignness of the dead.[10] People in Ho Chi Minh City express this logic when they claim, "They are just like us," or, colloquially, "As is the underworld, so is this world" (*Âm sao, dương vậy*), expressions that domesticates the dead by making visible their desires in the form of commodities and money. They remit their gifts to the "other world" through the ritual process of engulfing the material form in flames, even going so far as to write the name of the intended recipient on each note to ensure that it will arrive at its destination, much like one might fill out a form at Western Union. This project of configuration, in which the not-living are made visible in the form of the desires of the living, carries a risk. Both remittances and spirit money challenge the territorial conception of peoplehood. Overseas remittances symbolize a debt-bond paid by those who left Vietnam to those who remained. And this debt-bond was appropriated when US dollars entered into the ritual economy in the form of hell dollars (*đô-la âm phủ*) offered to ancestors, ghosts, and gods. The separation of these two worlds, of "them" and "us," as we will see, is not so easily maintained.

HELL DOLLARS AND THE PROBLEM OF GHOSTS

Spirit money is part of a broad range of votive offerings (*hàng giấy tiền mã*, literally, "paper goods and spirit money"). These include everyday household items such as age-specific and gender-specific clothing, and prestige items such as cell phones, multistory houses, and even Honda motorbikes. The range of spirit money is just as noteworthy: sheets of "dynastic coins," đồng notes with the portrait of the Jade Emperor, even gold bars with the SJC (Saigon Jewelry Company) imprint. However, it was the almost perfect replication of the US hundred dollar bill that blurred the boundary between "commerce" and "ritual," "real" money and "spirit" money. Once brought

4.2   A perfect replica of the hundred-dollar bill.

4.3   The back side of the replica replaces "The United States of America" with Ngan Hang Dia Phu, "Bank of Hell."

from the marketplace to the altar, these objects are no longer market goods but symbolic vehicles that transmit prayers to the spirits with the hope that those spirits will provide blessings.

By the early 1990s, the image of US hundred-dollar bills appeared on offerings for the spirits of ancestors, temple deities, and forsaken persons. These notes were almost exact reproductions of US hundred-dollar bills (figs. 4.2 and 4.3). Unlike the đồng version of spirit money, hell dollars carried the portrait of Benjamin Franklin, not the God of Hell. Hell dollars did have one noticeable distinction: the phrase "United States of America" on real-world dollars was replaced by Ngân Hàng Địa Phủ, or "Bank of Hell," on spirit dollars.

The appearance of foreign currency in these rituals was by no means novel. In the early twentieth century, people used replicas of the Mexican silver dollar, and later the Indochinese piastre, for offerings. At the Temple of the Goddess of the Treasury (Bà Chúa Kho Temple), traders refer to "Goddess money" (*tiền của bà*), coins made of foil placed on top of a simple bamboo frame. The image pressed onto the coins was that of the piastre issued by the Bank of Indochina in 1906 that circulated until after World War II. Indigenous critiques of the practice of offering spirit money likewise came from Vietnamese intellectuals in the 1920s and 1930s who condemned it as wasteful and inappropriate for the modern world.[11]

Hell dollars, like US dollars, unsettled the very differences that specific currency objects were supposed to secure. Anthropologist Heonik Kwon described how in central Vietnam, the universalizing value of the US dollar threatened the imperial hierarchy of the underworld that had been preserved by maintaining different ritual currencies for gods, ghosts, and ancestors.[12] By offering hell dollars to both gods and ghosts alike, people broke down the hierarchy of status. In the inventory of practices that signified national culture, offerings of hell dollars likewise threatened to overturn the hierarchy of "us" and "them" that secured the legitimacy of the Vietnamese state, a predicament not lost on government officials. As with real dollars, officials attempted to restrict the circulation of hell dollars. In the mid-1990s, a government delegation recommended that hell dollars be banned as a superstitious practice.[13] Spirit money, the delegation advised, should be limited to replicas of gold, an appropriate symbol of national tradition.

Officials and ordinary Vietnamese have vied with one another to control the meaning of these symbolic exchanges.[14] Officials have promoted a sense of public memory and peoplehood that is unitary, even though the very project of public memory and national identity can never be contained. Economic reforms have not only enhanced the position of households but have also revived ancestral rites. These rites, in turn, have generated a structural opposition in the form of nameless ghosts.[15] In Vietnamese cosmology, ghosts are those spirits whose grievous deaths cannot be properly commemorated, although they can be partially appeased by invoking the spirit world. Anonymous ghosts, for example, may become temple spirits through regular offerings of money. Ritual and ceremonial practices resolve "unclaimed experience," including physical dislocation and familial disintegration, and a sense of loss and bereavement is transformed through acts of recognition.

The Vietnamese social landscape is haunted by the ghosts of those excluded from the national narratives of heroism, a problem especially acute in southern Vietnam.[16] Hell dollars embody the contradictions of state-based commemoration and popular understandings of wealth, a contradiction manifested above all in state cemeteries where martyrs (men and women commemorated for having fought and died for national liberation) are buried. State cemeteries are common along what was once the Ho Chi Minh Trail, a vital supply link between northern Vietnam and the southern front during the war. The trail has since been expanded into a national highway to provide additional transit routes connecting the northern and southern regions. A banker in southern Vietnam who had already expressed a strong criticism of overseas remittances described his trip on the new highway as part of an official delegation in 2002. He and the other delegates had stopped by a cemetery, where they noticed the hell dollar offerings. The banker then brought this to the attention of a former Vietnamese prime minister, thus underscoring how even though hell dollars are part of popular culture, they are still constructed as a problem for governing the economy.

Hell dollars could no more be banished from the gravesites of martyrs than real US dollars could be eliminated from the marketplace. Their appearance did, however, raise the specter of counterfeits. Some ordinary Vietnamese were cautious when handling hell dollars, lest they be accused of passing counterfeit dollars. I once purchased a stack of hell dollars from a vendor who ran a small stall at a marketplace in District Four without paying much attention to the appearance of the notes. I later gave them to a friend, who noticed that the bills were exact replicas of US hundred-dollar bills. She warned me that the police might arrest anyone who handled those bills on the suspicion they were producing counterfeit dollars. Her fear that the hell dollars would be perceived as counterfeit bills anticipated the surveillance of state officials who attempted to limit the production of these ritual offerings through accusations that traders were trying to pass the notes off as money in the marketplace.

Anxiety over spirit money being perceived as counterfeit money raises a question: Is the origin of money's symbolic value vested in the secular state? The eagerness with which people see spirit money as "counterfeit" can be attributed to something ghostly in modern national culture.[17] US dollars arrive through the transnational kinship networks of stretched families and are then symbolically offered to ancestral spirits and ghosts. Dollars in both exchanges constitute acts of remembering and serve as an instrument of collective memory that is unauthorized by the Socialist Republic of Vietnam.[18] Overseas Vietnamese compromise the official national ideology that "all the peoples of Vietnam are united within the boundaries of the country."[19] And their gifts of dollars compromise the state-based project of creating a unified territorial currency. Dollars as gifts to kin and spirits thus constitute an alternative form of remembrance to the state's commemoration of heroes.

When Mr. Thiệu picked up a few of the hell notes left for his friend, he did so as one might pick up a souvenir, a reminder of a specific place and time. Mr. Thiệu seldom received money from the United States, although his estranged wife and his three daughters lived in California. His wife had fled the country with their eldest daughter, telling him only that she was traveling to northern Vietnam to visit her parents. Years later, when she sponsored the other two daughters' move to the United States, he learned that she was in California. A few people were puzzled as to why Mr. Thiệu appeared so poor given that his family resided in the United States. Alienated both from his family and from the revolutionary Vietnamese state, Mr. Thiệu resembled a living ghost. By picking up those hell dollars, he collapsed the distinction between the two worlds. Bùi Giáng's money blurred the social boundaries that separate one form destined for the world of spirits from the form that circulates among the living. By taking the bills off the gravesite, Mr. Thiệu embodied the figure of a forsaken spirit (*cô hồn*), one for whom "fake" dollars could be transformed into real ones.

REMEMBER THE SOURCE

The Lunar New Year (Tết Nguyên Đán) is grounded in rituals that reenact the importance of returning "home" as the origin of value. Ancestors are invited to return for the three days of Tết, and since 1994 hundreds of thousands of people who reside in other countries have also returned for the Lunar New Year. Tết is also symbolized by the circulation of money. What then do popular rituals around money tell us about the source of its value?

In the days leading up to my first celebration of Tết in Ho Chi Minh City in 2001, commercial activities spilled into the streets. Vendors stocked their kiosks and stalls with goods to sell to workers, who earned a bonus month's pay for the holiday. Homeowners rushed to complete construction and renovation projects. The price of gold rose as people settled their debts before the year's end.

But on the first day of the year, the city streets were strangely empty. They had been swept clean of rubbish. The usually gridlocked traffic was light. Even the rows of vendors who had crowded the sidewalks in the weeks leading up to the holiday had vanished. The city's silence underscored that most people hailed from a place other than Ho Chi Minh City. It also marked a transformation in the place of money. Some people locked their cash in a drawer so as not to spend any money for the first few days. Other people refrained from sweeping their houses lest they also sweep out the good luck. If the preceding days emphasized commerce, then Tết itself signaled the disavowal of money's alien and alienating qualities through its conversion into a gift.

In Ho Chi Minh City, people greet each other with the popular saying "May you prosper" (*Phát tài*) and give small envelopes filled with cash. Popular greetings invoking material prosperity contrasted with long-standing customs in northern Vietnam, where outright wishes for prosperity at the New Year had been banned in the 1950s. People were instead encouraged to wish each other good health and a long life; even the gifts of money offered in red envelopes were encoded as celebrating the occasion for becoming a year older (*mừng tuổi*) rather than as a symbol of wealth. In Ho Chi Minh City, these gifts of "lucky money" were accompanied by the enormously popular greeting "Wishing you wealth and prosperity" (*Phát tài phát tướng*).

In the first days of the Lunar New Year, money circulated as a material sign to make evident the social hierarchy. Parents gave (*cho*) envelopes to their children; adult children presented (*tặng*) envelopes to their elderly parents; and people offered (*biếu*) money to temple spirits. These gifts of money did not circulate in only one direction. The head monk at a Buddhist temple in District Six printed out small slips of paper to give visitors, each with a fortune for the coming year. Each slip was affixed to a two-hundred-đồng note, a symbol of the multiple sources of blessings that were bestowed on the recipient. The monetary souvenirs from this temple were insignificant but nevertheless signaled money's privileged role as a sign of prosperity and blessing for the New Year. Despite the almost joyous celebration of these ritualized exchanges, state-sponsored campaign banners and billboards cautioned citizens to be frugal, a reminder that clashed with the powerful moral imperative to "remember the source."

Overseas Vietnamese, even when they do not return, are still included within this economy of remembrance. While the steady increase of returning Vietnamese demonstrates how strong the draw of the homeland is, many people participate in the New Year by remitting money to kin and near-kin.[20] Yet the concerns expressed by some Vietnamese Americans resembled those expressed by the secular state. One woman in her early twenties complained that although her family sent hundred-dollar bills to more than twenty relatives, the recipients were no longer satisfied with that gift. "It's only enough for one night out," she said, drawing on the city's reputation for nightlife to devalue the size of her gift. Another woman discovered on a return trip to Vietnam that the money she had remitted to buy her brother a motorbike for the Lunar New Year had been diverted to gambling. Both the official campaigns to encourage frugality and the vernacular criticisms of givers expose the public secret that these gifts are nothing more than money.

When making offerings at temples during the first days of the Lunar New Year, people will mingle "real" money with "spirit" money. The real money is usually a five-thousand- or ten-thousand-đồng note they place alongside the other offerings—stacks of spirit money, flowers, and fresh fruit. The amount of money on the plate is usually insignificant, a practice people explain by pointing out that larger amounts would attract thieves. After the incense has burned down, people considered the offerings to have been consecrated into "blessings" or lộc, the counter gifts from the spirits. People then burn the spirit money, but the other money, the real money, is theirs, money for keeping, not for spending. These notes are kept as physical representations of the blessings granted by the temple spirits—some people place these notes on their altars at home, while others gamble on the serial numbers on the notes. The paper money converted into lộc, I was told again and again, was "capital" (vốn) that had the power to beget more money. "Don't spend the note, don't lose it, don't give it away," people cautioned me, as if the note in its singularity represented the plentitude of the sign—pure money.

INCURRING DEBTS

Even more potent than lộc, the blessings from spirits, is borrowed money. Through popular religion, borrowed money is invested with supernatural powers. In this conversion, money conspires with popular religion to generate capital.

Two of the most popular temples that people visit to seek loans from temple deities are Bà Chúa Xứ (Lady of the Realm) in the town of Châu Đốc in southern Vietnam and Bà Chúa Kho (Goddess of the Treasury) outside Hanoi. The popularity of these temples extends far beyond their locality.

Television broadcasts and state-run newspapers report on the throngs of worshipers who visit these temples during the first lunar months of the new year to seek good fortune.

During the first three months of the lunar New Year, people flock to Bà Chúa Kho to ask for blessings from the temple spirit and to borrow money. While the temple draws its potency from its association with commerce, folklorist Nguyễn Minh San claims that the actual devotees of the Bà Chúa Kho include "cadres, Party members, and intellectuals," who arrive with the wish of becoming wealthy, or at least better off than they were before.[21] The sheer popularity of the temple in the 1990s led to the curtailing of offering spirit goods (for example, televisions, clothes, cars, and motorbikes). Temple keepers requested that devotees offer spirit money and paper votive ingots.[22] But even with such restrictions, the ashes of people's ritual offerings piled up behind the temple gates, the material remains of their gifts to the underworld.

On one occasion on which I accompanied people to the temple, no one in the group dared borrow money from the temple spirit for fear of incurring a debt they could not repay. They instead purchased flowers, fruit, and spirit money to offer to the temple deity in return for some blessings. One man expressed apprehension about the ritual procedures, fearing that he might accidentally incur a debt with the temple deity. He even backed away when a woman who worked on the temple grounds asked him to choose a piece of paper with a mimeographed fortune on it. He later confided to me that even though he had avoided borrowing money from the Lady, he still returned to the temple the following lunar year to return the Vietnamese đồng notes he had received. When I asked why he had done so, he replied that the temple deity would regard the gift as a loan and thus demand repayment from him.

Blessings are part of the perpetually regenerating flow that constitutes hierarchical relations between the living and the dead. Loans, by contrast, are contractual. People who borrow money from the Lady set the terms of the contract with the expectation that by the end of the lunar year, as is customary, the loan will be repaid in its entirety. One man explained that the ritual had procedures, "just like a bank." People who borrow money from the Lady hire a scribe to write a petition in "scholar's characters" (for example, Chinese characters) that lays out the loan's denomination and the terms of its repayment. Because it is symbolic, the debt can be denominated in any form, including real or spirit money. Once the contract specifying the terms of the loan and its repayment had been written, petitioners then climb the temple steps with their ritual offerings of cans of beer, steamed chicken, and stacks of hell dollars, including bills attached to sticks, in imitation of the popular tree with branches that signify "good fortune" (lộc). In these displays, the plentitude of the natural world is symbolized by a golden branch, which is ultimately replaced by images of US dollar bills as the source of abundance.

Borrowers thus initiate the loan and the terms of its repayment, in contrast to the debt-bond that structures filial obedience and thus can never be repaid. But many people believe there is still a risk that the temple deity might be dissatisfied with the terms of repayment, which compels them to give back far more than the original terms. Such acts of repayment constitute the temple's built structure, as the pillars on temple gates are engraved with the names of devotees who both repaid their loans and made significant donations to the temple itself. The temple stands as a monument to credit and debt relations associated with market expansion, its popularity a sign of demand for investment capital. Yet some people still refused to enter into a debt relation with the temple deity. Several women who earn their living by escorting urban dwellers through the ritual process claimed that they never borrowed money from the temple deity for fear that they would be considered "greedy." Unlike the blessings bestowed by temple deities and ancestors, these loans are unforgivable: "Even though there are no official documents that one has borrowed money, like other social contracts, almost no one dares escape this debt. Everyone is of the heart and mind that if they do not repay the Lady, then they will suffer losses."[23] Thus, the ritual served a pedagogical purpose by reminding people to adhere to the contractual terms of the loan.

On a hill overlooking Bà Chúa Kho stands another shrine. Several friends in their twenties and I followed a path that led out the temple gates, past the piles of ashes from the offerings, to a small shrine. The shrine sheltered an altar with a large white bust of Hồ Chí Minh. In front of this bust were offerings of fruit, flowers, and a few boxes of crackers. On a small table in front of the altar was a supply of joss sticks for worshippers to offer to Hồ Chí Minh's spirit.

When we arrived, the temple keeper was sweeping up fallen leaves from the yard in front of the shrine. We were the only visitors at that time, and he put down his broom to recount the story of why the shrine was built. It had been constructed by villagers in 1997, in the wake of urban dwellers from Hanoi flocking to the temple, and was a tribute to Hồ Chí Minh, who had twice visited the village. The first time had been to praise the villagers for their work in shooting down US aircraft during the war, and the second time had been to inspire them to rebuild the dam that had burst due to annual flooding.

As I stepped into the shrine, the others did not follow me but remained outside the temple. A friend whispered to me, "The temple could be fake," but this time she was not trembling, as she had in front of the altars at the temple down below. Another woman, an active member of the Communist Youth League, also looked uneasy in front of the temple. She too felt it could be a fake. Without another word, we then walked back down the hill to Bà Chúa Kho.

The shrine dedicated to Hồ Chí Minh did not attract the throngs of worshippers that crowded into the various halls of the temple below. The small shrine seemed out of place in an atmosphere that was thick with the smoke of incense and burning offerings. People's fear that the shrine might be "fake" invoked a public discourse about authenticity when religious practices were conflated with commodification, "buying and selling spirits" (*buôn thánh bán thần*). Official and popular discourses vacillate between promoting traditional customs (*phong tục truyền thống*) and condemning acts of superstition (*mê tín dị đoan*). Critics argue that the ritual offerings are wasteful, acts of destruction without adequate return, a specter of consumption that does not lead to social reproduction. The very category of "superstition" (*mê tín*, literally, "blind belief") conjures up a whole range of practices that invoke supernatural agency. These practices—including fortune telling, calling spirits, and mediumship—are at odds with official visions of the sovereign human subject, both modern and rational.

Popular religion thrives on power that cannot be fully incorporated into the state's representations of its own authority. By borrowing money from temple deities, people express the belief that capital is beholden neither to one's kin nor to the revolution. Hell dollars seem to elude the efforts of the state to harness the popular energies of devotion and the attention of the masses. By contrast, the images on Vietnamese money commemorate Hồ Chí Minh, the first president of the Democratic Republic of Vietnam. Standardized portraits of Hồ Chí Minh gaze out over spaces dedicated to state power—school classrooms, police stations, and hospitals. People carry the same portrait in their pockets on the state-issued currency. As an icon of the communist revolution in Vietnam, people do not call forth Hồ Chí Minh's image for personal gain. They turn instead to other sources for monetary blessings.

State officials and scholars agree that popular religious practices bolster Vietnam's national cultural heritage by invoking values such as filial piety and gratitude. Nguyễn Minh San argues that the customs around Bà Chúa Kho reinforce the cultural imperative to "remember the source." The debt to the fatherland, like that of parent and child, is represented as enduring and perpetually regenerating. Bà Chúa Kho stands as an alternative source for generating confidence and credit, an exemplary model in the Vietnamese Communist Party's attempt to foster a "rich people and strong country."[24] How is the practice of seeking blessings and incurring debts from saints reconciled with the state's goal of promoting economic development? As wealth in reform-era Vietnam is becoming increasingly privatized, the very forms of indebtedness are being transformed. These new forms include loans contracted with temple spirits. They are also embodied by a new form of exclusion figured by marginalized youth in Ho Chi Minh City.

LIVING GHOSTS

In the seventh lunar month, which usually falls in late August, people observe the Hungry Ghosts Festival. The festival is widely celebrated throughout Asia as a time when the gates of the underworld open, and the forsaken, hungry, and discontented ghosts wander the earth. These spirits, or *cô hồn*, in contrast to ancestors, are not commemorated within households but outside in the city streets, where people make offerings to these forsaken spirits, not to rescue or transform them but to draw on their wild and uncultivated potency.

The popularity of the festival is rooted in its importance to both ancestral cults and Buddhism.[25] During this month, the Buddhist festival Vu Lan is also celebrated on the eve of the full moon and commemorates the transformation of a forsaken ghost into a monk's own mother. In Ho Chi Minh City, festival attendees pin artificial white or red flowers to their shirts to signify whether their mother is living or dead, reaffirming the importance of filial piety over a more generalized abstract notion of community.

On the streets, the efficacy of the ritual lies in attracting a crowd, living representatives of the spirits who jostle each other as they wait restlessly for the offerings to "snatch." Households offer food as well as paper items, including currency, for these spirits. After lighting paper replicas of basic tunics and coins on fire, people toss out a little something for these living ghosts—pastel-colored candies, peanuts, pieces of sugar cane, oranges, or

4.4 Making offerings to hungry ghosts on the seventh lunar month, 2001.

money—to attract a crowd. Sometimes, though, offerings are made in parks as people gather for early morning exercise (fig 4.4).

In Ho Chi Minh City, the forsaken spirits are not represented by women. The meaning of *cô hồn* is ambiguous. People refer to ghosts that may be incorporated into kin structures as *cô bác* (aunts or uncles). By contrast, ancestors are referred to as *ông bà*, indicating a more direct line of descent.[26] While *cô* is an attribute meaning "lonely," "forsaken," or "abandoned," it also is a term of address used for women. These two meanings come together in the socially constructed category of the unmarried woman. The gendering of these figures in central Vietnam recognizes the burden women bear in biological and social reproduction, a burden that is not memorialized in the symbolic dominance of paternal ancestors and thus may return to haunt the living. In Ho Chi Minh City, forsaken spirits are packs of boys who roam the lanes and alleys of the city wearing nothing but shorts and sandals, in search of households that call forth these spirits. These living ghosts are not drawn by votive offerings. They are uninterested in the heaps of paper tunics and "tattered money" that will be burned in front of the house. The living ghosts (*cô hồn sống*) want only one thing—money.

During the seventh lunar month in 2001, I followed these living ghosts around District Five as they gathered in front of houses rumored to have prepared offerings for these hungry spirits. My guide was a resident of District

Five, where he had also taken to the streets in his youth. He recalled with pleasure the danger as grown men would shove the younger children aside to grab a few notes of money on the ground. In the 1970s and early 1980s, people tossed coins to the ground to summon these spirits. As the coins hit the ground, people claimed that the sound of the metal against the pavement attracted spirits. When I was there, coins were no longer in circulation. People instead tossed onto the ground small-denominated Vietnamese đồng notes folded into triangles. Unlike the red envelopes that circulated at Tết or the clean notes that people placed on altars, these notes were often ratty and torn, spare change that was almost worthless. The notes were folded up, disguising their denomination, but were nevertheless recognizable as money. It was the sight of this money being tossed into the street that lured these living ghosts.

Young and restless with anticipation for the moment when money would be tossed into the air, these living ghosts represented the wildness of money (fig. 4.5). As I watched, a man who laid out offerings on the street then disappeared into the house and reappeared in a window on the second floor. From a distance, he tossed out offerings to the living spirits gathered near the flames of the burning tunics and money that were now descending to the underworld. The flames of the bonfire leapt into the sky, illuminating a terrifying scene of arms and torsos grabbing the paper notes that fell from the

4.5   Boys and a few girls, the "living ghosts" of Ho Chi Minh City, chase after spare change, 2001.

sky. I had been standing behind my motorbike, my back to the wall, but as the boys scrambled to grab a few notes, they pushed my motorbike back, pinning me to the wall. After a few minutes, the money had all been snatched, and the boys unfolded the triangular notes, quickly counting up how much they had garnered. The thrill was not in the sum of money, which amounted to a few thousand đồng, but in the snatching and pushing others out of the way. The other offerings—nuts, tangerines, and cakes wrapped in banana leaves—were left in the street.

It was against this wild and undomesticated form of wealth, then, that the household needed to be secured. Worshipping forsaken spirits during the seventh month is still honored by some households, but the custom of tossing money into the streets is becoming increasingly rare as homeowners shut the gates of their homes to these living ghosts. One man shooed away the hordes of young boys, claiming that this year he would not toss real money into the streets but instead offer only spirit money. The boys lingered, uncertain whether he would really carry out this threat. All of a sudden, money floated in the air. The boys leapt up, grabbing pieces of paper that were floating down into the street. Then the rush of activity abruptly stopped. The money was indeed spirit money, of no use to these living ghosts. Someone had tossed the notes into the air to stir up the crowd. Slowly the packs of boys wandered in different directions in search of another house that still honored forsaken spirits.

Several household owners told me that they no longer carried out the custom of tossing money because earning money was now harder than it had been only a few years earlier. One household owner in District Five, standing in front of the open door to his house and exposing new models of motorbikes parked inside, told the young men to leave. He limited his offerings of goods—tunics and money—to the ghosts of the underworld. The denunciation of being "stingy" (kẹo) is a risk that accompanies the privatization of wealth. Those people who carried out the tradition insisted that the ritual expenditures were minimal and that the ritual brought amusement to otherwise bored youth. These were the proprietors of small businesses— hair salons, noodle shops, and cyclo services—that depended on the support of their neighbors. Those household owners who limited their sacrifices to "real" ghosts and their monetary offerings to "spirit" money demonstrated the ways in which monetary flows were creating new forms of connection and disconnection. The living ghosts—young men who roamed the streets of Ho Chi Minh City—embodied this form of disconnection as wealthier households closed their doors with the claim that they could no longer afford to offer real money.

As we have seen, spirit money and overseas remittances are vehicles for the expression of moral economies and the constitution of personhood in reform-era Vietnam. Both demonstrate money's power in creating and maintaining socially sanctioned forms of indebtedness. But even spirit money, and especially hell dollars, may be misrecognized as counterfeits. The work of distinguishing real money from spirit money, just like distinguishing us from them, requires cultural work. Failure to secure such distinctions leads to a collapse in the spheres of exchange that organize people's identity. Hell dollars thus stand as an ambiguous sign of the changing order of morality and the marketplace in Ho Chi Minh City. People gleefully expose these dollars as counterfeits and snatch them from gravesites. In the economy of national remembrance, the circulation of dollars is a highly valued sign that overturns imperial rank but violates the meaning of heroic sacrifice in the name of national independence.

FIVE

THE QUALITIES OF MONEY

O RDINARY people in Ho Chi Minh City have vastly increased the available supply of money by using different currencies. But even while they transact with multiple currencies, their concerns over the quality of money have paradoxically restricted its circulation. This has led not to a unified concept of "money" but rather to a reinforced popular understanding that gold, dollars, and đồng circulate as do other commodities in the marketplace.[1] And, as with other commodities, people evaluate these varieties in terms of their qualities, shaping their circulation and attracting the attention of bankers, government officials, and even development experts. People's concerns with the multiple qualities of money should not be construed as a failed project of modernity; these concerns instead show how people's experiences with money cannot wholly be explained by Western economic models. By qualifying money, people attempt to control how money counts in the context of market-driven reforms and expose how these everyday acts coincide with and even subvert attempts to govern the economy.[2]

A PILE OF CASH

In Ho Chi Minh City, the prices of apartments and houses are usually listed in gold bars. Prices for motorbikes, the privileged sign of mobility and personal autonomy, are advertised in dollars. But because prices are given in dollars or in gold does not mean that people transact only in these forms. The city's expanding marketplace has created new conditions for converting value across otherwise disparate money forms.

In 2002, I spent many evenings at a small motorbike shop owned by one of my neighbors, Mr. Hiếu. The shop was readily identified by the row of shiny new Honda motorbikes on the sidewalk. A weather-beaten Master-Card sign was posted on the wall of the shop. The owner claimed that no one had ever used a card to purchase a motorbike. His customers paid him in cash. By posting the logo on his shop, he was declaring his membership in a globalizing consumer economy in which the barriers imposed by different national currencies have been eliminated by digitized payment networks. In his own wallet, Mr. Hiếu carried several cards that resembled credit cards. While they were not linked to electronic payment networks, they did give him discounted prices at high-end hotels and supermarkets around the city.

Mr. Hiếu started his business as a truck driver in the late 1980s. On his routes, he brought used motorbikes across the border from Cambodia and Laos, which he then repaired and resold to city residents. By the mid-1990s, he was selling only new motorbikes. And while he had initially resisted selling Chinese motorbikes, knockoffs of the most popular Honda models, by 2002, his resistance had waned. Because Mr. Hiếu was so oriented to the status conferred by imported goods, I was surprised at how indifferent he was to the medium of payment.

One evening a young man and young woman came into the shop to settle payment for a new motorbike. The man had stopped by earlier in the afternoon and chosen a Honda model for the price of forty-five million đồng, about three thousand US dollars. The woman carried a black plastic bag, from which she took several stacks of 100,000-đồng notes. From the pocket of his jean shorts, the man pulled two gold bars issued by the Saigon Jewelry Company and several hundred-dollar bills. The couple then put the pile of paper money and gold on Mr. Hiếu's desk in the middle of his small showroom.

Mr. Hiếu reminded his customer of the price they had agreed upon in Vietnamese đồng. Without calling attention to the pile on his desk, he picked up the telephone to inquire about the day's exchange rate. He did not inform his customers of the exchange rate, foreclosing an opportunity for further negotiation. He then tapped the gold bars on his desk, fingered the hundred dollar bills, and held both the bars and the hundred-dollar bills up to the light. He pulled out a bill and noted wryly that the edges were burned. He then placed the stacks of Vietnamese đồng in an electric money counter.

As Mr. Hiếu calculated and converted value across these three monetary forms, the young man glanced nervously around the showroom. He pointed to the sleek mobile phone on the desk. "How much?" he asked. He then glanced toward the wall, where another bike was suspended above the model he was purchasing. Mr. Hiếu acknowledged the young man's desire by quoting a price several times higher than for the model he had selected earlier that afternoon. "Choose a color," Mr. Hiếu told the young man with a tone of impatience as he filled out the registration paperwork and one of his employees filled the motorbike's tires with air. After the man and women drove off on their new motorbike, I asked Mr. Hiếu why he hadn't minded the different currency forms. He shrugged and said that it was all just money.

QUALITIES OF CASH

Consumers are active agents who do not merely purchase products but also determine the value of products, generating an "economy of qualities."[3] These qualities often disrupt prevailing regimes of value in capitalist economies, in which notions of authenticity are derived largely in relation to brand cultures. Economies of quality are especially visible in developing countries such as Vietnam, where consumers have not yet been disciplined by branding as a form of authentication.[4] People instead assess branded goods according to different matrices of value that reflect their rapid exposure to the global consumer economy. The Honda brand, for example, did not secure value for Vietnamese consumers who instead qualified the vehicles based on their serial numbers, which identified whether a particular motorbike had been manufactured in Japan, Thailand, or China. Motorbikes produced in Japan, for example, were more highly valued than identically branded objects produced in China or Vietnam, at least in 2002. By privileging the place of production rather than the brand itself, Vietnamese consumers drew on their local knowledge of production and position in the global economy.

People in Ho Chi Minh City are likewise attentive to the different currencies in circulation. Currency exchange booths are plentiful in Ho Chi Minh City. Newspapers and evening television reports announce the đồng's daily exchange rate in US dollars, gold, and even euros. Banks display their rates on digital screens, and gold shops post their prices on large whiteboards facing the street. But these pricing mechanisms function as technologies of abstraction that remove these objects of value from their "social and practical contexts."[5] For many people in Ho Chi Minh City, such contexts are indispensable for establishing confidence and trust. Far from displaying the coherence of money, the visibility of these exchange rates instead underscores its fluctuations.

Most people prefer to buy and sell currencies in outside markets rather than in the formal and highly regulated banks. One such exchange I regularly visited was located in Bến Thành marketplace, one of Ho Chi Minh

City's landmarks and a popular destination for tourists. The small booth was in a stall tucked among other stalls, the shelves bare except for a few bottles of household cleaner and insect spray. The customers who lined up to exchange currencies there were not foreigners but other vendors. Every vendor I talked to agreed that the woman who operated the booth sold money "at the right price." Her credibility, however, was personal, not bureaucratic; it did not extend beyond the specific social space where she worked. When I brought a friend who needed to purchase German marks to her stall, he was later chastised by his mother and older sisters. Why, they asked, hadn't he contacted a money dealer through his family's network? What if he had been given counterfeit bills and had landed in jail on his trip to Germany?

Scholarly understandings have emphasized money's "purely quantitative quality."[6] Vietnamese consumers and vendors actively qualify that which is said to be defined *only* by quantity. In this regard, money does not circulate as a token of general trust that allows social interactions to proceed simply and confidently. People do not routinely accept the money handed them; they rely on their own judgment regarding the credibility of particular notes. The qualities of cash—its appearance, its feel, even its denomination—shape people's confidence in its performance as money. Upon receiving cash, sellers will rub the notes between their fingers, verifying the note by its feel, or hold it up to the light to see if the watermark of Hồ Chí Minh's portrait is crisp or blurred. Some vendors reject paper notes that have been taped or burned along the edges, handing them back to the buyer. When receiving change, buyers will quickly count the cash they receive, pulling out notes that appear worn or tattered for possible rejection.

Notes that have been in circulation for a few months have creases down the middle from being constantly folded and unfolded. People count notes by grouping them in stacks of nine and then folding the tenth note down the middle and tucking it over the rest. This technique allows people to count each stack, and then the number in each stack, sometimes pulling out a note they find objectionable and requesting another one. Other people commented on the damp, limp notes that are passed from hand to hand. Many people carry their money close to their bodies—in the rolls of their pants, in envelopes tucked into their shirts, or in scarves they clutch tightly as they make their rounds at the market. Wearing money close to one's body is a sensible precaution against pickpockets and purse snatchers. But when people purchase something, the notes are transformed into a profane substance, something to be discarded rather than held closely. People toss notes carelessly to vendors, even onto pieces of raw meat and fish displayed in the markets. "Never give a large bill to the woman who sells fish sauce," was one piece of advice I received. The woman insisted that the odor of the sauce soaks into the note, so it is better to give that vendor the correct change. By observing how people handle money, a woman in Ho Chi Minh City suggested, one can tell whether they value money or not. But such an equation is difficult to make in a city where many people have lived through periods of deprivation and where cash itself is still so highly valued.

Just what is at stake in these everyday inspections is puzzling. After all, a ten-thousand-đồng note that shows wear does not depreciate to eight thousand đồng, just as a worn dollar bill is not devalued to eighty cents. These inspections recall the crisis of confidence sparked by "clipped coins" in previous centuries. When coins circulated as commodity money and were valued by the weight and purity of their material substance, people would shave or clip bits off the coin, thus reducing its actual weight relative to its assigned value. In an effort to resolve the crisis, state authorities issued nominal or representational currency. Representational currency emphasized money's symbolic function over its material substance. Even as those coins and later notes become worn, tattered, or torn, their inscribed value remains constant.

In Vietnamese marketplaces, however, measurements are still subject to negotiation. Sellers often settle disputes over price by tossing in an onion or a bunch of fresh herbs. And they sometimes refuse notes offered in payment by their customers. Supermarkets, by contrast, provide a different experience for consumers. Vegetables and fruit are often wrapped tightly in plastic, their fixed prices displayed openly on the cellophane.[7] Yet even supermarkets cannot resolve the recurrent problem of providing correct change. Cashiers often run out of change and substitute a stick of chewing gum or a piece of candy in place of a few hundred đồng.

Currency inspections are also not limited to markets. The State Bank of Vietnam also participates in this economy of qualities. As late as 2002, the bank did not have any procedures for replenishing the physical stock of paper notes, which reinforced the popular conception that the material quality of money mattered. Posters displayed enlarged photographs of Vietnamese paper notes that were "below standard," including images of those that were ripped, taped together, written on, burned, or even chewed by rats. Substandard notes, the poster instructed, should be withdrawn from circulation; below-standard currency, although not counterfeit, had through constant circulation exhausted its credibility. But people were not instructed about what to do should they find themselves holding a note they suspected to be below standard or counterfeit. Consequently, people in Ho Chi Minh City monitored their own money supply to ensure that what they accepted would in turn be acceptable to someone else. Through these routine inspections, people called into question the credibility of the currency structure itself, rendering visible the "ineffable presence of these fetish objects."[8]

These inspections undermine a common assertion about money and modernity, namely that money circulates as an almost Durkheimian embodiment of religious faith in society itself. Georg Simmel, in his sociological treatise *The Philosophy of Money*, likewise described money as an objective manifestation of faith in the sociopolitical organization and order.[9] Inspections of currency call into question that faith. Those worn, ripped, and torn notes have not exhausted their credibility as representations of money; they signal the exhausted credibility in the social order that presumably guarantees their validity.

COUNTERFEITS

In 2002, people inspected fifty-thousand-đồng notes carefully to ensure that the notes they accepted did not have one of the telltale signs of counterfeiting. Some fifty-thousand-đồng notes were declared counterfeit because the word "đồng" was missing a hatch mark on the letter "d," turning "đồng" into "dồng." A man with close ties to the State Bank suggested to me that those notes were not actually counterfeits but simply misprints. The problem, he suggested, was not criminal intent but bureaucratic negligence.

This public concern about below-standard and counterfeit currency in circulation contrasts with capitalist societies, in which the money supply is constantly monitored by financial institutions. In these societies, the physical stock of currency is replenished and renewed in ritualized procedures that underwrite people's confidence in money, as described in chapter 1. Such a system, however, is premised on cash reentering the banking system, where it is monitored for its physical qualities and then multiplied through the production of credit money. In Ho Chi Minh City, people draw on the power to monitor currency in their everyday transactions. By flipping through stacks of paper money, pulling out unacceptable notes, and demanding substitute notes of equal value but better quality, people do not demonstrate the taken-for-granted trust so often ascribed to representational currency.

How people handle notes they suspect are counterfeit depends on their location within the national economy. A clerk at a consulate in Ho Chi Minh City described how he had withdrawn his salary from a bank and then purchased a ticket to Saigon. When the sales agent informed him that two notes were unacceptable, he then "threw them away." I pressed him to explain what he meant by "throwing them away," and he described how he spent them in a nightclub where no one would inspect them closely. By contrast, a man born in Saigon who had served with the Army of the Republic of Vietnam and later worked repairing small appliances received a fifty-thousand-đồng note in payment for fixing a small electronic fan for thirty thousand đồng. He gave the man a twenty-thousand-đồng note in change and a working fan. Later, when he tried to purchase something, he realized that the note was counterfeit. He also "threw the note away," because he feared that the police would accuse him of counterfeiting.

Paper currency that passes from one hand to another is "true" in the sense that it works as money.[10] Yet people's fears about being accused of counterfeiting reinforces popular perceptions that some citizens are recognized as worthy subjects and others are accused of being fakes. The epithet *ngụy quyền*, often translated as "puppet government," circulated as a slogan to disparage the legitimacy of the Republic of Vietnam. The anxiety of being misrecognized lingered as the older man whose age and accent linked him to pre-1975 Saigon worried that he would be accused of having produced the counterfeit bill. By contrast, the younger man from Hanoi passed the note—albeit in darkened circumstances, but unafraid that the note's suspect quality would rub off on him.

With the expanding marketplace, the problem of confidence in the money supply has become increasingly apparent. In the moment a seller or buyer refuses to accept a note because of its quality, the note loses its "cover," its social force to represent money. But not even technology can definitively establish which currency objects are real and which are fake. Some vendors depend on machines to assess the authenticity of particular notes. These machines, however, utter incomprehensive sentences. On one occasion, when I asked the teller what the machine had just said, she replied that although she didn't understand the words because they were in Chinese, she was sure that the machine had announced that it had detected a counterfeit bill.

People in the city pay attention to the appearance of money in other ways as well. The quality of money is even more pronounced in transactions in which cash rejuvenates social relations and reaffirms hierarchies through gifting practices. In these exchanges, people's concerns with the quality of money do not diminish. Gifts of money, people insist, should possess a particular quality: newness.

NEW MONEY

In the marketplace, people are as wary of cash as they are of other commodities. But cash in Ho Chi Minh City is not limited to the marketplace. People incorporate cash into ritual and ceremonial exchanges, momentarily personalizing currency by transforming it into a gift. Whether such gifts are denominated in dollars or đồng, most people insist that they possess the quality of newness.

In the weeks leading up to the new year, people clean out their houses, and buy new clothes and other consumer goods. They also distribute "new money," often lavishly. "New money" refers to crisp, new bills that do not show signs of wear. Like flowers in bloom, new money signifies potentiality and prosperity. The flow of new money begins before the end of the year. Employees receive their year-end bonuses in the form of new notes. People also trade old notes for new ones at the banks. During the first days of Tết, people tuck new notes into red envelopes and pass them out as tokens of good luck. People emphasize the importance of offering new money to temple spirits, calling attention to the appearance of the paper notes rather than their objective value.

As the issuer of new money, the State Bank of Vietnam plays a role in this popular practice. In 2002, in anticipation of the new year, I went to the bank with old notes, as I had done the year before. Newspapers the year before had announced that the banks were stocked with new money in preparation for the new year so that people could exchange old notes for new ones. When I arrived at the bank, the teller informed me that no new notes had been issued in Ho Chi Minh City. She pointed to a sign posted by her window announcing that the State Bank of Vietnam had issued no new money in Ho Chi Minh City after it had determined that the city had "harvested" too much money during the year. No new currency, other than the drab two-thousand-đồng note, would be issued. The bank teller confided that the printing presses in Ho Chi Minh City had been sent up to Hanoi. Money in Ho Chi Minh City was therefore both abundant and scarce.

As word of the State Bank's decision not to issue new money for Tết spread throughout the city, people resigned themselves to giving old notes instead of new ones. They reassessed the quality of newness with different calculations. One woman, who had given her son several green 100,000-đồng notes in 2001, decided instead to give him a single red 10,000-đồng note. Once the notes were stripped of their newness, she saw the objective value and calculated that she had been giving her son too much money. And giving him too much money, she reasoned, was dangerous because she did not know how he would spend it. A man in his fifties, by contrast, reckoned that because everyone wanted money, the ritual required only that the traditional red envelope be new. These calculations revealed that the quality of newness was merely a guise that distracted both the giver and receiver from the objective value of the exchange.

Concealing money in envelopes to diminish the objective value of a gift is a common strategy that people use to convert commodities into gifts. These strategies momentarily obscure the vectors of calculation that underlie the economies of obligation and recognition.[11] In Japan, people also use qualities of newness to encode the significance of monetary gifts. Life-cycle events such as weddings and births are signified by giving new bills lying face up; funerals are marked by gifts of crumpled money lying face down.[12] By wrapping money in an envelope or dressing it as new, money's objective value is covered over.

In Ho Chi Minh City, the very word "envelope" (*phong bì*) has since become a euphemism for monetary transactions. The envelope both conceals and reveals—everyone knows money is inside the envelope, and the only remaining question is how much. The gift may be an addressed envelope with a wedding invitation, a red envelope with gold embossing given at Tết, or simply a small piece of paper quickly tucked over some cash just before being pressed into the hand or pocket of the recipient. In the popular media, however, the practice of gift giving is lampooned to highlight the ironies of how sociality has become saturated with money.[13] Cartoons depict newly married couples dressed in the familiar envelope with red and blue margins, or bosses accepting envelopes from their employees. Cash transactions are culturally masked as gifts, exposing the calculative dimensions of a gift economy.

Yet the envelope has another function. The temporal delay that inaugurates a transaction as a gift rather than a payment also shields the currency from immediate inspection. When people receive money as a gift, they rarely count it on the spot or inspect the quality of the notes. No one relates stories of receiving counterfeit notes as a gift or rejects the notes she or he receives and demands cleaner ones. That people did not tell me such stories was not, of course, evidence that people were not worried about receiving counterfeit notes. It merely suggests that discourses of counterfeiting belong to the marketplace.

CASH AND MOBILITY

How people handle cash challenges scholarly understandings of money that have largely been conceived within already capitalized societies. Economists, for example, assume that, for fiduciary currencies such as the Vietnamese đồng and the US dollar, the quality that matters is quantity. As we have seen, the qualities people attribute to money, while unrelated to its nominal value, still structure the circuits through which money moves. These evaluations demonstrate the limits of Western economic models premised on the paradigmatic model of a singular, unified monetary system. Everyday habits of handling money cannot be explained by the disciplinary powers of banking and the state in the West.[14]

In Ho Chi Minh City, people prefer cash. People keep cash "outside" state-owned financial institutions, thus restricting the creation of credit money, a constitutive element of capitalism. People rely on alternative payment networks, sources of credit, and forms of debt that are not validated by monetary authorities. While these alternatives are not backed by institutionalized guarantees, they defy the assertion that cash settles accounts only in the here and now. People raise money through a variety of credit schemes, including employee pools and rotating credit associations, or *hụi*, as a social forum for generating cash. Participants in a pool bid on the right to collect a given pot of money. Ideally, each participant will collect the pot once during the round, but these credit associations are not institutionalized, so some participants might disappear before the *hụi* line is complete.

But there are costs to the city's cash-and-carry economy. The emphasis on cash, for example, extracts a price in terms of delivering and collecting payments. In the afternoon, the city streets are crowded as people rush home or deliver payments for goods delivered earlier in the morning. Mr. Minh owns a small noodle shop in District Eight. In the late afternoon, he drives his blue Honda Cub motorbike around the central districts of the city to collect payment from small shops. I accompanied him on his route at times. When we would arrive at the various corner shops, he would collect the payment without much discussion. His route was the same every day. He had a list of names written in pencil in a small notebook and collected payments entirely in cash. Mr. Minh entrusted his payment system to his own labor and an old but reliable Honda Cub. In so doing, he showed how the city's cash economy restricted the expansion and circulation of monetary value even as it compelled people to move.

Mrs. Chín, whom I introduced in chapter 2, depended on personal relations to purchase pork on credit and then repay when she appeared in the marketplace the following day. Her reputation in the marketplace had been the parting gift of a friend who had emigrated to Canada after introducing Mrs. Chín to her former customers and acquainting her with the wholesale market. Since then, Mrs. Chín has relied on extended payments. She provides her customers with pork in the morning, and in the late afternoon they return with their payments. Mrs. Chín and her two daughters rarely take note of who has paid. They instead collect the cash receipts in a tin can. In the evening, they dump the cash on the floor, where they sort the bills into denominations, which are easily identifiable by their different colors. They then count the piles using the conventional method of bundling nine notes marked by a tenth note folded in half. Like many other women who make their living in the marketplace, Mrs. Chín counts the bundles by thumbing through stacks at an astonishing speed. The following morning, when Mrs. Chín returns to the pork market, she pays for her previous day's purchase.

Both Mr. Minh and Mrs. Chín's payment networks are entirely cash based. While their transactions are profit oriented, they rely on personal, rather than institutional, relations of credit to maintain their businesses. It is the interval of time, sometimes half a day and other times a week, that maintains these ongoing relations of trust and obligation, keeping the city's transactional networks in motion and its streets congested with traffic. Yet these daily errands depend on moving around the city to settle debts. This physical labor is compounded by the đồng's relatively low value in the city's markets. People not only carry around thick stacks of đồng notes but spend much time counting those notes. The State Bank of Vietnam has periodically responded to the quality of quantity by introducing đồng notes of ever-higher value.

BIG MONEY

In Ho Chi Minh City's widespread cash economy, denomination itself is a quality that matters. The value of the Vietnamese đồng, as we have seen, is measured in relation to its "alternative," the US dollar, but also in terms of its purchasing power in Ho Chi Minh City's rapidly expanding consumer market. Until September 2000, the largest note in circulation was the 50,000-đồng note (approximately US$3.35). People relied on shorthand ways to refer to price. When purchasing petrol for their motorbikes, people often said "ten đồng" or "five đồng," dropping the "thousand." Prices in the thousands or even millions underscored the currency's low value in the city's marketplace.

The đồng's low exchange value but high face value is a residue of devaluation. In 1985, the five-hundred-đồng note was the largest note in circulation. Twenty years later, a five-hundred-đồng note could buy a glass of iced tea at a streetside food stall in Ho Chi Minh City. The one-đồng notes, now divested of their exchange value, are sold as curios and collectibles in souvenir shops. Even the hundred-đồng note has dropped out of circulation in the city, and most people dismiss the two-hundred-đồng note as something to spend only in the countryside.

Transacting with Vietnamese currency in any significant amount has entailed handling large stacks of notes. Even in the mass media, articles about the currency are usually accompanied by photographs of bank tellers counting piles of đồng notes, emphasizing the currency's materiality. In an effort to address this problem, the State Bank of Vietnam issued a 100,000-đồng note (US$6.70) in 2000. The series was printed with the year "1994," which sparked speculation that the note had been printed in 1994 but withheld from circulation for fear of triggering inflation.

Most people were first introduced to the 100,000-đồng note as an enormous image on a poster in a bank or in newspaper ads accompanied by descriptions of its features: its dimensions, color, and various security features. It was weeks before I saw an actual note in circulation. The first time was with Mr. Hiếu, the motorbike dealer, who pulled out his wallet to show me several of the bills. A woman selling lottery tickets, just as curious about the notes as I was, approached us. Mr. Hiếu then held out one of the bills and offered to buy five lottery tickets at two thousand đồng each. The woman's face fell; her curiosity turned into shock as she realized she would have to produce change for the transaction. She went around to people sitting at the food stalls to see if anyone had change for a 100,000-đồng note. No one did. The dealer kept his 100,000-đồng note, and I was left paying for the lottery tickets with my small change.

People were initially reluctant to use the supersize notes. The 100,000-đồng note was simply too much money for most streetside purchases. Vendors or taxi drivers who accepted the notes often had to find other people with change, which took time and restricted the circulation of money. Handling these notes in public also risked displaying too much economic power. Some people relied on bargaining strategies in which they claimed to have little money, a claim that would be called in doubt by pulling out a 100,000-đồng note. In other cases, transactions with the note often produced a remainder. People nearby might beg for change, making moral claims on the remainder. For this reason, beggars often gathered in spaces where such money appeared—petrol stations, parking lots, and even temples.

The circulation of "big money" exposed its disciplinary powers in the city's cash economy. In some spaces of the city, big money indicated status and power. Mr. Hiếu, for example, displayed the 100,000-đồng notes in his wallet while also offering to purchase lottery tickets, a gesture that demonstrated that he not only possessed big money but that he could also afford to give it away. Other residents rarely saw a 100,000-đồng note. And when they did, the high-value notes often compelled them to engage in additional labor to acquire change for their customer.

But within two years, not even the 100,000-đồng note satisfied Ho Chi Minh City's expanding marketplace.

PLASTIC MONEY

The introduction of the 100,000-đồng note in 2000 did not resolve the problem of confidence in the national currency. Within a few months of its introduction, state-run newspapers carried stories about counterfeit notes in circulation. Some observers called for the State Bank to produce a higher-quality đồng note, one that would use the latest technologies to guarantee its authenticity and preserve its value. The spectrum of security devices included watermarks, holograms, and other elaborate techniques used by central banks to preserve the artifice of state-issued currencies. Without these additional security measures, experts warned, Vietnamese currency would not meet the demands of the marketplace.

On December 7, 2003, the State Bank of Vietnam again issued new money. The new money included two newly designed notes, a 50,000-đồng note and a 500,000-đồng note. This time, the newly issued money was made of tear-proof polymer deemed appropriate for a national economy in which more than half of all transactions were in cash. The polymer notes were promoted as being almost indestructible. They did not tear easily, and so could hold up even to the popular practice of folding a note in half to mark a bundle of ten notes. Economists heralded the new notes as facilitating economic growth in Vietnamese terms, and journalists praised them as evidence of the State Bank's effort to improve the quality of Vietnamese currency.

Most of the people I talked to in December 2003 were perplexed, even anxious, about the side effects of the new currency on the *value* of the Vietnamese đồng. The newly issued 500,000-đồng note was a Vietnamese version of "big money," but many people feared it summed up too much economic value given the average monthly salary. One man pointed out that the newly issued note was equal to his monthly salary. "I'll only receive one note," he lamented, which in his billfold seemed an inadequate representation of his labor. The 500,000-đồng note renewed people's fears of inflation. The escalating face value of paper money—first the 100,000-đồng note, and then the 500,000-đồng note—reminded people of the inflation of the late 1980s. At that time, soon after the State Bank had issued higher denominations, the low-value đồng notes had fallen out of circulation once they were rejected by vendors as worthless.

This time when the State Bank issued the new 500,000-đồng note, it also issued coins in three different denominations. The coins were intended to offset the shock of the 500,000-đồng note. Coins can remain in circulation far longer than paper, so the value of these coins suggested a symbolic effort to protect the value of the Vietnamese đồng. These coins, including the new but almost insignificant two-hundred-đồng coin, anticipated the use of vending machines and other self-service devices. In spite of their heft and shiny appearance, people regarded the coins, especially the two-hundred-đồng coin, as worthless. "What will it buy?" people asked as they held the new coin, weighing the worth of the coin against its heft in their pocket.

While people expressed their concerns, the introduction of the new currency was a well-attended and talked-about event. People lined up at banks to trade their old Vietnamese notes for the new polymer notes and coins. As I stood in a line to exchange my money, the manager of the bank approached me to ask how much money I wanted to exchange, led me into a glass-enclosed office, and offered to let me purchase as much new money as I wanted. As I was walking toward the office, one of the bank's security guards whispered a request that I exchange money for him. The bank's supply of coins was limited, he explained, and might run out before he had a chance to get a collection of the newly issued coins for himself.

By the end of that week, many banks had experienced a run on their stock of new money. Most no longer had any more plastic money or coins to exchange. The bills and coins did not immediately appear in circulation, at least not in market transactions. People instead passed the new notes and coins out as curios and gifts. A few people suggested that they would send the coins abroad as gifts to family members. Others accumulated the polymer notes in anticipation of the upcoming Lunar New Year celebration.

When I returned to Ho Chi Minh City in 2007, people were using the coins but pointed out the difficulties in managing the different substances of money. The coins were inconvenient and easy to lose. But it was the new bills—the 200,000-đồng note and the 500,000-đồng note—that manifested the growing inequality exposed by cash. Some people regularly transacted with 200,000-đồng notes, especially people who received their salaries through automatic teller-machine withdrawals. But other people told me that they rarely saw, much less handled, the notes. The physical money in circulation signaled more than economic value; it also indexed growing inequality.

In 2007, the State Bank announced that in August the old 100,000-đồng and 50,000-đồng notes made of paper would be withdrawn from circulation and only the newly issued polymer notes would be accepted. Within days, some vendors refused to accept the old bills. The State Bank responded with edicts stating that the old notes were still current and that not accepting them violated state law.

ENROLLING BANK CUSTOMERS

Ordinary people often carry significant quantities of cash. These stacks of currency cannot fit in one's pocket, the place where Karl Marx argued that people try to turn the social power of money into private power.[15] People instead carry their bulky cash in their handbags, backpacks, and satchels, which contributes to widespread anxiety about theft and purse snatchings. On several occasions, my handbag's strap was cut as I was riding on a motorbike. When I described the events to Vietnamese acquaintances, several had similar stories to tell. But while I lost an amount of money equivalent to twenty to thirty dollars, they lost sums in the thousands of dollars.

Experts and government officials are likewise concerned with the high percentage of cash transactions. International lenders such as the International Monetary Fund and the World Bank have urged the Vietnamese government to create new payment systems for ensuring that monetary transactions are ordered and legible. Relying on cash, they argue, encourages corruption, slows down the payment system, and restricts economic growth. The predominance of cash transactions reinforces Vietnam's status as a less-developed nation, easily corrupted by the unregulated circulation of money in the country's expanding economy. Cash, recast as loose, undetermined, unregulated, and traceless, has become a target for regulation in the country's anticorruption drive. But there are a number of obstacles to bringing outside money or cash into the institutional system of banked payments, namely popular mistrust of the state banking sector.

Like other cities in Asia, Ho Chi Minh City is situated both at the center and at the margins of the financial world, a fact that is evident in the number of global banks that have established branches in the city. The return of Hong Kong Shanghai Banking Corporation in Ho Chi Minh City in 1995, for example, triumphantly signaled the country's integration into the global capitalist economy. Its headquarters in the city now stand as one of the city's distinctive landmarks. But most Vietnamese citizens were prohibited from opening accounts at these institutions until quite recently.

Only in the mid-1990s were retail-oriented banks established for Vietnamese citizens. These banks offered financial services to consumers, including payment instruments such as debit cards that anticipated new consumption patterns. Economists and bankers regard Vietnam as one of Asia's most "underbanked economies," a reference to the low percentage of the population that regularly uses bank services. In Thailand, 75 percent of the population is banked, but in Vietnam only 15 percent of the population is estimated to have an account, and only 10 percent actively use those accounts.[16] These figures do not, of course, account for people's participation in informal networks of credit based on kinship or place-based relations. But they have helped spur the growth of both domestic and foreign consumer and retail banking institutions, evident in Ho Chi Minh City, where more than eighty banks have established branches.[17]

One of these retail banks is the Asia Commercial Bank, widely known by its acronym, ACB. Despite its English title, the bank is not a foreign-owned bank but a joint-stock bank headquartered in Ho Chi Minh City. It heavily promotes its own bank cards, in association with a chain of supermarkets and a fleet of taxis, thus coupling new forms of payment and mobility. Many of its advertisements make reference to the global consumer economy in which shopping is not a daily errand but a source of pleasure and an expression of selfhood.[18] While these bank cards appear to offer Vietnamese citizens membership in a globalized economy, they are not linked to global payment systems; they remain tethered to a local economy in which cash is ultimately the means of settling debt.

Private domestic banks now offer Vietnamese citizens an alternative to state-owned banking. They woo new customers by offering competitive rates for gold, US dollars, euros, and Vietnamese đồng deposits. They also advertise lotteries or "lucky draws" for high-status consumer goods such as televisions and motorbikes to attract domestic savers into the banking system. But what banks have required is a way to connect consumers to their cash. Automated Teller Machines (ATMs) provided a link to connect consumers with their cash via the banking sector by promising twenty-four-hours-a-day secure access.

The first international ATM was installed by the Hong Kong Shanghai Banking Corporation (HSBC) in Ho Chi Minh City in 1996. Vietcombank had installed two ATMs in Ho Chi Minh City in 1994, but the machines could be used only by customers of that bank. The people I interviewed in 2003 still recalled that the Vietcombank machines were chronically out of order or out of cash. The ATMs installed by HSBC, by contrast, dispensed both US dollars and the Vietnamese currency, until the State Bank required that all ATMs dispense only the national currency. Even as late as 2001, the

5.1   A cluster of ATMs in Ho Chi Minh City, 2007.

only functional ATMs in Hanoi, the capital city of Vietnam, belonged to foreign-owned banks.[19]

When I returned to Ho Chi Minh City in 2007, I was surprised by the sheer number of ATMs around the city (fig. 5.1). The total number of machines was estimated to be 3,800 at the time, and almost 6.5 million cards had been issued. By 2010, the number of machines had tripled to 10,200, while over 23 million cards had been issued.[20] Most of the machines, however, were clustered in urban centers around major supermarkets and department stores, and outside bank branches.

The increasing number of ATMs was a governing strategy to create a banked payment system premised on the order of advanced capitalist societies. The machines were advertised in promotional literature and the mass media as a convenient portal to a global consumer economy. Capitalist societies were constructed as an idealized model against which the pathologies of Vietnam as a less-developed nation could be understood. Yet people seemed to respond to the ATMs favorably. Several people even claimed that household robberies were on the decline because people no longer had to store their money at home. One man pulled out several ATM cards, dexterously explaining how he used the cards to separate and encode different circuits of exchange—one card to access his salary, and another for receiving money sent from family members living outside Vietnam. Not everyone was eligible for this new form of economic subjectivity. Some employees at municipal agencies were paid irregularly, depending on the project, unlike employees at foreign firms, who had regular salaries that were deposited in bank accounts. The distinction between government and foreign employer began to change.

The Vietnamese state passed a decree in 2007 that required state employees and pensioners to receive their payments through bank deposits.[21] The state-sponsored decree was a key event in turning "unbanked" citizens into "banked" customers (fig. 5.2) by enrolling citizens in *domestic* banks as a postreform strategy for governing the Vietnamese economy. While this campaign of "banking the unbanked" appeared to be premised on financial inclusion, the decree was part of a broader governing strategy to ensure that state transactions were legible, traceable, and legitimate. The directive was initially limited to Hanoi, Ho Chi Minh City, and several other major cities, with the goal of establishing twenty million personal bank accounts and reducing cash payments to 18 percent. While ATMs appealed to a global imaginary, they were still entrenched in a specific economic culture. Within

5.2　A newly chartered bank in Ho Chi Minh City advertises YouHouse and YouCar, "for a happy way of life," 2007.

only a few weeks of implementing this policy, the ATM was transformed from a venue of readily accessible cash to a technological failure.

SORRY, OUT OF CASH

Like the 100,000-đồng note, ATMs were introduced to residents through the state-run media. Newspapers carried stories linking the ATM to the values of capitalism. In the months leading up to 2008, ATMs were promoted as quick, secure, and convenient ways of accessing cash. Machines were set up in supermarkets and outside banks around Ho Chi Minh City. People began to line up in front of the machines to withdraw cash shortly before the Lunar New Year. Within weeks, the heavily promoted ATM was no longer lauded as a machine of convenience; it was ridiculed as a throwback to the subsidized era.

The subject of discourse around the machines soon shifted to the users' frustrations. People waited in long lines to try to access their funds from a machine that was either broken or out of cash. The meaning of "ATM" was transformed into a new moniker, *à thấy mệt*, or "so damn tired." These complaints exposed that ATMs were still mired in their domestic monetary context: people waited in long lines only to find the machines were empty. The ATM, which had once appealed to the desires of global economic integration, now instead left people standing in front of a screen that read "out of cash."

The push to get people to use ATMs in Ho Chi Minh City resembled the "top-down model" of campaigns in China. In her ethnography of the Shanghai stock market, anthropologist Ellen Hertz argues that these campaigns are often referred to as "waves," in order to generate the appearance of popular acceptance.[22] This model can be applied to the Vietnamese government's decree to enroll civil servants and pensioners into the domestic banking sector. The people who lined up to withdraw cash from ATMs in the first months of 2008 did not do so as willing consumers; they had been conscripted as bank customers. Expanding the retail banking sector was achieved not by consumer choice but rather by state decree.

The overall number of ATMs in Ho Chi Minh City in 2007 was still extremely low, even by regional standards. People had been accustomed to receiving their salaries in cash as a lump sum, so most wanted to withdraw all their salary all at one. Some found that they could not withdraw their entire salary because banks required customers to maintain a minimum balance. In other cases, the ATM could only dispense bills in fixed amounts. Most machines were stocked with 200,000-đồng notes; thus people could only withdraw their money in those increments. Moreover, most of the machines were clustered in the central districts of the city. People who lived in the outer districts had to travel to withdraw cash, often searching over the weekend for a machine stocked with cash.

The sheer demand for cash from these machines generated another failure—the ATM running out of cash. The phrase *hết tiền* ("out of money") is often used as an explanation or alibi for why someone cannot carry out an obligation or a duty. The phrase can usefully be regarded as a socially significant explanation. Yet the ATM's being out of cash was perceived as a moral transgression in that the machine refused to yield "my money." The dilemma of the out-of-cash ATM was a failure on the part of banks to keep the machines supplied.

ATMs in Ho Chi Minh City promised a secure and convenient way to access cash, but they were soon a new site of insecurity around the city's cash economy. Some people suspected that the machines would be stocked with counterfeits, leaving the person who withdrew those bills no recourse to exchange them for higher-quality ones. Newspapers printed stories of people who had lost their ATM cards or had discovered that their bank accounts had been wiped out. One of the first widely reported stories of loss focused on the employee of a security company whose wallet had been stolen, along with her ATM card. The bank's investigation ultimately determined that she was responsible for any charges on her stolen card because her PIN number was the same as her birthday, which was readily available on the personal identification card she carried with her ATM card.

Bank officials quickly attributed the failure of the ATM system not to the technology but rather to the everyday habits of Vietnamese citizens and the city's overcrowded streets. Bank officials claimed restocking the machines was delayed by the congested city traffic. These arguments reinscribed ATMs within their domestic context but failed to address the moral dimensions of banking in an economy structured around cash.

Since 2008, mass-mediated representations of ATMs have shifted from emphasizing the values of convenience, access, and security to portraying the terminals as sites of danger. ATM booths as places where cash emerges render the user both visible and vulnerable. Some customers now hire security guards to accompany them to and from ATMs. Rumors circulate of how thieves wait at both gold shops and ATMs, two places associated with large sums of cash. These fears have been used to promote other forms of technology in which cash never appears. One of these technologies is the point-of-sale terminal, and it is this machine that the State Bank of Vietnam now promotes as the new national payment space for its banked population.

Point-of-sale terminals are not the only noncash payment services available to the banked population in Vietnam. Other services, particularly mobile banking, Internet banking, and home banking, provide services that draw on people's existing habits around using technology. These new payment spaces are linked to the production of new economic citizens, who become identified as virtuous and modern by their participation in these spaces. How ordinary citizens are persuaded to identify themselves as bank customers, and how they refuse those identifications, makes visible the contested infrastructure of money. Even as the Vietnamese state is actively attempting to "nationalize" the payment space of these new networks, Vietnamese citizens, to the extent that they identify themselves as consumers, want to do so as full members of a global economy. These networks draw on the technology and services associated with the global consumer economy, but in ways that reinscribe consumers within a domestic payment space.

The ATM failed for reasons that illuminate the social infrastructure of money in Ho Chi Minh City. Even though the ATM was initially framed by the social imaginary of global capitalism, the everyday habits around storing and spending cash contributed to its breakdown. As ATMs were linked to the state-sponsored campaign to enroll people as bank customers, people invoked critiques that echoed complaints of the subsidized period from the late 1970s—long lines and shortages of cash. ATM networks, rather than liberating Vietnamese consumers, instead demonstrated that they were still mired in the domestic money context. This failure points to why people have developed strategies to elude the regulatory landscape in Ho Chi Minh City.

SIX

DODGING, OR STREET-LEVEL STRATEGIES FOR PERSONAL GAIN

I N 2007 red banners heralding the country's accession to the World Trade Organization lined the streets of Ho Chi Minh City. Newly chartered banks redefined the city's skyline. Billboards advertised new residential complexes yet to be built. And department store displays sparkled with high-end imported goods. How were ordinary people negotiating their own prospects for personal gain within this highly monetized city that gleamed with such promise of prosperity? By dodging, artfully eluding the bureaucratic and regulatory apparatuses that govern the economy.[1] By characterizing as "dodging" the strategies people employed for personal gain, I try to avoid the general tendency to either characterize them as resistance or designate them as corrupt. Rather, seen in the ethnographic spirit, "dodging" helps elucidate people's strategies of mobility that characterize their efforts to realize personal gain in Vietnam's largest city.

GETTING AROUND THE CITY

Ho Chi Minh City's astonishing growth has strained the city's infrastructure. And, just as cash hinders the expansion of economic growth, as we saw in chapter 5, so do the clogged city streets and narrow bridges. In an effort to spur economic growth by facilitating the movement of traffic, municipal authorities with funding from international organizations such as the World Bank have implemented large-scale construction projects around the city. Roadways have been widened by tearing down buildings, and bridges have been built over the city's canals and waterways to connect once disparate points in the city. These projects, insofar as they facilitate the mobility of some groups rather than others, are critical sites for understanding how the culture of circulation is being reordered in Ho Chi Minh City.

One of the many streets widened to accommodate the city's mobile population was Nam Kỳ Khởi Nghĩa, a main artery connecting the city's financial district to Tan Son Nhut International Airport. The street, made nearly twice as wide as its original fourteen meters, is now a spacious avenue with broad sidewalks. No landmark remained untouched in expanding the roadway. Even the gate to the Vĩnh Nghiêm Pagoda was ceremoniously lifted and moved back several meters to accommodate the expansion. The road was a showcase for the city's transnational capitalist class—foreign investors, government officials, and Vietnamese entrepreneurs. Their travel from the international air terminal to the city's financial center would no longer be hindered by the city's legendary traffic—at least this was how several people described the project to me in 2007, each of whom accompanied me to see the widened boulevard as a model of the city's changing infrastructure. The widened boulevard boasted the services of a globalizing economy—villas housing elegant cafés with underground parking, multistoried English-language schools open late at night, and newly chartered banks gleaming with the promise of prosperity. But widening Nam Kỳ Khởi Nghĩa was not a project designed to facilitate the movement of ordinary Vietnamese. Nor was it intended to improve the livelihoods of those residents who earned scant incomes on the boulevard's sidewalks. In fact, the state-sponsored project only marginalized the vendors who pushed carts and bicycles loaded with baskets of fruit, and old men and women who wandered from café to café selling state-issued lottery tickets.

Despite the promise of the newly widened boulevard to enhance mobility, the project was plagued by delays. The Ho Chi Minh City People's Committee chairman finally promised that the project would be completed before the Lunar New Year in 2010. But by the end of that year, the roadway was still clogged with traffic. For residents, the city's constant state of repair has meant devising new routes and alternative strategies to dodge the very projects intended to facilitate movement. And one of those strategies has been relying on motorbikes, not on cars, to get around.

Motorbikes are the most widely used form of transportation in Ho Chi Minh City. More than any other form of motorized vehicle, motorbikes are appropriate to the scale of everyday life in Ho Chi Minh City. Unlike automobiles and trucks, motorbikes are not bound to the grid of city streets (fig. 6.1). People park their motorbikes on sidewalks, maneuver them through

6.1　Pulling up on a motorbike to shop on the outskirts of Hòa Bình Market, 2007.

narrow alleyways, and even leave them in the front rooms of their homes for safekeeping. Unlike bicycles, motorbikes promise mobility without physical exertion, accelerating with a twist of the handle and braking with a slight tap on the foot pedal. People's reliance on motorbikes has not, however, translated into improved traffic.

Motorbikes, much like US dollars, signal the complex relationship between the city's newly liberalized markets and subject formation. Early indicators of rising household incomes and socioeconomic status, the number of motorbikes in the city has risen exponentially since the mid-1990s.[2] By 2007, the number of motorbikes in Ho Chi Minh City was an estimated 3.1 million.[3] The sheer number of motorbikes on the city streets has paradoxically inhibited the very mobility and autonomy that the motorbike as commodity promised. Recent estimates suggest that the sheer number of motorbikes and other vehicles on city streets has slowed traffic down to a crawl; the average speed of traffic in Ho Chi Minh City dropped from thirty kilometers per hour in 1975 to a slow ten kilometers per hour in 2007.[4]

The surge in motorbike ownership and the accompanying traffic crisis provide insight into the problems of governing Vietnam's postreform economy. In early 2004, the government attempted to control traffic by limiting the number of motorbikes a resident could own. This campaign, known as "one person, one motorbike," outright banned the registration of new motorbikes in the center of Hanoi, the country's capital city. Middle-class residents and lawyers in Hanoi challenged the ban by claiming that their right to own property was protected by the 1992 Vietnamese constitution and civil code. By focusing on "the right to be free to own, register, and ride one's own motorbike," the protests privileged consumption practices and private property over broader political demands.[5]

In Ho Chi Minh City, by contrast, people did not invoke state law, at least in 2002. They relied instead on strategies of dodging. Drivers would pull their bikes up on the sidewalk to bypass congested traffic, drive the wrong way down one-way streets, and carry three and sometimes four adults on the back of a motorbike. Even red traffic lights had little authority in keeping a mass of motorbikes at a stop. After enough motorbikes had gathered at a red light, the vehicles would move forward like a phalanx into oncoming traffic. Since then, demand for regulating traffic has come from different fronts— foreign investors who championed motorbike safety helmets, international organizations that pledged funding for infrastructure improvements, and municipal authorities who sponsored traffic safety campaigns. But the city's problem remains more than a technical one for municipal authorities to resolve. It instead requires a social order that establishes and maintains regularized distances between motorists and governs their movement in predictable ways. Governing traffic, like governing the economy, requires new forms of regulating who (or what) has the right-of-way.

State-sponsored projects to facilitate the movement of traffic, such as the widening of Nam Kỳ Khởi Nghĩa, imposed new forms of distinction based on the mode of transportation. Thus the emphasis on mobility, fluidity, and autonomy disenfranchised less valued modes of transport. Cyclos and pedicabs, pushcarts, and eventually even motorbikes were sidelined to facilitate the mobility of private cars. What mattered was the size and speed of one's motorized vehicle. People dodged these constraints on motorbikes as a way of realizing the very freedom promised by the market reforms.[6] But there were limits on their success, as seen by state-led efforts to facilitate the movement of privately owned cars. Still, Ho Chi Minh City's streets were a stage for displaying the dodging strategies people used for getting around the city.

In the late afternoon, just when the streets of the city were the most congested, barefoot young boys darted through traffic. As they nimbly dodged motorbikes and other vehicles, they waved mimeographed sheets listing the day's winning lottery numbers. People purchased a sheet for two hundred đồng and then pulled over to the side of the road to scan the winning numbers. Even without these sheets, the day's numbers were impossible to miss. They were posted everywhere—on large boards by the side of the street, in the following day's newspaper, and, by 2007, on the radio and television as well as via texts directly to mobile phones (fig. 6.2). By 2012, the streetside appearance of the numbers subsided as people relied on mobile networks to learn the outcome of the day's game.

People still talk about lottery tickets in terms of "buying an opportunity" (*mua cơ hội*) or "buying hope" (*mua hy vọng*). One man justified his daily habit of buying lottery tickets as "the opportunity, the chance to win." He carried his lottery ticket in the same pocket as his cash, mingling the two, as if the ticket represented another form of currency. Other people purchased lottery tickets after making offerings at temples, often with the paper notes that symbolized the "blessing" (*lộc*) they had just received or betting

6.2   Posting the day's winning lottery numbers, 2007.

on the notes' serial numbers. Still others bought a ticket after having done a good deed, such as volunteer work. Some people would purchase a packet of ten tickets and then distribute them to their friends or to the workers at a café. Lottery tickets did not appeal to everyone in the city; some purchased the tickets out of sympathy for the seller, while others simply shook their heads, and the ticket sellers moved on.

Sellers appeared almost everywhere. On ferries and in narrow alleyways, in marketplaces and inside noodle shops, sellers held out packs of lottery tickets. By contrast, vendors in Hanoi sold tickets from established locations. A few sellers explained to me that if they stood still, they would sell nothing, so they felt compelled to walk the streets of the city until midnight. These sellers had come to escape the limited income-generating activities in the countryside, and they soon learned that pursuit of money in the city required that they stay in motion.

Lotteries are not new in southern Vietnam, but their promotion reflects the postrevolutionary emphasis on personal wealth over national development. Before 1975, the Saigon-led government had organized a national lottery; anticipation would descend over the city on Tuesday afternoons as people listened for the announcement over the national broadcast system. After 1975, the national lottery was abolished as part of a campaign to outlaw gambling as a bourgeois vice. But by 1980, lotteries were again in vogue as provinces in southern Vietnam promoted them under the slogan of "welfare lotteries" (số xổ phúc lợi) with the proceeds promised to those people who appeared to be suffering. This economy thus turned embodied suffering— elderly women without other means of support, children who had dropped out of school, or men with physical handicaps—into vehicles for selling "hope." The tickets themselves promoted private wealth and consumption. Tickets printed before 1975 touted images of national development, such as rice paddies and monumental architecture, whereas tickets in the 1980s depicted imported commodities (figs. 6.3 and 6.4). One such ticket, which displayed a JVC television next to a Honda Cub motorbike, one of the first motorbikes to be imported to postwar Vietnam, read, "Win the lottery and buy imported goods!" By the 1990s, tickets carried images of young women, flowers, sleek cars, and lavish villas, signifiers of the "good life" that wealth would bestow.

Most residents were skeptical about the actual legitimacy of lottery tickets, just as they were about paper money. Even casual players who only occasionally purchased tickets expressed doubt that the state-sponsored companies

6.3   Lottery ticket from 1960.

6.4   Lottery ticket from 1987.

actually printed *winning* tickets—at least not tickets that matched the "special numbers" that paid a top prize of fifty million đồng (approximately US$3,300) in 2002. Other people warned me that tickets might be fake or even expired. Despite these warnings, I never observed anyone inspect the date on the ticket they purchased. Most buyers appeared more attentive to the cash they received as change from the seller.

The circulation of lottery tickets was a cover for a more popular and lucrative form of playing called *số đề*, or "playing the numbers." Players did not purchase an actual ticket but registered their chosen numbers with a bookie. They bet that a two-, three-, or even four-digit number would appear at the "head" or "tail" of the list, or even "straight down," meaning that the number would appear anywhere on the list. A two-thousand-dong lottery ticket in which the last two numbers appeared on the top of the list yielded a paltry twenty thousand dong. In đề, a thousand-dong bet could yield seventy thousand đồng. And, as playing the numbers did not require holding an actual ticket, people bet on the numbers of any of the organized lotteries in Vietnam.

On one occasion, I watched as a friend played đề using the numbers of the address of a temple she had just visited—"12" and "21." She led me downstairs from the fifth-floor apartment where she lived to a street corner where an older man was sitting on a lawn chair. She told him she wanted to play those numbers down the entire list of eighteen possibilities. Each number cost one thousand đồng, for a total of 36,000. He wrote down the numbers on a yellow piece of paper with a small piece of carbon paper for his own records. To my surprise, the number "12" appeared as the first number listed for the Đồng Nai lottery. My friend took home 72,000 Đồng.

Agents for số đề are familiar to people in the neighborhood. Most hold other streetside jobs—selling cigarettes, operating small amusement rides for children, or brewing coffee. Agents, people pointed out, are not the "bosses." They are simply hired to record the numbers and collect the money. With new communications technology, however, placing bets was also changing. One man placed his bets by mobile phone. After placing several bets for me, he then suddenly refused. His first excuse was that betting was illegal. When I explained that I would not report him to the authorities, he pointed out that betting was immoral. I countered that I enjoyed the risk as much as he did. But his final and irrefutable reason was that the bets I placed were simply too low.

Playing the numbers is a strategy for dodging restrictions imposed by the official game. People are not limited to the numbers printed on official state-produced tickets. They can choose their own numbers and bet on their appearance in different places. Similar motivations for profits have been attributed to Chinese villagers who bet on the numbers issued by the Hong Kong lottery.[7] The villagers were suspicious that the winning numbers were *not* generated at random, but rather than reject the lottery because of their suspicions, these villagers believed that the winning numbers could be divined by either luck or destiny. Villagers thus interpreted their participation in the underground lottery as an investment that carried risk—not as a game of chance.

Insofar as playing the numbers and participating in underground lotteries depends on people's disbelief in the legitimacy of the official lottery, it also generates rumors of who actually profits from these pools. A few of the players I interviewed insisted that big-time players bribed the officials who organized the lotteries, paying up to two hundred taels of gold for a specific number to appear on the top or bottom of a list, claims that further blurred the distinction between the state-sponsored lottery and its unruly privatized version. These rumors were not limited to southern Vietnam. Elsewhere in Asia, people have linked the involvement of crime syndicates to state-based lotteries, indicating how these lotteries as generators of wealth have not yet been domesticated.[8]

Not everyone plays lottery or its underside, *số đề*. Some people regard both the state-sponsored lottery and its privatized version as tossing away one's money. Even long-term players have taken stock of their winnings and losses and then given up their daily habit. Still others only play when they wanted to test their luck. But for people who play on a daily basis, the numbers signify the conversion of chance into risk, an element that can be calculated. These players manage risk in different ways. Some believe that the correct number can be divined through dreams or by calling spirits.

The correlations are wholly conventional, and people who play on a daily basis can readily name which image corresponds to which number. A man in his forties who regularly plays *số đề* recalled a dream in which he stomped on a large rat. That day he did not play the numbers that corresponded to a rat, but when that number appeared on the top of the list, he resumed playing. Through these associations, the dream world becomes a source of possible winning numbers. I found it odd that the combination "oo" did not correspond to any image. Nor did any number correspond to the image of Hồ Chí Minh. When I asked a frequent player which number corresponded with Hồ Chí Minh, he laughed and replied, "Hồ Chí Minh is just money, to dream of Hồ Chí Minh is to dream of money."

CASINO CAPITALISM

The dodging strategies of residents who play *số đề* demonstrate risk-taking behavior that is linked to late capitalism and the global transformation in state-sponsored fiscal regimes. In the 1970s, national governments became increasingly involved in gambling as a strategy for generating revenue. State-sponsored lotteries have since become indispensable fiscal instruments in many countries, including Britain and the United States, where gambling and lotteries were once banned. As fiscal instruments, lotteries are not directed toward redistribution by taxing wealth; rather, they signal a reordering of whose wealth could be appropriated by the state and under what conditions.[9] Even Vietnam now uses gambling as a fiscal policy. By 1999, official lottery ticket sales amounted to US$100 million.[10] Ten years later, the sale of lottery tickets had skyrocketed to US$1.771 billion, or 2.1 percent of the gross domestic product.[11]

Gambling is not limited to the fiscal strategies of territorial states. Just as states have absorbed gambling into their fiscal order, so has global finance expanded through highly speculative markets and digital technologies that have vastly accelerated currency conversions. This reordering has been called "casino capitalism" and is characterized by loosened capital controls and a dismantling of a Weberian ethos of capitalism in which individuals defer immediate gratification by investing in productive enterprises.[12] Gambling and its short-term horizon of wealth maximization have become iconic of money's reproductive power to enrich some people and impoverish others.[13]

As the moral divide between gambling and investing has lessened, both sovereign states and their citizens have come to rely on new strategies for economic gain. In Romania, for example, people justified their participation in Caritas, a pyramid scheme in the mid-1990s, as a form of redemption for the suffering they endured under socialism.[14] Investment in the scheme generated new distinctions in money as citizens began to dissociate money as a simple representation of their labor, distinguishing instead between "my money," or the initial sum they have invested, and "their money," the return on that investment. People had confidence in Caritas in large part because its founder was closely tied to the Romanian state, thus granting the scheme some legitimacy in their eyes. In Africa, the mining of resources have brought hard currency but few other benefits to local populations; even though prosperity may be elusive, its promise appears within reach, motivating a desperate scramble for wealth in which people "pursue magical means for otherwise unattainable ends."[15]

Underground lotteries in Ho Chi Minh City, by contrast, are popular precisely because people imagine themselves evading or dodging the limits on winning imposed by official state-run lotteries. The popular emphasis on buying hope could be likened to wishfulness, where people are invested not in the moment of winning or losing but in the possibility of personal enrichment. However, the emphasis on buying hope overlooks the active role of many players who construct the numbers as *knowable*, either through the proper interpretation of signs, as an outward manifestation of merit or good luck, or through blessing bestowed by the world of the spirits. This cultural premise is not limited to *số đỏ* players in Ho Chi Minh City. In Thailand and Taiwan, gamblers have appealed to supernatural beings to reveal winning lottery numbers.[16] Yet the underground lottery, like the baptism of money, should not be explained simply as a superstitious practice or an occult economy. Such an argument reinforces the institutional strategies associated with global capital that attempt to distinguish the rational from the irrational and the sanctioned from the unsanctioned by overlooking how economists make similar predictions regarding price movements or economic growth.[17] In this regard, *số đề* is an instructive cultural-form by which one can understand localized interpretations of investment and prosperity in Ho Chi Minh City today.

FROM *SỐ ĐỀ* TO *SỐ ĐỎ*

After 1975, Vietnamese who had been involved in commerce were shunned as "speculators" and "profiteers." Speculators (*đầu cơ*) were condemned for hoarding commodities based on their future selling price, while profiteers raised prices beyond what could be morally justified. With economic reform, these activities have been rehabilitated as entrepreneurial. The labor of small investors—both those who succeed and those who fail—is critical in creating new commodity forms and markets in Ho Chi Minh City. And, like *số đề* players, these small investors also rely on dodging even as they appeal to state officials to legitimate their transactions.

In Ho Chi Minh City's real estate market, buying and selling property is restricted to "land-use certificates," or *số đỏ*. Foreign investors, while barred from participating fully in the extensive yet unruly market for land titles, also rely on dodging, including using the names of domestic partners or even marriage as a strategy. Domestic investors, however, are the ones who forged new relationships to land through the use of land-use certificates. Like the numbers in *số đề*, the buoyant real estate market depends on state-issued documents, but buyers and sellers both dodge bureaucratic hurdles by not officially transferring titles and relying instead on personally issued documents. By wresting the value of land from a social matrix that has tied the householder to the land and a state matrix that has retained control over designating ownership, domestic investors have generated new value around the buying and selling of land-use certificates.

Land has been closely tied to the politics of identity in Vietnam. In villages in northern Vietnam, communal land holdings provide revenue for ritualized exchanges. Patrilineal kin groups, for example, often designate plots of land to fund ritual expenditures and support temples that show the collective strength of the patrilineage. In southern Vietnam, the tradition of communal land holdings is far weaker.[18] These regional differences have also shaped real estate activity. In Ho Chi Minh City, people buy and sell properties even when ownership is not properly documented by state agencies; they rely instead on the recognition and enforcement of contracts by a range of alternative institutions, including appeals to the world of spirits.[19]

No place has generated more interest in buying and selling land-use certificates than District Two, which lies just across the Saigon River from the commercial and financial heart of Ho Chi Minh City. Despite its proximity to the city's center, much of the land is still designated as agricultural or farm land. Rumors circulating in 2001 had it that the Japanese government intended to finance a tunnel under the river that would connect the largely rural District Two with District One, the heart of the city. Domestic investors had already anticipated that the district would become a coveted location for the city's growing middle class, and the rumor fueled interest among city residents and led to a rapid increase in the price of these land-use certificates.

One such investor was Thúy, a woman from northern Vietnam who had lived in southern Vietnam since the late 1970s. She earned a small livelihood on the edge of Ho Chi Minh City's main district, but her main income was a pension she received as a former member of the army. Many of her acquaintances were well positioned in the city and included high-ranking managers at state-owned enterprises as well as police officers. Not all of Thúy's friends boasted of such institutional affiliation. Thúy was also close friends with a married couple who lived in District Eight and identified themselves as ethnically Chinese. It was this couple, notably the wife Yến, who provided her with money to invest in the city's bubbling market for land-use certificates while Thúy's wide-ranging contacts would identify which areas would turn a profit in short order.

On several occasions, I accompanied Thúy on the ferry across the Saigon River, a short trip but one that made the district seem all the more remote from Ho Chi Minh City's glamorous shopping and financial center. The ferry was a quintessential form of public transformation: there were people on bicycles, pushing cyclos and three-wheeled vehicles filled with various sundries. Vendors plied the ferry and waiting area, hawking cigarettes and lighters, lottery tickets, and small bags of peanuts. Mostly, however, people sat on idling motorbikes. On the other side of the river, just behind a wall of tattered billboards, the urban landscape gave way to countryside. Women walked down dirt paths with shoulder baskets filled with banana-leaf-wrapped cakes. In the distance, the tall buildings of Ho Chi Minh City rose up like majestic structures, and the large container ships in Saigon Port were reminders of the population's instatiable appetite for imports.

Thúy had pooled money with Yến to purchase a small plot of land. They had agreed to purchase the land for four hundred million đồng earlier in 2001. The two women paid a deposit of three hundred million đồng and received the land title (sổ đỏ) in return. Anticipation of the rezoning of land in District Two had driven prices up, and Thúy estimated that the plot was worth almost eight hundred million đồng. The seller now refused to transfer the land title into Thúy's name. While she held the actual land-use certificate, without a clear title she could not resell the land at a profit.

Early one morning in December 2001, I accompanied Thúy and Yến to District Two. Their destination was a small courthouse, where they hoped to resolve the issue of the land's title. I expressed surprise to see Thúy sitting on a new Honda Dream motorbike, rather than on her secondhand Angel. She was wearing a new bracelet and ring, both of which gleamed with the purity of twenty-four-karat gold but seemed out of character with her usual frugal self-presentation. She quickly explained that the Honda motorbike had been made in Thailand and that the jewelry was borrowed. Her appearance underscored how the display of wealth—gold bangles and imported motorbikes—established personal credibility in the city. But her explanation also suggested that those appearances could also deceive.

The courthouse was located down a dusty alleyway, not in a stately building, as I had imagined. In the front yard were parked several upscale motorbikes and a run-down car. A few people were sitting on benches. Thúy approached a man sitting at a desk, flipping cursorily through a pile of hand-written petitions. Thúy explained that she had been told that the sellers had an appointment that morning with him regarding the sale, and she wanted to know how the case would be resolved. He asked her why she needed the land, but she didn't answer. "Go home," he advised.

She rushed outside, and as she explained her side to both Yến and me, her story became more complicated. Thúy had served in the army, and several of her friends who now worked for the city's police force had promised her that if the court did not resolve the matter, they would officially confiscate the land-use certificate so that the seller could not sell the land at any price. But Thúy wanted to either buy the land for the agreed-upon price or have her money refunded twofold, as stated by the law. She now used the only currency she had—the name of an official. She called an inspector for the district and informed him that she knew "Mr. Thảo," a high-ranking official in the court system and, coincidentally, the brother-in-law of a close friend. The inspector immediately agreed to meet us that afternoon.

When we met the inspector at a café, Thúy gave him a copy of the land-use document, a piece of paper that listed the details—the name of the land-use holder, the size of the plot, the district and ward, and a small map of the area with the plot marked in red ink. "What street leads to this plot?" the inspector asked. Neither woman knew. "What do you intend to do with the land?" he pressed. They were silent. The inspector laughed at having exposed that their interest in the land lay in its potential profit, not its actual location.

FICTIONAL PRICES

Like countless other small-time investors, Thúy's interest in District Two was motivated by the desire to cash in on the city's changing landscape. But her prospects for profit were overshadowed by larger processes overtaking Ho Chi Minh City. The frenzy over purchasing land had not yet transformed the actual landscape of that part of District Two, but it had driven up prices. This speculative activity drew sharp criticism from municipal authorities. City officials condemned the illegal land transfer cases, claiming that they destabilized the city's economic growth, although more than two billion US dollars reportedly changed hands in the illegal trading of three thousand hectares of land.[20] The government declared the speculative bids a "fiction" that was undermining the orderly development of District Two.[21] By the summer of 2002, the city government brought an abrupt halt to buying and selling land in District Two, leaving would-be investors such as Thúy holding a land-use document but not the right to sell.

Like số đề players who rely on numbers generated by the state's games, investors like Thúy depend on state-issued documents and state develop-ment projects to provide the infrastructure needed to realize their profits.

Thúy had bet on the municipal government's capacity to transform the city into a developed and modernized metropolitan area. She had faith in the promise of state-led development, and she believed that the tunnel would be built, connecting the two sides of the river, but still she avoided cumbersome legal processes so that she could realize greater profits.[22]

Nevertheless, Thúy relied on the bonds of personal dependency in order to elude bureaucratic hurdles such as transferring the title. In so doing, she confounded claims that the expansion of markets creates objective relations among individuals who relate to one another only through market prices and money.[23] People exchange title, while authentic, through processes that are not quite legal, relying on their uncanny knack for converting their personal relations into duly signed and stamped documents that have passed through the hands of court clerks and inspectors.

Eventually, I came to doubt Thúy's claim to the status of investor. The trip to the courthouse in District Two appeared to me to be a straightforward case of both parties wanting to profit from a piece of land's sudden increase in value. As I followed her on several more excursions to District Two, I saw her role instead as that of a *cò,* or "broker," who works the edges of these land transfers, often in the name of her "husband," whom she claims owned the land. On our excursions, she could barely contain her glee at the thought of so much undeveloped land. In her eyes, the gold on the arms of the women was proof of their participation in the lucrative world of real estate. But whenever we were accompanied by potential buyers of her "land," she could not remember where a specific property was located, and relied instead on local motorbike drivers, who merely drove us around in circles.

The next time Thúy invited me to accompany her, the details became murkier. She called me to see if I wanted to accompany her to Đồng Nai, just outside Ho Chi Minh City, where she claimed she owned a piece of land that she wanted to sell to a few friends who had just been introduced to her. We arrived at a house in the Phú Nhuận district, and a young woman pulled the iron gates open. The owner of the house appeared, a women in her early forties dressed in jeans, high heels, and a silk shirt. She wore sunglasses with the Giorgio Armani name inscribed on the frame. Thúy squeezed the woman's waist and complimented the woman on her figure. "Tennis," the woman responded, staking her position in the city's ever-changing landscape of status. A Toyota Camry was parked out front. Another woman appeared with a male driver. The two women, it turned out, were government officials. They were interested in purchasing the land to resell to their work units. They took no notice of me, except when the driver remarked that if the police stopped the car for merging into the lane dedicated to motorbikes so he could bypass trucks, the fine would be higher because a foreigner was in the car.

We drove down a well-paved road. The women marveled at the vacant land, ripe for development. They whispered that they would offer 250 million đồng. The map indicated that the land was designated "urban," which meant that it would be easier for them to sell it back to their work units at a profit. Thúy did not know where the plot of land was. She claimed that she had bought it only by looking on a map and did not have the paperwork with her. When we reached the end of the paved road, Thúy made a quick call on her mobile phone, and then five men in dark glasses appeared on motorbikes. She jumped on the back of one of the bikes, and the men led us down a bumpy road, over potholes, around water buffalo, and past slow-moving wagons. Thúy suddenly waved her hand to ask the motorbikes to stop. It was pouring rain. She refused to go with them any further, declaring that they were only interested in showing the carload of people their own pieces of land. I realized at that moment that Thúy had no idea where the land she claimed to own was located. On the ferry boat back to the city, I asked her who actually owned the land. "What do you think of me?" she asked forlornly. She then repeated her story: her husband owned the land; he was a party member who had been sent away on business and had asked her to sell the land for him. She had never seen it, except on a map.

After her failure to resolve the land-title dispute through her connections to various officials and state-appointed inspectors, Thúy decided to visit a fortune-teller in District Five with Yến and me in tow. When we arrived the room was dark, although some light leaked in from the window. A woman sat at a table with a small stack of five or six books and a deck of cards under a tortoise shell in front of her. "What direction does your apartment face?" she asked Thúy, who remained silent. Thúy lived in an apartment building, so she confessed that she didn't know. Nor did she know on what day she had been born. All she wanted to know was whether she would be able to sell a piece of land. Thúy then complained that all year she had met with misfortune (*xui*). The fortune-teller shook her head as she explained that misfortune is a particular condition that can be alleviated by the proper rituals; it is not the same as plain bad luck. Misfortune, the fortune-teller explained, is the accidental nature of things that brings about bad results, not the willful misconduct that results in a bad investment. Thúy grew visibly irritated by the fortune-teller's refusal to agree with her assessment that she had met with misfortune (which could be remedied by appeals to the spirit world) rather than bringing bad luck on herself. As the woman listed events that could count as misfortune, Thúy abruptly asked her how much she owed, left the money on the table, and walked out.

Speculative investors in Ho Chi Minh City's property markets rely on personal relations, much like residents who purchase a number to play *số đề*. Thúy leveraged her connections, dropping the names of high-ranking officials with whom she had tentative social relations and making appeals to divine or supernatural intervention to pull off her increasingly ill-fated transactions. For Thúy, both the District Two courthouse and the fortune-teller stood as unwilling and unsympathetic participants in her efforts to capitalize on the city's rapid transformation.

How should Thúy's strategies at personal enrichment be classified? Labeling the unregulated exchange of land-use certificates "illegal" would deny the force of these would-be investors in recoding land as a commodity in Ho Chi Minh City. It would also deny how these transactions are creating new frontiers for generating wealth in the city. The securities market and the real estate market in Ho Chi Minh City move in tandem, both fueled by rising asset prices as the city gradually liberalizes financial services. By 2006, the VN-Index, the securities exchange in Ho Chi Minh City, had captured the attention of city residents. And, like *số đề*, these markets, while sanctioned by the state, were not fully controlled by the state. Both players and brokers vied for greater gains than those authorized by the Vietnamese state.

THE RISE AND FALL OF THE VN-INDEX

Ho Chi Minh City's burgeoning real estate market was not the only financial arena that offered residents new possibilities for generating wealth. The VN-Index, which opened in Ho Chi Minh City in July 2000, is the larger of Vietnam's two securities indices. At that time, only two firms listed were state-owned companies, and most of the people I knew had no interest in buying securities. Instead, they were interested in those games whose outcome could not be known in advance, much as Clifford Geertz described in his classic analysis of the Balinese cockfight. Geertz argued that interest in the fight was highest when the cocks were evenly matched, but that interest waned when observers could predict the outcome in advance. Potential investors in 2002 were likewise uninterested in how the state-owned enterprises were valued on the VN-Index, but by 2007 people in Ho Chi Minh City were talking about nothing but the VN-Index.

By the beginning of 2007, just as Vietnam was celebrating its accession to the World Trade Organization, the VN-Index hit the one thousand mark. Its increase from one hundred in 2002 to more than one thousand solidified Ho Chi Minh City's reputation as a popular "emerging market" for foreign investors. And the new heights achieved by the VN-Index served as a promise to many city dwellers that they would finally reap the benefits of membership in the global economy.

The city's charged stock exchange and real estate markets appeared to be far removed from Ho Chi Minh City's streetside trade in lottery tickets, but in actuality they were not. The lottery provided a spectacle for capital as well as a model for dodging the state's effort to cap the winnings. The electronic display of rising and falling prices of the VN-Index resembled the ever-changing numbers of the state-run lottery. And just as people could request lottery numbers be sent to their mobile phones as text messages, so could they request stock prices.

In 2007, the city's rhythms were structured around the movement of the VN-Index. In the early mornings, men dressed in white shirts gathered around the numerous stalls that served noodles or beverages to glean information about the city's growing stock market. Young boys ran from stall to stall selling papers containing scant information about the listed companies and the previous day's market prices. People purchased newspapers and swapped information about which stocks were likely to register gains. During the day, people congregated in the rooms of domestic investment firms to watch the prices move. Price changes in the exchange were posted three times a day, unlike in most stock exchanges, where buying and selling is done in real time. Domestic investors clustered in the investment houses, watching the screens as the prices were posted.

The rapid gains on the VN-Index spurred people to participate as investors. As in Shanghai, private schools opened to instruct city residents in the language of the securities market, and the shelves of bookstores were lined with translations of books on how to invest in the stock market. Anthropologist Ellen Hertz described a similar fever in Shanghai in 1992 in her ethnography of the stock market, one sparked by a government-sanctioned campaign, not a natural call of capitalism embodied by the uncanny commercial nature of the Chinese.[24] In Ho Chi Minh City, however, the government attempted to cap the daily gains.

Government controls over price fluctuations were more tightly regulated with the VN-Index in Ho Chi Minh City than with the HN-Index in Hanoi. While prices on the HN-Index could fluctuate within a 10 percent range, the prices on the VN-Index could only fluctuate by 5 percent. For this reason, many people turned to over-the-counter or unlisted exchanges that were not subject to the state-imposed trading ban of 5 percent. Some brokers estimated that the over-the-counter market was three times as big as that of official trades. By using unlisted exchanges, people were relying on the same means of escaping controls that figured into the black market premium for US dollars in the 1980s and into the popularity of *số đề*.

These new financial markets also generated interest in new social types: the stockbroker, the banker, and the investor. Whereas *số đề* players were often depicted in the state-run press as wretched figures, these new types were figures to be celebrated and emulated (fig. 6.5). Even the city's cultural houses provided showcases for its banking and financial sectors. One event I attended was a singing competition among employees of the twenty or so Vietnamese investment houses. The songs were of two genres—the revolutionary and the romantic. The young securities agents established themselves as the vanguard of youth, calling on other young people to "step into the future." In these performances, participating in the securities market was a heroic endeavor, collapsing previously irreconcilable narratives of revolution and capital accumulation.

6.5   Young securities brokers celebrating the VN-Index with a song, 2007.

In a similar fashion, foreign institutional investors were also "stepping into the future" represented by Vietnam's astonishing economic growth. By the summer of 2007, institutional investors had put Ho Chi Minh City on the circuit of cities to visit. Events were organized at downtown hotels to welcome the "indirect investor" who arrived to seek out investment opportunities. Restrictions on foreigners purchasing shares had just been lifted, although their fees were higher and the minimum account balance was substantially larger.

I was also caught up in the citywide exuberance of buying and selling shares. The young brokers who worked at the securities firms assured me that I would profit from my investments. Vietnam had not yet become a destination for "hot money," or very liquid assets that search for the highest yields. Domestic investors profited instead from state policies that were intended to expand the banking sector. These newly chartered banks offered customers financial instruments, which included mortgages to purchase high-end apartments and loans to purchase stock on the city's exchange. The rise in asset prices as measured by the VN-Index had performative power as the country's membership in the World Trade Organization attracted even more investors, both domestic and foreign, and pushed asset prices even higher.

Most stock analysts I spoke with did not rely on the Western models they had been taught in training programs, often in Singapore, Australia, or the United States. One stock analyst described how she evaluated companies based on her "feelings." When I pressed her to explain, she said that in Singapore most investors made decisions based on what they saw in the marketplace—what people were buying, what they were talking about. It was very "direct." While she had learned how to think that way as well, it wasn't enough in Vietnam, because people the still believed in "relations and rumors." These relations and rumors, like the dream signs of *số đề*, provided an alternative model of pricing and investing at the frontiers of capitalism.

Wealth generated on the VN-Index, like that of the underground lottery, was not domesticated. People whispered rumors of how newfound wealth ended in tragedy. Several people recounted a similar story of how a young woman, unbeknownst to her family, amassed a significant fortune through buying and selling stock. She was then killed in a car or motorbike accident. These rumors engendered a moral economy, one in which excessive wealth led to self-destruction. By 2007, HSBC and Morgan Stanley were already discussing a bubble in asset prices, both on the VN-Index and in the real estate market. These rumors were suspiciously like those that circulated of the self-destruction of the young woman who could not control the wealth she had suddenly accumulated. By spring 2009, the VN-Index had dropped below 250, turning what had been one of the world's best-performing stock markets into one of the worst.

PROSPERITY IN POSTREFORM VIETNAM

The euphoria that surrounded Vietnam's accession to the World Trade Organization in 2007 evaporated with the rapid contraction of the global economy. This time, however, the crisis was located not on the frontiers of capitalism but in its heartland, the United States. In Ho Chi Minh City, the rapid conversion of money across different social domains that had fueled economic growth came to an abrupt halt. Buyers who had purchased shares on the VN-Index and newly constructed apartment buildings were often highly leveraged, a gamble by the Vietnamese state to expand the domestic banking sector. Thus in a largely cash-based economy, residents in the city found themselves debt-bound by the very markets that had promised financial freedom.

Not everyone was leveraged in the same way. Small-time investors such as Thúy had raised money through long-distance kinships. Thúy had received some of her money from a sister who lived in Japan. In the end, however, she was left holding a certificate that was of no value. Her cash, she cried, was unrecoverable because it had been turned into gold jewelry or a new motorbike. These two objects were widely regarded as signifiers of personal wealth, thus Thúy characterized her loss not in terms of the vagaries of the real-estate market but as the seller's personal enrichment.

People's strategies for realizing private gain in Ho Chi Minh City cannot be explained by reference to the forms of capitalism that characterized Saigon in the 1960s or the 1970s. These strategies instead need to be situated within the new fiscal orderings that have changed capital markets around the world. Through dodging strategies, people navigate the regulatory landscape and still keep money in motion. People place bets on state lotteries without buying tickets, purchase property without proper titles, and invest in over-the-counter securities in an attempt to realize greater wealth. Dodging state-based restrictions, as we have seen, still depends on alternative social institutions. In their quest to realize personal gain through lotteries, real estate, and the stock markets, people appeal to both government officials and supernatural beings. Keeping money in motion was central to the promise of prosperity and wealth creation that people believed would follow in the wake of reforms. In this way, personal gain depends not only on those institutions that are sanctioned as market based but also on those institutions that capitalist ideologies construct as being external to economy, including kinship and the supernatural.

Some US economists have blamed the global financial crisis on the propensity of Asians to save rather than spend. They advocate that Asians consume more and save less. This overlooks the fact that, in the years leading up to the crisis, such global imbalances contributed to new sources of wealth. Just as the US government and the American people received low-cost imports and ready financing for mortgages that help expand the consumption-led US economy, Asian countries reinforced their export-led development strategy. The rapidly growing export economy in Vietnam fueled an image of prosperity, an image that attracted both foreign and domestic investors and engendered new opportunities for generating wealth as well as debt. Dodging was a strategy to realize personal gain in a highly monetized city where people still regularly evaded state-imposed regulations for governing the economy. But dodging should not be reduced to resistance; residents in fact depended on the state apparatus to issue official lottery numbers, land-registration certificates, and cap gains on the VN-Index. Nor should these strategies be regarded as corrupt. They instead reflect the streetside sensibilities that allow people to realize the promise of reform summed up by the Vietnamese government's own slogan: "Rich People, Strong Country."

EPILOGUE

Vietnam's admission to the World Trade Organization in 2007 came more than twenty years after the Vietnamese Communist Party launched Đổi Mới (Renovation). The following year, the threat of the collapse of global financial institutions triggered a crisis that originated not in Asia but in the heartland of capitalism, the United States. Unlike the collapse of socialism in Eastern Europe in 1989, however, the financial crisis has not (at the time of this writing) launched a wholesale restructuring of national economies. No image equivalent to the collapse of the Berlin Wall has yet come to symbolize this crisis.[1] Crisis management has focused on stabilizing and restoring credit markets and financial institutions rather than reforming and restructuring them.[2] What, then, of societies where the financialization of everyday life does not run so deep? How does this translate to other economic cultures, those in which the scope and stretch of financial institutions in everyday life is shallower and more contested?

Dreaming of Money in Ho Chi Minh City is an ethnographic monograph about events that took place in the years leading up to the financial crisis. It tells of monetary pluralism rather than tightly wound institutional bets, of the sensuous pleasures of cash rather than the calculations of derivatives. And it tells about the morality of money in a country that has struggled to remain independent from the two countries that have come to define the economic crisis, China and the United States.

For many economists, the financial crisis is framed as a morality play of two societies—an overconsuming and indebted United States and an export-producing, foreign-reserve-hoarding China. But this scenario overlooks important dynamics within both countries, particularly the ideological privileging of home ownership in the United States and state-led growth in China. Even the chairman of the US Federal Reserve acknowledged that, in regard to those countries that pursue strong export-led growth backed by large current account surpluses and ample foreign-exchange reserves, the lessons for Asian countries are not clear.[3] In an export-driven world, weakened currencies are seen as leverage to enhance productivity. The Chinese government has resisted calls to let the renmibi appreciate, but it has taken steps to create offshore markets based in Hong Kong to enhance the liquidity of the currency. The fates of the US dollar and the euro are not so certain. Confidence in the US dollar has been boosted by the sovereign debt crisis in the euro zone, which has made apparent the costs of abandoning monetary sovereignty. Ireland and Greece can no longer resolve debt problems by devaluation, as the euro has been turned into the instrument for disciplining populations who never benefited from the financial bets that triggered the crisis.

These emergent possibilities reinforce the major claim of this book, namely that global monetary policies underwrite cultural politics of identity as much as they point to possible avenues for future inquiry. What I have argued is how ordinary citizens on the streets, in homes and alleyways, and across territorial borders have shaped the social imaginary of money, demonstrating why monetary politics cannot be reduced to Western models and concepts. Money must be unbundled from its particular guises that depend on specific political institutions, policies, intellectual practices, and even physical stock to support its circulation. Currencies may be recalled by state authorities, their role as a measurement of value eroded by increasingly higher-denominated bills being put into circulation, their status as a store of value overturned by political events. Considering people's experiences with the failures of currency—the steep devaluations, the forced reforms, the unstable prices—their orientations to money's transformative power is all the more remarkable. Whether the 2008 financial crisis will lead to "decoupling," a radical reordering of power among developed and developing countries, is beyond the scope of this book, but what is clear is that currencies will not lose their power to mediate the cultural politics of identity. Within money resides the magic of modernity made all the more powerful when it is revealed as mere artifice.[4]

MONETARY PLURALISM

Residents of Ho Chi Minh City recognize that not all money is created equal and that its pluralism entails different obligations, risks, and opportunities. Money in its different guises—Vietnamese đồng, US dollars, gold bars, and votive offerings—mediates the cultural politics of identity in Ho Chi Minh City. And by handling different forms of money, people make claims about national integrity, political legitimacy, and membership in globalizing markets. Reducing these dynamics of pluralism to expressions of choice and efficiency would deflate this long history of how people have both defined and redefined themselves in relation to the symbolic inventory of money.

Ho Chi Minh City has long been characterized by a highly pluralized and deeply monetized culture. In the eighteenth century, Saigon rivaled Bangkok as a political and economic center.[5] It was later associated with Chinese merchants and the trading area of Chợ Lớn (Great Market). In the 1920s French banks and other commercial interests financed public works, turning the city into a prominent metropolis of French Indochina. By the 1960s, the United States government financed an urban middle class as a cultural line of defense against the expansion of communism. Today the city is an epicenter of foreign investment and global manufacturing. As this book has demonstrated, money cannot be reduced to a particular Western modernity order around the "market economy, public sphere, and the self-governing of people."[6]

In this book I have not simply described people's street-level experiences. I have aligned these experiences with the structuring and restructuring of global politics, which may be understood as "tournaments of value" among political authorities over the nature of money. As we saw in chapter 1, the "currency question" of the colonial period exposed the instability of the metropole's mastery over Indochina.[7] The 1945 August Revolution spawned competing currencies to signal allegiance to different political regimes and moral communities. Red dollars exposed the Republic of Vietnam's dependency on the US economy. But even the introduction of a unified currency by the Socialist Republic of Vietnam in 1978 failed to resolve the problem of value as the đồng's rapid depreciation led residents to seek alternative currencies.

The dual-price policies in the postwar period magnified the gap between the state-subsidized sector and the market-based sector, as described in chapter 2. These pricing policies made visible the state's project of using family backgrounds to distribute the rights of full citizenship. The currency reforms in 1975, 1978, and 1985 were likewise not simply attempts to refashion currency but political projects to remake citizens in a new society. Money, however, provided an alternative regime of value, subverting the revolutionary project. Subsequent reforms passed by the State Bank of

Vietnam, adjustments imposed by multinational financial institutions such as the International Monetary Fund and the World Bank, and the demands of foreign investors only partly explain the street-level experiences that I've documented here. The resolution of these tournaments has consequences for the lives of people in Ho Chi Minh City, but it cannot wholly explain the "more mundane realities of power and value in ordinary life."[8]

It is common for economic experts to see the city's entrenched cash economy as an obstacle to growth. Certainly, people's attention to the qualities of money restricts its circulation. While government officials and technocrats promote noncash payment systems, many residents still prefer to transact with cash. Cash offers an important quality—anonymity—that is sacrificed by networked payment systems. But people value its other qualities as well. Designating specific notes as "new" and "big" is also a way of measuring national integrity in a city rapidly drawn into globalizing markets by making residents' desires visible within a hierarchy of the developed and developing worlds.[9] Dismissing the historical and cultural reasons why residents transact with cash only reinstates this hierarchy and overlooks how the social imaginary of money has been generated within an alternative modernity project.

NEW SUBJECTIVITIES IN SOUTHEAST ASIA

How do the findings of this particular ethnographic case study of money in Ho Chi Minh City contribute to understanding Southeast Asia, a region whose national histories have been situated on the frontiers of global capital? The role of money in mediating the new subjectivities underway in Ho Chi Minh City resembles broader processes underway in Southeast Asia. As residents in the region have been drawn into rapidly growing economies, money has partly supplanted other constructions of cultural inheritance. People attribute a supernatural quality to money that cannot be reduced to either Marx's commodity fetishism or Simmel's spiritualization of money.[10] Across Southeast Asia, the spiritualization of money has been expressed not by the processes of money shedding its material residue but rather by acts that transform money into objects for sacralization, as evidenced in the offerings made by members of El Shaddai in the Philippines, the fastening of paper notes on trees in northern Thailand, and the offerings of simulated dollars to ghosts in Vietnam.[11] In these practices, money is "singularized," or withdrawn from circulation as a way of expressing its place in social reproduction.[12] In Ho Chi Minh City, people draw on the mediating power of money to appease ghosts, fulfill kin-based obligations, and divine winning lottery numbers. These activities subvert what capitalist discourses of the economy seek to secure, namely the "neat categorizations"—the economic and non-economic, the monetary and nonmonetary, the public and private—upon which an "ordered discourse of capitalism" depends.[13]

While the national currencies of Thailand, Indonesia, and Malaysia all underwent significant devaluations in 1997–98, Vietnam's relatively late entrance into global financial markets likewise shielded it from the volatility of the Asian financial crisis. In the subsequent decade, the Vietnamese state liberalized financial services and expanded the banking sector as part of its commitment to join the World Trade Organization in 2007. Boosted by the country's growing trade with the United States, the opening of Vietnam's securities markets to foreigners and its loose monetary policies helped propel economic growth to levels not seen since the financial crisis.

The emphasis on "keeping" dollars distinguishes Vietnam from these other countries in Southeast Asia. If dollarization in Vietnam, Cambodia, and Laos can be regarded as a structural legacy of US military intervention, it is a legacy now sustained by the diaspora. The massive transfer of wealth via kin-based networks stretched across national boundaries equals, if not exceeds, the financing provided to the Republic of Vietnam by the United States in the late 1960s. The complex economy of Vietnamese personhood embodied by the flow of those dollars is expressed by the paradoxical claim that dollars are for "keeping," as we saw in chapter 4. Dollar bills both mediate kin-based networks and connect citizens to the global economy. If the global dollar in Ho Chi Minh City arrived as an expression of kin-based obligations, it stayed in circulation as a symbol of a newly globalizing economy in which status is designated by foreignness. People "keep" dollars in circulation despite state-led efforts to require citizens and enterprises to convert those dollars into Vietnamese đồng.

Yet the liberating effects of money have also stimulated anxiety about membership in the nation. As we have seen, the values and meanings of money have been deeply entwined with the region's political history, embodied in stretched families, enhanced by commodity consumption, and emboldened by the persistent use of US dollars, especially when communicating with spirits. The popular concern with counterfeits and fakes is a symptom of these competing moral orders. People understand all too well that designations of value are not fixed; particular histories and social biographies matter. This popular knowledge runs counter to commodification in which economic value is constituted by the objects' mutual exchangeability. The discourse of counterfeits make apparent people's anxieties about this process of abstracting value, anxieties expressed by people's preoccupations with substandard national money and counterfeit spirit money. If people in southern Vietnam say that to dream of Hồ Chí Minh is to dream of money, it is because money, like the revolution, offers an infrastructure for reassembling the self and the nation.

NOTES

NOTES TO INTRODUCTION

1   Anthony Giddens, *The Consequences of Modernity* (Stanford, CA: Stanford University Press, 1990), 26.

2   Eric Klinenberg, *Heat Wave: A Social Disaster in Chicago* (Chicago: University of Chicago Press, 2002), 11.

3   Karl Polanyi, *The Great Transformation* (Boston: Beacon Press, 1957), 24.

4   Trinh Quang Do, *Saigon to San Diego: Memoir of a Boy Who Escaped from Communist Vietnam* (New York: McFarland & Company, 2004), 67–68. In this memoir, the author describes how he and his classmates sang the revised lyrics with "great relish." In this version, the singer describes finding a bag of money with four thousand dollars (*bốn ngàn đô*) and Uncle Ho calling out, "Give it all to me!"

5   Keith Hart, *Money in an Unequal World: Keith Hart and His Memory Bank* (London: Texere, 2001), 6.

6   Jean-Joseph Goux, *Symbolic Economies: After Marx and Freud* (Ithaca, NY: Cornell University Press, 1990), 127.

7   Vo Dai Luoc, "The Fight against Inflation: Achievements and Problems," in *Reinventing Vietnamese Socialism: Doi Moi in Comparative Perspective*, ed. William S. Turley and Mark Selden (Boulder, CO: Westview Press, 1993), 107.

8   See the book epigraph for one version of the poem.

9   Karl Marx proposed that the money form itself was a commodity whose function was to abstract, concretize, and replace the value of other commodities in the marketplace. And while money metabolized the circulation of commodities, it also obscured the source of value, human labor, as people came to see money as a thing in itself, an object of wealth and power. Marx identified this process as fetishization. What is important in Marx's analysis is not just the illusory quality of the monetary system or what he called a misrepresentation of social reality, but rather how that illusory quality led to the expansion of the system. Karl Marx, *Capital*, vol. 1 (New York: Vintage Books, 1977), 125–244. By contrast, Georg Simmel theorized that the widening circulation of money led to its objective existence and that money's indeterminacy and detachment from its own origins was a condition of individual freedom. Georg Simmel, *The Philosophy of Money* (New York: Routledge, 1978).

10   Jane Guyer, *Marginal Gains: Monetary Transactions in Atlantic Africa* (Chicago: University of Chicago Press, 2004), 51.

11   Stefan Senders, "What Do You Want Me to Do, Bang My Head against the Wall? Reflections on Having and Not Having in the Field," in *Money: Ethnographic Encounters*, ed. Stefan Senders and Allison Truitt (Oxford: Berg Press, 2007), 83–92.

12   Hồ Chí Minh, *Thực Hành Tiết Kiệm và Chống Bệnh Tham Ô, Lãng Phí, Chống Bệnh Quan Liêu* [How to economize and resist the scourges of greed, wastefulness, and bureaucracy] (Ho Chi Minh City: Chính Trị Quốc Gia, 1999).

13   Shaun Kingsley Malarney, *Culture, Ritual, and Revolution in Vietnam* (London: RoutledgeCurzon, 2002).

14   William J. Duiker, *Vietnam Since the Fall of Saigon* (Athens: Ohio University Center for International Studies, Center for Southeast Asian Studies, 1985), 10.

15   Martin Gainsborough, *The Changing Political Economy of Vietnam: The Case of Ho Chi Minh City* (New York: Routledge, 2003).

16   William S. Turley and Brantly Womack, "Asian Socialism's Open Door: Guangzhou and Ho Chi Minh City," in *Transforming Asian Socialism: China and Vietnam Compared*, ed. Anita Chan, Benedict J. Tria Kerkvliet, and Jonathan Unger (Lanham, MD: Rowman & Littlefield, 1999), 111.

17   Li Tana, "The Water Frontier: An Introduction," in *Water Frontier: Commerce and the Chinese in the Lower Mekong Region, 1750–1880*, ed. Nola Cooke and Li Tana (Lanham, MD: Rowman & Littlefield, 2004), 9.

18   Trần Bạch Đằng, "Tính năng động, sáng tạo của người Việt sống trên đất phương Nam" [The dynamic and creative character of Vietnamese in the southern region], in *Nam Bộ Đất Người* [Southern land and people], ed. Lửa Huỳnh, Hội Khoa học Lịch sử Thành Phố Hồ Chí Minh [Institute of History, Ho Chi Minh City] (Ho Chi Minh City: Nhà Xuất Bản Trẻ, 2002), 5–15.

19   Philip Shendon, "Reaching for the Good Life in Vietnam," *New York Times*, January 5, 1992.

20   Michael Herzfeld, *Cultural Intimacy: Social Poetics in the Nation-State* (New York: Routledge, 1997).

21   Peter North, *Money and Liberation: The Micropolitics of Alternative Currency Movements* (Minneapolis: University of Minnesota Press, 2007), 3.

22   Keith Hart, *Money in an Unequal World: Keith Hart and His Memory Bank* (New York: Texere, 2001).

23   David Graeber, *Debt: The First 5,000 Years* (Brooklyn: Melville House, 2011).

24   Mary Poovey, *Genres of the Credit Economy: Mediating Value in Eighteenth- and Nineteenth-Century Britain* (Chicago: University of Chicago Press, 2008).

25   Viviana A. Zelizer, *The Social Meanings of Money: Pin Money, Paychecks, Poor Relief, and Other Currencies* (Princeton, NJ: Princeton University Press, 1997).

26   Karen Strassler, "The Face of Money: Currency, Crisis, and Remediation in Post-Suharto Indonesia," *Cultural Anthropology* 24, no. 1 (2009): 68–103.

27   Robert J. Foster, "Bargains with Modernity in Papua New Guinea and Elsewhere," *Anthropological Theory* 2, no. 2 (2002): 233–51.

28   Alaina Lemon, "'Your Eyes Are Green Like Dollars': Counterfeit Cash, National

Substance, and Currency Apartheid in 1990s Russia," *Cultural Anthropology* 13, no. 1 (1998): 22–55.

29 Douglas Rogers, "Moonshine, Money, and the Politics of Liquidity in Rural Russia," *American Ethnologist* 32, no. 1 (2005): 63–81.

30 Jennifer Dickinson, "Changing Money in Post-Socialist Ukraine," in *Money: Ethnographic Encounters*, ed. Stefan Senders and Allison Truitt (New York: Berg, 2007), 27–42.

31 Katherine Verdery, "Faith, Hope, and Caritas in the Land of the Pyramids: Romania, 1990–1994," *Society of Comparative Study of Society and History* 34, no. 4 (1995): 625–69.

32 W. G. Wolters, "The Euro: Old and New Boundaries in the Use of Money," *Anthropology Today* 17, no. 6 (2001): 8–12.

33 Thomas Malaby, "Making Change in the New Europe: Euro Competence in Greece," *Anthropological Quarterly* 75, no. 3 (2002): 592.

34 Anna Tsing, *Friction: An Ethnography of Global Connection* (Princeton, NJ: Princeton University Press, 2005), 57.

35 Maurice Bloch and Jonathan Parry, "Introduction: Money and the Morality of Exchange," in *Money and the Morality of Exchange*, ed. Jonathan Parry and Maurice Bloch (Cambridge: Cambridge University Press, 1989), 19.

36 Jean Comaroff and John L. Comaroff, "Millennial Capitalism: First Thoughts on a Second Coming," *Public Culture* 12, no. 2 (2000): 292.

37 Margaret Somers and Fred Block, "From Poverty to Perversity: Ideas, Markets, and Institutions over Two Hundred Years of Welfare Debate," *American Sociological Review* 70, no. 2 (2005): 260–61.

38 Saskia Sassen, *Territory, Authority, Rights: From Medieval to Global Assemblage* (Princeton, NJ: Princeton University Press, 1996), 157.

39 Mitchell M. Dean, *Governmentality: Power and Rule in Modern Society* (London: Sage Publications, 1999); and David Harvey, *A Brief History of Neoliberalism* (Oxford: Oxford University Press, 2005), 5–38.

40 Vicente L. Rafael, *The Promise of the Foreign: Nationalism and the Technics of Translation in the Spanish Philippines* (Durham, NC: Duke University Press, 2005), 5.

41 Bill Maurer, *Mutual Life, Limited: Islamic Banking, Alternative Currencies, Lateral Reason* (Princeton, NJ: Princeton University Press, 2005); and Peter North, *Money and Liberation: The Micropolitics of Alternative Currency Movements* (Minneapolis: University of Minnesota Press, 2007).

42 Bloch and Parry, "Introduction," 23–30.

43 Yves Dezalay and Bryant G. Garth, *The Internationalization of Palace Wars: Lawyers, Economists, and the Contest to Transform Latin American States* (Chicago: University of Chicago Press, 2002), 14.

44 Tony Day, "Ties that (Un)Bind: Families and States in Premodern Southeast Asia," *Journal of Asian Studies* 55, no. 2 (1996): 388; and Charles F. Keyes, Helen Hardacre, and Laurel Kendall, "Introduction: Contested Visions of Community in East and Southeast Asia," in *Asian Visions of Authority*, ed. Charles F. Keyes, Laurel Kendall, and Helen Hardacre (Honolulu: University of Hawai'i Press, 1994), 1–18.

45 Katherine L. Wiegele, *Investing in Miracles: El Shaddai and the Transformation of Popular Catholicism in the Philippines* (Honolulu: University of Hawaiʻi Press, 2005); Alan Klima, "Spirits of 'Dark Finance' in Thailand: A Local Hazard for the International Moral Fund," *Cultural Dynamics* 18, no. 1 (2006): 33–60; Peter Jackson, "The Enchanting Spirit of Thai Capitalism: The Cult of Luang Phor Khoon and the Post-Modernization of Thai Buddhism," *SouthEast Asia Research* 7, no. 1 (1999): 7–60; and Heonik Kwon, "The Dollarization of Vietnamese Spirit Money," *Journal of the Royal Anthropological Institute* 13 (2007): 73–90.

46 Peter Jackson, "Royal Spirits, Chinese Gods, and Magic Monks: Thailand's Boom-Time Religions of Prosperity," *SouthEast Asia Research* 7, no. 3 (1999): 245–320.

47 Hy V. Luong, ed. *Urbanization, Migration, and Poverty in a Vietnamese Metropolis: Hồ Chí Minh City in Comparative Perspectives* (Singapore: NUS Press, 2009); and Dominique Haughton, Jonathan Haughton, and Nguyen Phong, eds., *Living Standards during an Economic Boom* (Hanoi: Statistical Publishing House, 2001), are excellent analyses that do examine these categories.

NOTES TO CHAPTER 1

1 Keith Hart, "Heads or Tails? Two Sides of the Coin," *Man* 21, no. 4 (1986): 647. David Graeber, *Debt: The First 5,000 Years* (New York: Melville House, 2011), 73, extends the metaphor of the two sides of the coin to question two origin stories: that of money as a commodity and that of money as an IOU. What is important in Graeber's analysis is how the nation itself has generated the idea of the primordial debt, a debt that constitutes our identity as citizens of particular nation-states that we can never repay (71).

2 Popular interest in collecting money in Vietnam has been accompanied by several books in Hội Tem Thành Phố Hồ Chí Minh [Stamp Association of Ho Chi Minh City], *Một Trăm Năm Tiền Giấy Việt Nam* [One hundred years of paper money in Vietnam] (Ho Chi Minh City: Trẻ, 1994). The book is published in four languages—Vietnamese, English, French, and Chinese—with full-color photos of the specimens.

3 Nguyễn Thị Hạnh, "Giấy bạc cụ Hồ ở Nam Bộ trong kháng chiến chống Pháp" [Venerable Ho's notes in the South during the war against the French], in *SàiGòn—Thành Phố Hồ Chí Minh Thế kỷ XX: Những vấn đề lịch sử—văn hóa* [Saigon—Ho Chi Minh City in the twentieth century: Historical and cultural issues], ed. Nguyễn Thế Nghĩa and Lê Hồng Liệm (Ho Chi Minh City: Nhà Xuất Bản Trẻ, 2000), 120.

4 The introduction of state-issued currencies depended on casting other monetary forms as fictions or counterfeits, or as primitive. Shells, brass rods, cattle, privately issued notes, and even silver coins simply could not compete with the institutional power of centralized political authorities to force their coins into circulation through the policies of taxation.

5 Jean Bodin, *On Sovereignty: Four Chapters from the Six Books on Commonwealth* (Cambridge: Cambridge University Press, 1992), 59.

6 Richard Von Glahn, "The Origins of Paper Money in China," in *Origins of Value:*

The Financial Innovations That Created World Capitalist Markets, ed. William N. Goetzmann and K. Geert Rouwenhorst (Oxford: Oxford University Press, 2005), 65–90, 66.

7   Von Glahn, "Origins of Paper Money," 69.

8   Man-houng Lin, *China Upside Down: Currency, Society, and Ideologies, 1808–1856* (Cambridge, MA: Harvard University Press, 2006), 5.

9   Alexander Woodside, "Territorial Order and Collective-Identity Tensions in Confucian Asia: China, Vietnam, Korea," *Daedalus* 127, no. 3 (1998): 191–220.

10   Jane Guyer, *Marginal Gains: Monetary Transactions in Atlantic Africa* (Chicago: University of Chicago Press, 2004).

11   Charles Robequain, *The Economic Development of French Indo-China* (London: Oxford University Press, 1944), 137–38.

12   Martin J. Murray, *The Development of Capitalism in Colonial Indochina, 1870–1940* (Berkeley: University of California Press, 1980), 114.

13   Ann Laura Stoler, "Rethinking Colonial Categories: European Communities and the Boundaries of Rule," *Comparative Studies in Society and History* 31, no. 1 (1989): 134–61.

14   Susan Strange, "The Politics of International Currencies," *World Politics* 23, no. 2 (1971): 215–31.

15   Robequain, *Economic Development of French Indo-China*, 139.

16   Virginia Hewitt, "A Distant View: Imagery and Imagination in the Paper Currency of the British Empire, 1800–1960," in *Nation-States and Money: The Past, Present, and Future of National Currencies*, ed. Emily Gilbert and Eric Helleiner (New York: Routledge, 1999), 97–116, 99.

17   David Del Testa, "Workers, Culture, and the Railroads in French Colonial Indochina, 1905–1936," *French Colonial History* 2 (2002): 181–98, 187.

18   Stoler, "Rethinking Colonial Categories," 635.

19   Murray, *Development of Capitalism*, 124.

20   David Marr, "Concepts of 'Individual' and 'Self' in Twentieth-Century Vietnam," *Modern Asian Studies* 34, no. 4 (2000): 787.

21   Van Nguyen-Marshall, *In Search of Moral Authority: The Discourse on Poverty, Poor Relief, and Charity in French Colonial Vietnam* (New York: Peter Lang, 2008), examines the formation of discourses around poverty and poor relief in colonial Tonkin and northern Vietnam as a lens for competing claims of moral authority between colonial officials and Vietnamese intellectuals.

22   James C. Scott, *The Moral Economy of the Peasant: Rebellion and Subsistence in Southeast Asia* (New Haven: Yale University Press, 1976), 88.

23   Murray, *Development of Capitalism*, 130.

24   Andrew Hardy, "The Economics of French Rule in Indochina: A Biography of Paul Bernard (1892–1960)," *Modern Asian Studies* 32, no. 4 (1998): 807–48.

25   Martin Thomas, "Albert Sarraut, French Colonial Development, and the Communist Threat, 1919–1930," *Journal of Modern History* 77, no. 4 (2005): 917–55.

26   David G. Marr, *Vietnam 1945: The Quest for Power* (Berkeley: University of California Press, 1995), 33.

27 "Giấy bạc 500$" [$500 note] *Cứu Quốc,* November 21, 1945, 1.

28 Hồ Chí Minh, "Chủ-tịch Hồ hô hào" [President Ho's appeal], *Cứu Quốc,* September 17, 1945.

29 Lê Đình Hanh, "Vài nét về ủy ban tổng phát hành giấy bạc Việt Nam Trung Bộ" [Several features of the committee for issuing money in Central Vietnam], in *Một Thời Không Quên* [An unforgettable time], vol. 2 (Hue: Nhà Xuất Bản Thuận Hoá, 2000), 29.

30 Trần Dương and Phạm Thọ, *Lưu Thông Tiền Tệ ở Nước Việt-Nam Dân Chủ Cộng Hòa* [The circulation of money in the Democratic Republic of Vietnam] (Hanoi: Sự Thật, 1960), 46.

31 Virginia Hewitt, *Beauty and the Banknote: Images of Women on Paper Money* (London: British Museum, 1994), 6.

32 Trần Quốc Dụ, Nguyễn Hữu Thuận, and Nguyễn Bá, *Đồng Bạc Tài Chính Đồng Bạc Cụ Hồ, 1945–1954* [Financial notes, Venerable Ho's money, 1945–1954] (Hanoi: Nhà Xuất Bản Tài Chính, 2000), 99.

33 Ann Laura Stoler, "Imperial Debris: Reflections on Ruins and Ruination," *Cultural Anthropology* 23, no. 2 (2008): 191–219, 194.

34 Alaina Lemon, "'Your Eyes Are Green Like Dollars': Counterfeit Cash, National Substance, and Currency Apartheid in 1990s Russia," *Cultural Anthropology* 13, no. 1 (1998): 22–55, 24.

35 Jonathan R. Zatlin, *The Currency of Socialism: Money and Political Culture in East Germany* (Oxford: Oxford University Press, 2008), 22.

36 Zatlin, *Currency of Socialism,* 22.

37 Ibid., 24.

38 Howard A. Daniel, *The Catalog and Guidebook of Southeast Asian Coins and Currency,* vol. 2, part 3, *Democratic Republic of Viet Nam Coins and Currency* (Lexington, VA: News Gazette, 1995), 26.

39 Nguyễn Bích Huệ, *Đồng bạc Việt-Nam và các Vấn-đề Liên-hệ* [Vietnamese currency and related issues] ([Saigon]: Phạm Quang Khai, 1968).

40 Bernard B. Fall. "South Viet-Nam's Internal Problems," *Pacific Affairs* 31, no. 3 (1958): 241–60, 255.

41 Shaun Kingsley Malarney, "Festivals and the Dynamics of the Exceptional Dead in Northern Vietnam," *Journal of Southeast Asian Studies* 38, no. 3 (2007): 515–40.

42 Fall, "South Viet-Nam's Internal Problems," 246.

43 Herbert Friedman, "Vietnam War Propaganda Notes," *I.B.N.S. Journal* 21, no. 3 (1982): 79–80, 79.

44 Phil Edwards, "Hanoi's Liberation Money—Still in Storage," *World Coins* (1975), 42–53, 48.

45 Timothy Mitchell, "Fixing the Economy," *Cultural Studies* 12, no. 1 (1998): 82–101.

46 Janet Roitman, *Fiscal Disobedience: An Anthropology of Economic Regulation in Central Africa* (Princeton, NJ: Princeton University Press, 2005).

47 Huỳnh Bửu Sơn, "Đồng bạc Việt Nam qua một chặng đường dài" [Vietnamese currency down a long road], *Thời Báo Kinh Tế Sài Gòn,* April 27, 1995, 8.

48 *Sài Gòn Giải Phóng,* January 23, 1981.

49 Virginia R. Dominguez, "Representing Value and the Value of Representation: A

Different Look at Money," *Cultural Anthropology* 5, no. 1 (1990): 16–44, 19.

50   Vo Dai Luoc. "The Fight against Inflation: Achievements and Problems," in *Reinventing Vietnamese Socialism: Doi Moi in Comparative Perspective*, ed. William S. Turley and Mark Selden (Boulder, CO: Westview Press, 1993), 107.

51   Adam Fforde and Stephan de Vylder, *From Plan to Market: The Economic Transition in Vietnam* (Boulder, CO: Westview Press, 1996).

52   Hue-Tam Ho Tai, "Monumental Ambiguity: The State Commemoration of Hồ Chí Minh," in *Essays in Vietnamese Pasts*, ed. K. W. Taylor and John K. Whitmore (Ithaca, NY: Southeast Asian Program, Cornell University, 1995), 273.

NOTES TO CHAPTER 2

1   Timothy Mitchell, "Fixing the Economy," *Cultural Studies* 12, no. 1 (1998): 93.

2   Chris Hann and Keith Hart, *Economic Anthropology: History, Ethnography, Critique* (Cambridge: Polity, 2011), 171.

3   Hy V. Luong, "Gender Relations: Ideologies, Kinship Practices, and Political Economy," in *Postwar Vietnam: Dynamics of a Transforming Society*, ed. Hy V. Luong (New York: Rowman & Littlefield, 2003), 212.

4   James C. Scott, *The Moral Economy of the Peasant: Rebellion and Subsistence in Southeast Asia* (New Haven, CT: Yale University Press, 1976).

5   Iris M. Young, *Justice and the Politics of Difference* (Princeton, NJ: Princeton University Press, 1992).

6   Shaun Kingsley Malarney, "Festivals and the Dynamics of the Exceptional Dead in Northern Vietnam," *Journal of Southeast Asian Studies* 38, no. 3 (2007): 515–40.

7   Susan Gal, "A Semiotics of the Public/Private Distinction," *differences: A Journal of Feminist Cultural Studies* 13, no. 1 (2002): 86.

8   Veena Das and Deborah Poole, "State and Its Margins: Comparative Ethnographies," in *Anthropology in the Margins of the State*, ed. Veena Das and Deborah Poole (Oxford: James Currey, 2004), 15.

9   Helen F. Siu, "Grounding Displacement: Uncivil Urban Spaces in Postreform South China," *American Ethnologist* 34, no. 2 (2007): 329–50.

10   Siu, "Grounding Displacement," 330; and Li Zhang, "Spaciality and Urban Citizenship in Late Socialist China," *Public Culture* 14, no. 2 (2002): 311–34.

11   Hy V. Luong, "Urbanization, Migration, and Poverty: Ho Chi Minh City in Comparative Perspectives," in *Urbanization, Migration, and Poverty in a Vietnamese Metropolis: Hồ Chí Minh City in Comparative Perspectives*, ed. Hy V. Luong (Singapore: NUS, 2009), 13.

12   Andrew Hardy, "Rules and Resources: Negotiating the Household Registration System in Vietnam under Reform," *Sojourn* 16, no. 2 (2001): 187–212.

13   Hardy, "Rules and Resources," 190.

14   William J. Duiker, *Vietnam since the Fall of Saigon* (Athens: Ohio University Center for International Studies, Center for Southeast Asian Studies, 1985), 34.

15   "Lý lịch của tôi" [My personal background record], *Tuổi Trẻ*, no. 130, April 7–13, 1978, 10.

16   Duiker, *Vietnam since the Fall of Saigon*, 35.

17   Heonik Kwon, *After the Massacre: Commemoration and Consolation in Ha My and My Lai* (Berkeley: University of California Press, 2006), 23.

18   Keith Hart, "Informal Income Opportunities and Urban Employment in Ghana," *Journal of Modern African Studies* 11, no. 1 (1973): 67.

19   Jane Guyer, LaRay Denver, and Adigun Agbaje, *Money Struggles and City Life: Devaluation in Ibadan and Other Urban Centers in Southern Nigeria, 1986-1996* (Portsmouth, NH: Heinemann, 2002).

20   Janet MacGaffey and Remy Bazenguissa-Ganga, *Congo-Paris: Transnational Traders on the Margins of the Law* (Oxford: James Currey, 2000), 5.

21   Julia Elyachar, "Mappings of Power: The State, NGOs, and International Organizations in the Informal Economy of Cairo," *Comparative Study of Society and History* 45, no. 3 (2003): 571–605.

22   Such anxieties are not novel. Viviana Zelizer, *The Social Meanings of Money: Pin Money, Paychecks, Poor Relief, and Other Currencies* (Princeton, NJ: Princeton University Press, 1997), describes how advertisers in the early twentieth century constructed American women as consumers. Likewise, Mary Beth Mills, *Thai Women in the Global Labor Force: Consuming Desires, Contested Selves* (New Brunswick, NJ: Rutgers University Press, 2006), describes the pull female migrants felt from televised advertisements for which they were a target. With money in hand, these women had the means to participate in the commodity-mediated image of the modern Thai woman, but they also felt the moral obligation to fulfill their duties as good daughters.

23   "Bạn gái sử dụng tiền lương như thế nào?" [How do young women use money?], *Tuổi Trẻ*, August 22, 1985, 5.

24   Hardy, "Rules and Resources," 198.

25   Lisa Drummond, "Street Scenes: Practices of Public and Private Space in Urban Vietnam," *Urban Studies* 37, no. 12 (2000): 2377–91.

26   James Scott, *Seeing Like a State: How Certain Schemes to Improve the Human Condition Have Failed* (New Haven, CT: Yale University Press, 1998).

27   Elizabeth C. Dunn, "Standards and Person-Making in East Central Europe," in *Global Assemblages: Technology, Politics, and Ethics as Anthropological Problems*, ed. Aihwa Ong and Stephen J. Collier (Oxford: Blackwell, 2008).

28   Hy V. Luong, *Tradition, Revolution, and Market Economy in a North Vietnamese Village, 1925-2006* (Honolulu: University of Hawai'i, 2010); and Shaun Kingsley Malarney, *Culture, Ritual, and Revolution in Vietnam* (London: RoutledgeCurzon, 2002).

29   In *Thai Women in the Global Labor Force*, Mary Beth Mills described a similar scene in the dormitory rooms of Thai female migrants.

30   Hy Van Luong, "Wealth, Power, and Inequality: Global Market, the State, and Local Sociocultural Dynamics," in *Postwar Vietnam: Dynamics of a Transforming Society*, ed. Hy V. Luong (Lanham, MD: Rowman & Littlefield, 2003), 81–106.

31   There are numerous studies on this topic, including Daniele Belanger, "Son Preference in a Rural Village in North Vietnam," *Studies in Family Planning* 33, no. 4

(2002): 321–34; Nguyễn-võ Thu-hương, *The Ironies of Freedom: Sex, Culture, and Neoliberal Governance in Vietnam* (Seattle: University of Washington Press, 2008); and Jayne Werner and Daniele Belanger, *Gender, Household, and State: Renovation (Doi Moi) as Social Process* (Ithaca, NY: Cornell University Southeast Asia Program Publications, 2002).

32 Allison Truitt, "Hot Loans and Cold Cash in Saigon," in *Money: Ethnographic Encounters*, ed. Stefan Senders and Allison Truitt (Oxford: Berg Press, 2007), 57–68.

33 Georg Simmel, *The Philosophy of Money* (London: Routledge Press, 1978).

NOTES TO CHAPTER 3

1 Benjamin J. Cohen, *The Geography of Money* (Ithaca, NY: Cornell University Press, 1998).

2 Eric Helleiner, *The Making of National Money: Territorial Currencies in Historical Perspective* (Ithaca, NY: Cornell University Press, 2003), 12.

3 Jeffrey Frankel, "Still the Lingua Franca: The Exaggerated Death of the Dollar," *Foreign Affairs* 74, no. 4 (1995): 9.

4 Barry Eichengreen, in *Exhorbitant Privilege: The Rise and Fall of the Dollar and the Future of the International Monetary System* (Oxford: Oxford University Press, 2011), 4, draws attention to how French officials in the 1960s strongly protested the dollar's singular status as the world's currency as a system that supported American living standards.

5 Craig Kamin, *Biography of the Dollar: How the Mighty Buck Conquered the World and Why It's Under Siege* (New York: Crown Business, 2008), 99.

6 Ibid., 100.

7 Arjun Appadurai, "Introduction: Commodities and the Politics of Value," in *The Social Life of Things: Commodities in Cultural Perspectives*, ed. Arjun Appadurai (Cambridge: Cambridge University Press, 1986), 15.

8 George Dalton, "Primitive Money," *American Anthropologist* 67, no. 1 (1965): 44–65.

9 Tim O'Brien, *The Things They Carried* (Boston: Houghton Mifflin, 1990), 2.

10 Rosemary Coombe, "Embodied Trademarks: Mimesis and Alterity on American Commercial Frontiers," *Cultural Anthropology* 11, no. 2 (1996): 202–24.

11 William Allison, "War for Sale: The Black Market, Currency Manipulation, and Corruption in the American War in Vietnam," *War & Society* 21, no. 2 (2003): 145–46.

12 Jed Stevenson, "Coins," *New York Times*, March 3, 1991, section 1; part 2, 65.

13 Felix Belair, Jr., "Devalued Piaster Is Urged on Saigon," *New York Times*, June 28, 1970, 1.

14 John Ruggie, "International Regimes, Transactions, and Change: Embedded Liberalism in the Postwar Economic Order," *International Organization* 36 (1982): 379–415.

15 Chris A. Gregory, *Savage Money: The Anthropology and Politics of Commodity Exchange* (Amsterdam: Harwood Academic, 1997), 272.

16 By the late 1960s, European bankers established credit markets for "off shore dol-

lars." These dollars, unlike loans originating in the United States, were unregulated and untaxed. It was through the creation of the Eurodollar market, financed through "petrodollars," or dollar receipts deposited by oil-producing states, that the US dollar returned to its preeminent place in the international monetary regime.

17 Susan Strange, in "The Persistent Myth of Lost Hegemony," *International Organization* 41 (1987): 552–54, critiques what she calls the "persistent myth of lost U.S. hegemony" on several grounds. First, the myth places the United States on a par with other nation-states, thus obviating how institutions such as the Federal Reserve impose structural conditions on the international system. Second, the structural power of the United States has increased, not decreased, as a result of shifts in the international monetary system. In the international monetary order, greater stability rests on US institutions than on the institutions of multinational corporations.

18 Nguyễn Hữu Định, *Kinh Doanh Vàng tại Thành Phố Hồ Chí Minh: Chính Sách & Giải Pháp* [The gold trade in Ho Chi Minh City: Policies and issues] (Ho Chi Minh City: Nhà Xuất Bản Thành Phố Hồ Chí Minh, 1996), 114.

19 Toan Ánh, *Phong tục Việt Nam* [Vietnamese customs] (Ho Chi Minh City: Nhà Xuất Bản Đồng Tháp, 1998), 98.

20 Suzanne Brenner, *The Domestication of Desire: Women, Wealth, and Modernity in Java* (Princeton, NJ: Princeton University Press, 1998); and Annelies Moors, "Wearing Gold," in *Border Fetishisms: Material Objects in Unstable Places*, ed. Patricia Spyer (New York: Routledge, 1998), 208–23.

21 Martin Gainsborough, *The Changing Political Economy of Vietnam: The Case of Ho Chi Minh City* (New York: Routledge, 2003), 371.

22 Lisa Cliggett, "Gift Remitting and Alliance Building in Zambian Modernity: Old Answers to Modern Practices," *American Anthropologist* 105, no. 3 (2003): 543–52.

23 Raul Hernandez-Cross, *Canada-Vietnam Remittance Corridor* (Washington, DC: International Monetary Fund, 2005).

24 Susan Eva Eckstein, *Immigrant Divide: How Cuban Americans Changed the US and Their Homeland* (New York: Routledge, 2009).

25 Eckstein, *Immigrant Divide*, 223; Esther Whitfield, *Cuban Currency: The Dollar and "Special Period" Fiction* (Minneapolis: University of Minnesota Press, 2008), 5.

26 Melanie Beresford and Dang Phong, *Economic Transition in Vietnam: Trade and Aid in the Demise of a Centrally Planned Economy* (Cheltenham, UK: Edward Elgar, 2000).

27 Annette Weiner, *Inalienable Possessions: The Paradox of Keeping-while-Giving* (Berkeley: University of California Press, 1992).

28 Philip Cowitt, *World Currency Yearbook 1984* (Currency Data and Intelligence, 1985), 36.

29 Alaina Lemon, "'Your Eyes Are Green like Dollars': Counterfeit Cash, National Substance, and Currency Apartheid in 1990s Russia," *Cultural Anthropology* 13, no. 1 (1998): 22–55.

30 At the time I conducted this study (2000–2002), the exchange rate was 15,000 VND to one US dollar. By 2011 the official exchange rate was 20,200 VND to one US dollar.

31 Friedrich A. Hayek, *Denationalisation of Money: The Argument Refined,* Hobart Paper 70 (London: Institute of Economic Affairs, 1976).

32 Nguyễñ Xuân Óanh, *Đổi Mới Vài Nét Lớn của Một Chính Sách Kinh Tế Việt Nam* [Renovation and several important aspects of Vietnamese economic policies] (Ho Chi Minh City: Nhà Xuất Bản Thành Phố Hồ Chí Minh, 2000), 70.

33 In a series of reforms to stabilize the Vietnamese đồng, the State Bank of Vietnam initiated a two-year period of broad restructuring of foreign currency controls. In March 1989, the government devalued the Vietnamese đồng, nearly eliminating the black-market premium. It then increased interest rates for đồng-denominated savings accounts and unified the foreign-exchange rate to enhance the competitiveness of the đồng vis-à-vis the dollar. Finally, it allowed citizens to open foreign-denominated bank accounts to bring dollars into the state banking system.

34 Mario de Zamaroczy and Sophanha Sa, in *Economic Policy in a Highly Dollarized Economy: The Case of Cambodia* (Washington, DC: International Monetary Fund, 2003), 13, provide instructive comparative figures for levels of dollarization in the region. Economists estimate dollarization in China to be 9 percent, while in Thailand it is only 1 percent. Estimates of dollarization in these two countries is calculated on foreign-currency accounts and do not include cash that circulates outside the formal banking sector. By contrast, the level of dollarization in Cambodia is astronomically higher, estimated to be 96 percent of the total money supply.

35 Chu Thi Trung Hai and Paul M. Pickie, *Economic Transition in Vietnam: Doi Moi to WTO* (Asian Development Bank, 2006), 26, available at http://www.adb.org/documents/reports/consultant/economic-transition-in-vietnam/default.asp, accessed February 11, 2011.

36 Andreas Hauskrecht and Nguyen Thanh Hai, "Dollarization in Vietnam," paper prepared for the Twelfth Annual Conference of Pacific Basin Finance, Economics, Accounting, and Business, August 10–11, 2004, Bangkok, available at http://www.bus.indiana.edu/riharbau/RePEc/iuk/wpaper/bepp2004-25-hauskrecht-hai.pdf, accessed February 11, 2011.

37 Alan Klima, "Spirits of 'Dark Finance' in Thailand: A Local Hazard for the International Moral Fund," *Cultural Dynamics* 18, no. 1 (2006): 33–66; Peng Cheah, "Crises of Money," *positions* 16, no. 1 (2008): 189–219.

NOTES TO CHAPTER 4

1 Pierre Bourdieu, *Outline of a Theory of Practice* (Cambridge: Cambridge University Press, 1977), 177. Bourdieu critiques the prevailing discourse of economism, which, he argues, cannot escape a capitalist theory of value. He proposes instead that "practice never ceased to conform to economic calculation even when it gives every appearance of disinterestedness by departing from the logic of interested calculation (in the narrow sense) and playing for stakes that are non-material and not easily quantified."

2 Maurice Godelier, *The Enigma of the Gift* (Chicago: University of Chicago Press, 1999).

3   Andrew Lam, *Perfume Dreams: Reflections on the Vietnamese Diaspora* (Berkeley, CA: Heyday Books, 2005), 5.

4   erin Khuê Ninh, *Ingratitude: The Debt-Bound Daughter in Asian American Literature* (New York: New York University Press, 2011), 39.

5   Janet Lee Scott, in *For Gods, Ghosts, and Ancestors: The Chinese Tradition of Paper Offerings* (Seattle: University of Washington Press, 2007), 22–23, argues that an alternative translation is "paper horses," which is believed to have originated with figures of paper horses that were burned as symbolic substitutes for objects that were too valuable to be sacrificed. In Ho Chi Minh City, however, people use the term *mã* to identify goods that are worthless.

6   Hoàng Thế Chinh, "Đốt Vàng Mã—Một Sự Xa Xỉ," *Văn Hóa*, October 1, 1997, 6.

7   Mayfair Yang, "Putting Global Capitalism in Its Place: Economic Hybridity, Bataille, and Ritual Expenditure," *Current Anthropology* 41, no. 4 (2000): 477–510.

8   Oscar Salemink, "One Country, Many Journeys," in *Vietnam: Journeys of Body, Mind, and Spirit*, ed. Nguyen Van Hy and Laurel Kendall (Berkeley: University of California Press, 2003), 42.

9   Shaun Kingsely Malarney, "Festivals and the Dynamics of the Exceptional Dead in Northern Vietnam," *Journal of Southeast Asian Studies* 38, no. 3 (2007): 515–40.

10 Stephen Feuchtwang, *Popular Religion in China: The Imperial Metaphor* (Richmond Surrey: Curzon, 2001), 21–22.

11 Công Kiệm, "Sĩ Diện" [Prestige], *Khoa Học* [Science], October 1, 1932, 1–2.

12 Heonik Kwon, "The Dollarization of Vietnamese Spirit Money," *Journal of the Royal Anthropological Institute* 13 (2007): 73–90.

13 Lê Thị Hồng Phúc, "Cần có giải pháp đồng bộ đối với vấn đề vàng mã đồ mã" [Is an integrated policy necessary for votive offerings?], in *Tín Ngưỡng Mê Tín* [Spiritual beliefs] (Hanoi: Nhà Xuất Bản Thanh Niên, 1987).

14 Michael DiGregario and Oscar Salemink, "Living with the Dead: The Politics of Ritual and Remembrance in Contemporary Vietnam," *Journal of Southeast Asian Studies* 38, no. 3 (2007): 433–40; and Philip Taylor, "Modernity and Re-Enchantment in Post-Revolutionary Vietnam," in *Modernity and Re-Enchantment: Religion in Post-Revolutionary Vietnam,* ed. Philip Taylor (Singapore: Institute of Southeast Asian Studies, 2007), 1–56.

15 Heonik Kwon, *After the Massacre: Commemoration and Consolation in Ha My and My Lai* (Berkeley: University of California Press, 2006).

16 Thien Do, *Vietnamese Supernaturalism: Views from the Southern Region* (London: RoutledgeCurzon, 2003); Mai Lan Gustafsson, "The Living and the Lost: War and Possession in Vietnam," *Anthropology of Consciousness* 18, no. 2 (2007): 56–73; and Heonik Kwon, *After the Massacre: Commemoration and Consolation in Ha My and My Lai* (Berkeley: University of California Press, 2006).

17 James T. Siegel, *A New Criminal Type in Jakarta: Counter-Revolution Today* (Durham, NC: Duke University Press, 1998), 63–64.

18 Keith Hart, *Money in an Unequal World: Keith Hart and His Memory Bank* (London: Texere, 2001), 234.

19 Charles Keyes, "'The Peoples of Asia': Science and Politics in the Classification of

Ethnic Groups in Thailand, China, and Vietnam," *Journal of Asian Studies* 61, no. 4 (2002): 1190.

20 Kate Jellema, "Returning Home: Ancestor Veneration and the Nationalism of Doi Moi Vietnam," in *Modernity and Re-Enchantment: Religion in Post-Revolutionary Vietnam,* ed. Philip Taylor (Singapore: Institute of Southeast Asian Studies, 2007), 57–89.

21 Nguyễn Minh San, *Tiếp Cận Tín Ngưỡng Dân Dã Việt Nam* [Approaching popular religion] (Hanoi: Nhà Xuất Bản Văn Hoá Dân Tộc, 1998), 210.

22 Lê Thị Hồng Phúc, "Cần Có Giải Pháp Đồng Bộ," 187.

23 Nguyễn Minh San, *Tiếp Cận Tín Ngưỡng Dân Dã,* 232.

24 Ibid., 234.

25 Stephen F. Teiser, *The Ghost Festival in Medieval China* (Princeton, NJ: Princeton University Press, 1998).

26 Heonik Kwon, "The Dollarization of Vietnamese Spirit Money," 73–90.

NOTES TO CHAPTER 5

1 Georg Simmel, *The Philosophy of Money* (London: Routledge, 1978), 301, notes that the "cheapening of money" occurs when its role as a whole becomes more powerful and comprehensive. This process in turn depends on "confidence that the money that is accepted can be spent again at the same value," 178.

2 Mitchell M. Dean, *Governmentality: Power and Rule in Modern Society* (London: Sage Publications, 2009), 39.

3 Michel Callon, Cecile Meadel, and Vololona Rabeharisoa, "The Economy of Qualities," in *The Blackwell Cultural Economy Reader,* ed. Ash Amin and Nigel Thrift (Oxford: Blackwell, 2004), 58–80.

4 Elizabeth Vann, "The Limits of Authenticity in Vietnamese Consumer Markets," *American Anthropologist* 108, no. 2 (2006): 286–96.

5 James G. Carrier, "Abstraction in Western Economic Practice," in *Virtualism: A New Political Economy,* ed. James G. Carrier and Daniel Miller (Oxford: Berg, 1998), 25.

6 Georg Simmel, *Philosophy of Money,* 259.

7 James G. Carrier, in "Abstraction in Western Economic Practice," 35, describes these pricing mechanisms as a critical device for distancing consumers from their personal relations with sellers.

8 Michael Taussig, *Defacement: Public Secrecy and the Labor of the Negative* (Stanford, CA: Stanford University Press, 1999), 54.

9 Georg Simmel, *Philosophy of Money,* 178–79.

10 Bill Maurer, *Mutual Life, Limited: Islamic Banking, Alternative Currencies, Lateral Reason* (Princeton, NJ: Princeton University Press, 2005), 58.

11 Pierre Bourdieu, *Outline of a Theory of Practice* (Cambridge: Cambridge University Press, 1977), 171, asserts that it is the temporal lag that "enables the gift or counter gift to be seen and experienced as an inaugural gift of generosity, without any past or future, i.e., without calculation." Arjun Appadurai, "Introduction: Commodi-

ties and the Politics of Value," in *The Social Life of Things: Commodities in Cultural Perspective*, ed. Arjun Appadurai (Cambridge: Cambridge University Press, 1986), 12, follows Bourdieu in suggesting that this line of analysis helps restore the "calculative dimension to societies that are too often simply portrayed as solidarity writ small."

12 Katherine Rupp, *Gift-Giving in Japan: Cash, Connections, Cosmologies* (Stanford, CA: Stanford University Press, 2003), 56.

13 C. Fred Blake, "Lampooning the Paper Money Custom in Contemporary China," *Journal of Asian Studies* 70, no. 2 (2011): 449–69.

14 Jane I. Guyer, *Marginal Gains: Monetary Transactions in Atlantic Africa* (Chicago: University of Chicago Press, 2004), 4.

15 Karl Marx, *Grundrisse* (New York: Penguin, 1973), 157.

16 "Vietnam Braced for Retail Ramp-Up," *The Banker*, March 1, 2010.

17 The distinction between domestic and foreign banks has been blurred by several foreign banks buying shares in domestic banks and the newly acquired status of foreign banks that incorporate locally to acquire đồng-denominated savings and open more branches.

18 Daniel Miller, *A Theory of Shopping* (Ithaca, NY: Cornell University Press, 1998).

19 Machines were limited to dispensing a maximum of forty notes per transaction. At that time, the largest note in circulation was the 50,000-đồng note (approximately US$3.50). In 2003, the State Bank of Vietnam issued higher-denominated notes, including the 100,000 note, and then later the 500,000-đồng note and the 200,000-đồng note.

20 *Tuổi Trẻ*, "Bắt Đầu Dùng Chung thẻ ATM Tại 25 Ngân Hàng [A single ATM card at twenty-five banks], May 10, 2010, available at http://tuoitre.vn/PrintView .aspx?ArticleID=379679, accessed February 15, 2011.

21 "Salary Payments through Bank Accounts," Prime Minister of Vietnam's Directive no. 20/2007/CT-TTg, dated August 24, 2007, stipulated that those employees who get paid from the state budget must receive their salaries via bank accounts.

22 Ellen Hertz, *The Trading Crowd: An Ethnography of the Shanghai Stock Market* (Cambridge: Cambridge University Press, 1998).

NOTES TO CHAPTER 6

1 Some people in Ho Chi Minh City would refer to these strategies as *chui*, a popular term that conveys a covert quality. *Chui* is sometimes translated as "ducking" or "under the table," because it refers to slipping in between cracks. The word in Vietnamese is defined negatively, as an action that either violates regulations or is carried out with bad intent. However, legality is constituted from the perspective of authorities. Adam Fforde and Stephan de Vylder, *From Plan to Market: The Economic Transition in Vietnam* (Boulder, CO: Westview Press, 1996), instead emphasize how economic reforms have involved a more dynamic process in which certain "fence-breaking" activities are overlooked and then later authorized. Dodging also emphasizes individual efforts to circumvent restrictions by empha-

sizing movement and mobility, which are critical for understanding monetary activities.

2   Dominique Haughton, Jonathan Haughton, Sarah Bales, Truong Thi Kim Chuyen, and Nguyen Nguyet Nga, *Health and Wealth in Vietnam: An Analysis of Household Living Standards* (Singapore: Institute of Southeast Asian Studies, 1999); Hy V. Luong, "Wealth, Power, and Inequality: Global Market, the State, and Local Sociocultural Dynamics," in *Postwar Vietnam: Dynamics of a Transforming Society,* ed. Hy V. Luong (Lanham, MD: Rowman & Littlefield, 2003); and Mandy Thomas and Lisa B. W. Drummond, "Introduction," in *Consuming Urban Culture in Contemporary Vietnam,* ed. Lisa Drummond and Mandy Thomas (London: RoutledgeCurzon, 2003).

3   The Asian Development Bank estimates that, in 2007, private vehicles represented more than 93 percent of all trips in Ho Chi Minh City. Motorcycle ownership increased to 3.1 million motorbikes, an annual growth rate of 8.4 percent between 2004 to 2007. Private car ownership increased at an even faster rate of 20.7 percent. The municipal government is thus promoting a public transport network to stem the increase and ward off problems such as congestion, road dangers, and air pollution that affect megacities such as Bangkok, Manila, and Jakarta. Nguyen Van Quoc, *Socialist Republic of Viet Nam: Preparing the Ho Chi Minh City Urban Mass Rapid Transit Line 2 Project* (Hanoi: Asian Development Bank, 2010), 2–3.

4   *Tuổi Trẻ,* "Xe buýt TP.HCM: Trợ giá không đúng chỗ" [Buses in Ho Chi Minh City: Subsidies are not in the right place], March 27, 2007, available at http://www .tuoitre.com.vn/Tianyon/Index.aspx?ArticleID=193354&ChannelID=3, accessed May 1, 2007.

5   Mark Sidel, *Law and Society in Vietnam: The Transition from Socialism in Comparative Perspective* (Cambridge: Cambridge University Press, 2010).

6   The traffic crisis in Ho Chi Minh City exemplifies what Nguyễn-võ Thu-hương has pointed out as the challenge of governing the "newly privatized intimate desires of citizens and the kinds of 'social problems' such desires create"; Nguyễn-võ Thu-hương, *The Ironies of Freedom: Sex, Culture, and Neoliberal Governance in Vietnam* (Seattle: University of Washington Press, 2008), xiii. While the author focuses particularly on sex, the motorbike also points to a similar irony in that it conjures up consumerist desire and pleasure while also facilitating the very mobility that economic growth requires.

7   Joseph Bosco, Lucia Huwy-Min Liu, and Matthew West, "Underground Lotteries in China: The Occult Economy and Capitalist Culture," in *Economic Development, Integration, and Morality in Asia and the Americas,* ed. Donald Wood (Bingley, UK: Emerald, 2009).

8   Bosco, "Underground lotteries in China"; and Alan Klima, "Spirits of 'Dark Finance' in Thailand: A Local Hazard for the International Moral Fund," *Cultural Dynamics* 18, no. 1 (2006): 33–60.

9   Michael Neary and Graham Taylor, *Money and the Human Condition* (New York: St. Martin's Press, 1998), 81.

10 Manh Hung, "Number Could be Up on Small-Time Lottery Games," *Vietnam Investment Review,* March 8, 1999.

11 *Sài Gòn Tiếp Thị,* November 1, 2010.

12 Susan Strange, *Casino Capitalism* (New York: Blackwell, 1986), 1–3.

13 Michael Taussig uses this phrase when describing how a baptized bill continually returns to its owner with interest; Michael Taussig, "The Genesis of Capitalism amongst a South American Peasantry: Devil's Labor and the Baptism of Money," *Comparative Studies in Society and History* 19, no. 2 (1977): 137.

14 Katherine Verdery, "Faith, Hope, and Caritas in the Land of the Pyramids: Romania, 1990–1994," *Comparative Studies in Society and History* 34, no. 4 (1995): 625–69.

15 Jean Comaroff and John L. Comaroff, "Millennial Capitalism: First Thoughts on a Second Coming," *Public Culture* 12, no. 2 (2000): 284.

16 Alan Klima, "Spirits of 'Dark Finance' in Thailand," 33–60; and Robert P. Weller, "Bandits, Beggars, and Ghosts: The Failure of State Control over Religious Interpretation in Taiwan," *American Ethnologist* 12, no. 1 (1987): 46–61.

17 Alan Klima, "Spirits of 'Dark Finance' in Thailand," 34.

18 Hy Van Luong, *Tradition, Revolution, and Market Economy in a North Vietnamese Village, 1925–2006* (Honolulu: University of Hawai'i, 2010).

19 Annette M. Kim, "North versus South: The Impact of Social Norms in the Market Pricing of Private Property Rights in Vietnam," *World Development* 35, no. 12 (2007): 2080.

20 Nguyen Duong, "Officials Vow to Get Tough on Illegal Land Dealings," *Vietnam Investment Review,* October 28, 2002.

21 Jane Guyer, "Composites, Fictions, and Risk: Toward an Ethnography of Price," in *Market and Society: The Great Transformation Today,* ed. Chris Hann and Keith Hart (Cambridge: Cambridge University Press, 2009).

22 Nguyễn Hồng Quân, the minister of construction, estimated that 80 percent of land transfers were "underground" (*ngầm*), as reported in *Tuổi Trẻ* newspaper, September 19, 2003.

23 David Harvey, *The Urban Experience* (Baltimore, MD: Johns Hopkins University Press, 1989), 167.

24 Ellen Hertz, *The Trading Crowd: An Ethnography of the Shanghai Stock Market* (Cambridge: Cambridge University Press, 1998).

NOTES TO EPILOGUE

1 Jamie Peck, Nik Theodore, and Neil Brenner, "Postneoliberalism and Its Malcontents," *Antipode* 41, no. 1 (2009): 94–16.

2 David Harvey, "The Crisis and the Consolidation of Class Power: Is This *Really* the End of Neoliberalism?" *Counterpunch,* March 13–15, 2009, available at http://www.counterpunch.org/harvey03132009.html, accessed February 10, 2011.

3 Bernanke, Ben S. "Welcome Address: Asia and the Global Financial Crisis," in *Asia and the Global Financial Crisis,* ed. Reuvin Glick and Mark M. Spiegel (San Francisco: Federal Reserve Bank of San Francisco, 2009).

4 Michael Taussig, "Viscerality, Faith, and Skepticism: Another Theory of Magic," in

Near Ruins: Cultural Theory at the End of the Century, ed. Nicholas Dirks (Minneapolis: University of Minnesota Press, 1998), 221–56.

5   Li Tana, "The Water Frontier: An Introduction," in *Water Frontier: Commerce and the Chinese in the Lower Mekong Rgion, 1750–1880*, ed. Nola Cooke and Li Tana (New York: Rowman & Littlefield Publishers, Inc., 2004), 11.

6   Charles Taylor, *Modern Social Imaginaries* (Durham, NC: Duke University Press, 2003), 2.

7   Hy V. Luong, *Tradition, Revolution, and Market Economy in a North Vietnamese Village, 1925–2006* (Honolulu: University of Hawai'i Press, 2010), 81.

8   Arjun Appadurai defines "tournaments of value" largely in ritual terms, apart from the "routines of economic life." Arjun Appadurai, "Introduction: Commodities and the Politics of Value," in *The Social Life of Things: Commodities in Cultural Perspective* (Cambridge: Cambridge University Press, 1986), 21.

9   Philip Taylor, *Fragments of the Present: Searching for Modernity in Vietnam's South* (Honolulu: University of Hawai'i Press, 2000); and James Ferguson, *Global Shadows: Africa in the Neoliberal World Order* (Durham, NC: Duke University Press, 2006).

10 Karl Marx defines fetishism as concealing the social relations through which value is created as a value inherent in the thing itself; Karl Marx, *Capital*, vol. 1 (New York: Vintage Books, 1977), 163–77. Georg Simmel compares the growing spiritualization of money to the mental activity that is stimulated by money's function to unify diverse values under its sign, "an extension of its function to more and more objects and the consolidation of even more diverse values in this form." Simmel, in *The Philosophy of Money*, also documents moments in which the pluralism of money is simply "just money," but more often how people emphasize the incommensurability of currencies in particular domains and in relation to the institutional backers of currency. Georg Simmel, *The Philosophy of Money* (London: Routledge Press, 1978), 198.

11 Katherine Wiegele, *Investing in Miracles: El Shaddai and the Transformation of Popular Catholicism in the Philippines* (Honolulu: University of Hawai'i Press, 2005); Alan Klima, "Spirits of 'Dark Finance' in Thailand: A Local Hazard for the International Moral Fund," *Cultural Dynamics* 18, no. 1, 2006): 33–60; Peter Jackson, "The Enchanting Spirit of Thai Capitalism: The Cult of Luang Phor Khoon and the Post-Modernization of Thai Buddhism," *SouthEast Asia Research* 7, no. 1 (1999): 7–60; and Heonik Kwon, "The Dollarization of Vietnamese Spirit Money," *Journal of the Royal Anthropological Institute* 13 (2007): 73–90.

12 Igor Kopytoff, "The Cultural Biography of Things: Commoditization as Process," in *The Social Life of Things: Commodities in Cultural Perspective*, ed. Arjun Appadurai (New York: Cambridge University Press, 1986).

13 Timothy Mitchell, "Fixing the Economy," *Cultural Studies* 12, no. 1 (1998): 98.

BIBLIOGRAPHY

Allison, William. "War for Sale: The Black Market, Currency Manipulation, and Corruption in the American War in Vietnam." *War & Society* 21, no. 2 (2003): 135–60.

Anagnost, Ann. "From 'Class' to 'Social Strata': Grasping the Social Totality in Reform-Era China." *Third World Quarterly* 29, no. 3 (2008): 497–519.

Anderson, Benedict. *The Spectre of Comparisons: Nationalism, Southeast Asia, and the World*. London: Verso, 1998.

Andrew, A. Piatt. "The End of the Mexican Dollar." *Quarterly Journal of Economics* 1, no. 3 (1904): 321–56.

Appadurai, Arjun. "Introduction: Commodities and the Politics of Value." In *The Social Life of Things: Commodities in Cultural Perspectives*, ed. Arjun Appadurai, 3–63. Cambridge: Cambridge University Press, 1986.

———. *Modernity at Large: Cultural Dimensions of Globalization*. Minneapolis: University of Minnesota Press, 1996.

Babb, Sarah. "Embeddedness, Inflation, and International Regimes: The IMF in the Early Postwar Period." *American Journal of Sociology* 113, no. 1 (2007): 128–64.

Belanger, Daniele. "Son Preference in a Rural Village in North Vietnam." *Studies in Family Planning* 33, no. 4 (2002): 321–34.

Beresford, Melanie, and Dang Phong. *Economic Transition in Vietnam: Trade and Aid in the Demise of a Centrally Planned Economy*. Cheltenham, UK: Edward Elgar, 2000.

Bernanke, Ben S. "Welcome Address: Asia and the Global Financial Crisis." In *Asia and the Global Financial Crisis*, ed. Reuvin Glick and Mark M. Spiegel. Federal Reserve Bank of San Francisco, 2009.

Blake, C. Fred. "Lampooning the Paper Money Custom in Contemporary China." *Journal of Asian Studies* 70, no. 2 (2011): 449–69.

Bloch, Maurice, and Jonathan Parry. "Introduction: Money and the Morality of Exchange." In *Money and the Morality of Exchange*, ed. Jonathan Parry and Maurice Bloch, 1–32. Cambridge: Cambridge University Press, 1989.

Bodin, Jean. *On Sovereignty: Four Chapters on Six Books from the Commonwealth*. Cambridge: Cambridge University Press, 1992.

Bohannan, Paul. "The Impact of Money on an African Subsistence Economy." *Journal of Economic History* 19, no. 4 (1959): 491–503.

Bosco, Joseph, Lucia Huwy-Min Liu, and Matthew West. "Underground Lotteries in

China: The Occult Economy and Capitalist Culture." In *Economic Development, Integration, and Morality in Asia and the Americas*, ed. Donald Wood, 31–62. Bingley, UK: Emerald, 2009.

Bourdieu, Pierre. *Outline of a Theory of Practice*. Cambridge: Cambridge University Press, 1977.

Braudel, Fernand. *Civilization and Capitalism, 15th–18th Century*. London: Collins, 1981.

Brenner, Suzanne. *The Domestication of Desire: Women, Wealth, and Modernity in Java*. Princeton, NJ: Princeton University Press, 1998.

Callon, Michel, Cecile Meadel, and Vololona Rabeharisoa. "The Economy of Qualities." In *The Blackwell Cultural Economy Reader*, ed. Ash Amin and Nigel Thrift, 58–80. Oxford: Blackwell, 2004.

Canetti, Elias. *Crowds and Power*. New York: Continuum Publishing Corporation, 1962.

Capannelli, Giovanni, and Jayant Menon. *Dealing with Multiple Currencies in Transitional Economies: The Scope for Regional Cooperation in Cambodia, the Lao People's Democratic Republic, and Vietnam*. Mandalyuong City, Philippines: Asian Development Bank, 2010.

Carrier, James G. "Abstraction in Western Economic Practice." In *Virtualism: A New Political Economy*, ed. James G. Carrier and Daniel Miller, 25–47. Oxford: Berg, 1998.

Caruth, Cathy. *Unclaimed Experience, Trauma, Narrative, and History*. Baltimore: Johns Hopkins University Press, 1996.

Cheah, Peng. "Crises of Money." *positions* 16, no. 1 (2008): 189–219.

Chu Thi Trung Hau and Paul M. Dickie. *Economic Transition in Vietnam: Doi Moi to WTO*. Hanoi: Asian Development Bank, 2006.

Cliggett, Lisa. "Gift Remitting and Alliance Building in Zambian Modernity: Old Answers to Modern Practices." *American Anthropologist* 105, no. 3 (2003): 543–52.

Cohen, Benjamin J. *The Geography of Money*. Ithaca, NY: Cornell University Press, 1998.

Comaroff, Jean, and John L. Comaroff. "Millennial Capitalism: First Thoughts on a Second Coming." *Public Culture* 12, no. 2 (2000): 291–343.

Công Kiệm. "Sĩ Diện." Khoa Học, October 1, 1932, 1–2.

Conway, John. "Hanoi's Rice Bowl." *Newsweek*, October 13, 1975, 27.

Coombe, Rosemary. "Embodied Trademarks: Mimesis and Alterity on American Commercial Frontiers." *Cultural Anthropology* 11, no. 2 (1996): 202–24.

Cowitt, Philip. *World Currency Yearbook 1984*. Brooklyn: Currency Data and Intelligence, 1985.

Dacy, Douglas. *Foreign Aid, War, and Economic Development: South Vietnam, 1955–1975*. Cambridge: Cambridge University Press, 1986.

Dalton, George. "Primitive Money." *American Anthropologist* 67, no. 1 (1965): 44–65.

Das, Veena, and Deborah Poole. "State and Its Margins: Comparative Ethnographies." In *Anthropology in the Margins of the State*, ed. Veena Das and Deborah Poole, 3–33. Oxford: James Currey, 2004.

Day, Tony. "Ties that (Un)Bind: Families and States in Premodern Southeast Asia." *Journal of Asian Studies* 55, no. 2 (1996): 384–409.

Dean, Mitchell M. *Governmentality: Power and Rule in Modern Society*. London: Sage Publications, 1999.

Del Testa, David. "Workers, Culture, and the Railroads in French Colonial Indochina, 1905–1936." *French Colonial History* 2 (2002): 181–98.

Dezalay, Yves, and Bryant G. Garth. *The Internationalization of Palace Wars: Lawyers, Economists, and the Contest to Transform Latin American States*. Chicago: University of Chicago Press, 2002.

Dickinson, Jennifer. "Changing Money in Post-Socialist Ukraine." In *Money: Ethnographic Encounters*, ed. Stefan Senders and Allison Truitt, 27–42. New York: Berg, 2007.

DiGregario, Michael, and Oscar Salemink. "Living with the Dead: The Politics of Ritual and Remembrance in Contemporary Vietnam." *Journal of Southeast Asian Studies* 38, no. 3 (2007): 433–40.

Do, Thien. *Vietnamese Supernaturalism: Views from the Southern Region*. London: RoutledgeCurzon, 2003.

Dodsworth, John, Erich Spitaller, Michael Braulke, Keon Lee, Kenneth Miranda, Christian Mulder, Hisanobu Shishido, and Krishna Srinivasan. *Vietnam: Transition to a Market Economy*. Washington, DC: International Monetary Fund, 1996.

Dominguez, Virginia R. "Representing Value and the Value of Representation: A Different Look at Money." *Cultural Anthropology* 5, no. 1 (1990): 16–44.

Drummond, Lisa. "Street Scenes: Practices of Public and Private Space in Urban Vietnam." *Urban Studies* 37, no. 12 (2000): 2377–91.

Duiker, William J. *Vietnam since the Fall of Saigon*. Athens: Ohio University Center for International Studies, Center for Southeast Asian Studies, 1985.

Dunn, Elizabeth C. "Standards and Person-Making in East Central Europe." In *Global Assemblages: Technology, Politics, and Ethics as Anthropological Problems*, ed. Aihwa Ong and Stephen J. Collier, 173–93. Oxford: Blackwell, 2008.

Eckstein, Susan Eva. *Immigrant Divide: How Cuban Americans Changed the US and Their Homeland*. New York: Routledge, 2009.

Edwards, Phil. "Hanoi's Liberation Money—Still in Storage." *World Coins* 12 (June 1975): 42–53.

Elyachar, Julia. "Mappings of Power: The State, NGOs, and International Organizations in the Informal Economy of Cairo." *Comparative Study of Society and History* 45, no. 3 (2003): 571–605.

Errington, Shelly. "Recasting Sex, Gender, and Power: A Theoretical and Regional Overview." In *Power & Difference: Gender in Island Southeast Asia*, ed. Jane Monnig and Shelly Errington, 1–58. Stanford, CA: Stanford University Press, 1990.

Escobar, Arturo. "Power and Visibility: Development and the Invention and Management of the Third World." *Cultural Anthropology* 3, no. 4 (1988): 428–43.

Espeland, Wendy Nelson, and Mitchell L. Stevens. "Commensuration as a Social Process." *Annual Review of Sociology* 24 (1998): 313–43.

Fall, Bernard B. "South Viet-Nam's Internal Problems." *Pacific Affairs* 31, no. 3 (1958): 241–60.

Ferguson, James. *Global Shadows: Africa in the Neoliberal World Order*. Durham, NC: Duke University Press, 2006.

Fernandes, Leela. *India's New Middle Class: Democratic Politics in an Era of Economic Reform*. Minneapolis: University of Minnesota Press, 2006.

Feuchtwang, Stephan. *Popular Religion in China: The Imperial Metaphor*. Richmond, UK: Curzon, 2001.

Fforde, Adam, and Stephan de Vylder. *From Plan to Market: The Economic Transition in Vietnam*. Boulder, CO: Westview Press, 1996.

Flynn, Dennis Owen, and Arturo Giraldez. "Cycles of Silver: Global Economic Unity through the Mid-Eighteenth Century." *Journal of World History* 13, no. 2 (2002): 391–427.

Foster, Robert J. "Bargains with Modernity in Papua New Guinea and Elsewhere." *Anthropological Theory* 2, no. 2 (2002): 233–51.

———. "Your Money, Our Money, the Government's Money: Finance and Fetishism in Melanesia." In *Border Fetishisms: Material Objects in Unstable Spaces*, ed. Patricia Spyer, 60–90. New York: Routledge, 1998.

Foucault, Michel. *The Order of Things: An Archaeology of the Human Sciences*. New York: Vintage Books, 1970.

Frank, Andre Gunder. *Reorient: Global Economy in the Asian Age*. Berkeley: University of California Press, 1998.

Frankel, Jeffrey. "Still the Lingua Franca: The Exaggerated Death of the Dollar." *Foreign Affairs* 74, no. 4 (1995): 9–16.

Friedman, Herbert. "Vietnam War Propaganda Notes." *I.B.N.S. Journal* 21, no. 3 (1982): 79–80.

Gainsborough, Martin. *The Changing Political Economy of Vietnam: The Case of Ho Chi Minh City*. New York: Routledge, 2003.

———. "The Politics of the Greenback." In *Consuming Urban Culture in Contemporary Vietnam*, ed. Lisa Drummond and Mandy Thomas, 60–72. London: RoutledgeCurzon, 2003.

Gal, Susan. "A Semiotics of the Public/Private Distinction." *differences: A Journal of Feminist Cultural Studies* 13, no. 1 (2002): 77–95

Geschiere, Peter. *The Perils of Belonging: Autochthony, Citizenship, and Exclusion in Africa and Europe*. Chicago: University of Chicago Press, 2009.

Gibson-Graham, J. K. "Diverse Economies: Performative Practices for 'Other Worlds.'" *Progress in Human Geography* 32, no. 5 (2008): 613–32.

Giddens, Anthony. *The Consequences of Modernity*. Stanford, CA: Stanford University Press, 1990.

Gilbert, Emily. "Money, Citizenship, Territoriality, and the Proposals for North American Monetary Union." *Political Geography* 26, no. 2 (2007): 141–58.

Gilbert, Emily, and Eric Helleiner. *Nation-States and Money*. London: Routledge, 1999.

Godelier, Maurice. *The Enigma of the Gift*. Chicago: University of Chicago Press, 1999.

Goodman, Allan E., Randolph Harris, and John C. Wood. "South Vietnam and the Politics of Self-Support." *Asian Survey* 11, no. 1 (1971): 1–25.

Goux, Jean-Joseph. *Symbolic Economies: After Marx and Freud*. Ithaca, NY: Cornell University Press, 1990.

Graeber, David. *Debt: The First 5,000 Years*. New York: Melville House, 2011.

Gregory, Chris A. *Savage Money: The Anthropology and Politics of Commodity Exchange.* Amsterdam: Harwood Academic, 1997.

———. "Whatever Happened to Householding?" In *Market and Society: The Great Transformation Today,* ed. Chris Hann and Keith Hart, 133–59. Cambridge: Cambridge University Press, 2009.

Gustafsson, Mai Lan. "The Living and the Lost: War and Possession in Vietnam." *Anthropology of Consciousness* 18, no. 2 (2007): 56–73.

Guyer, Jane I. "Composites, Fictions, and Risk: Toward an Ethnography of Price." In *Market and Society: The Great Transformation Today,* ed. Chris Hann and Keith Hart, 203–20. Cambridge: Cambridge University Press, 2009.

———. *Marginal Gains: Monetary Transactions in Atlantic Africa.* Chicago: University of Chicago Press, 2004.

Guyer, Jane, LaRay Denver, and Adigun Agbaje. *Money Struggles and City Life: Devaluation in Ibadan and Other Urban Centers in Southern Nigeria, 1986–1996.* Portsmouth, NH: Heinemann, 2002.

Hann, Chris, and Keith Hart. *Economic Anthropology: History, Ethnography, Critique.* Cambridge: Polity, 2011.

Hardy, Andrew. "Architects of a Discourse? Scholars, Migrants, and the Notion of Home in Vietnam." In *Approaching Transnationalisms: Studies on Transnational Societies, Multicultural Contacts, and Imaginings of Home,* ed. Brenda S. A. Yeoh, Michael W. Charney, and Tong Chee Kiong, 301–20. Boston: Kluwer Academic Publishers, 2003.

———. "The Economics of French Rule in Indochina: A Biography of Paul Bernard (1892–1960)." *Modern Asian Studies* 32, no. 4 (1998): 807–48.

———. "Rules and Resources: Negotiating the Household Registration System in Vietnam under Reform." *Sojourn* 16, no. 2 (2001): 187–212.

Hart, Keith. "Heads or Tails? Two Sides of the Coin." *Man* 21, no. 4 (1986): 637–56.

———. "Informal Income Opportunities and Urban Employment in Ghana." *Journal of Modern African Studies* 11, no. 1 (1973): 61–89.

———. *Money in an Unequal World: Keith Hart and His Memory Bank.* London: Texere, 2001.

Harvey, David. *A Brief History of Neoliberalism.* Oxford: Oxford University Press, 2005.

———. *The Condition of Postmodernity.* Cambridge, MA: Blackwell. 1990.

———. "The Crisis and the Consolidation of Class Power: Is This *Really* the End of Neoliberalism?" *Counterpunch,* March 13–15, 2009. Available at http://www.counterpunch.org/harvey03132009.html. Accessed February 10, 2011.

———. *Spaces of Global Capitalism: Towards a Theory of Uneven Geographical Development.* London: Verso, 2006.

———. *The Urban Experience.* Baltimore, MD: Johns Hopkins University Press, 1989.

Haughton, Dominique, Jonathan Haughton, Sarah Bales, Truong Thi Kim Chuyen, and Nguyen Nguyet Nga. *Health and Wealth in Vietnam: An Analysis of Household Living Standards.* Singapore: Institute of Southeast Asian Studies, 1999.

Haughton, Dominique, Jonathan Haughton, and Nguyen Phong. *Living Standards during an Economic Boom.* Hanoi: Statistical Publishing House, 2001.

Hauskrecht, Andeas, and Nguyen Thanh Hai. "Dollarization in Vietnam." Paper prepared for the Twelfth Annual Conference on Pacific Basin Finance, Economics, Accounting, and Business, August 10–11, 2004, Bangkok. Available at http://www. bus.indiana.edu/riharbau/RePEc/iuk/wpaper/bepp2004-25-hauskrecht-hai.pdf. Accessed February 11, 2011.

Hayek, Friedrich A. *Denationalisation of Money: The Argument Refined.* Hobart Paper 70. London: Institute of Economic Affairs, 1976.

Helleiner, Eric. *The Making of National Money: Territorial Currencies in Historical Perspective.* Ithaca, NY: Cornell University Press, 2003.

Hernandez-Cross, Raul. *Canada-Vietnam Remittance Corridor.* Washington, DC: International Monetary Fund, 2005.

Hertz, Ellen. *The Trading Crowd: An Ethnography of the Shanghai Stock Market.* Cambridge: Cambridge University Press, 1998.

Herzfeld, Michael. *Cultural Intimacy: Social Poetics in the Nation-State.* New York: Routledge, 1997.

Hewitt, Virginia. *Beauty and the Banknote: Images of Women on Paper Money.* London: British Museum, 1994.

———. "A Distant View: Imagery and Imagination in the Paper Currency of the British Empire, 1800–1960." In *Nation-States and Money: The Past, Present, and Future of National Currencies,* ed. Emily Gilbert and Eric Helleiner, 97–116. New York: Routledge, 1999.

Hoàng Thế Chinh. "Đốt vàng mã--Một sự xa xỉ" [Burning paper—An extravagance]. *Văn Hóa,* October 1, 1997, 6.

Hồ Chí Minh. *Thực Hành Tiết Kiệm và Chống Bệnh Tham Ô, Lãng Phí, Chống Bệnh Quan Liêu* [How to economize and resist the scourges of corruption, wastefulness, and bureaucracy]. Ho Chi Minh City: Chính Trị Quốc Gia, 1999.

Hội Tem Thành Phố Hồ Chí Minh [Stamp Association of Ho Chi Minh City]. *Một Trăm Năm Tiền Giấy Việt Nam* [One hundred years of paper money in Vietnam]. Ho Chi Minh City: Nhà Xuất Bản Trẻ, 1994).

Holston, James, and Arjun Appadurai. "Cities and Citizenship." *Public Culture* 8 (1996): 187–204.

Humphrey, Caroline. "Traders, 'Disorder,' and Citizenship Regimes in Provincial Russia." In *Uncertain Transition: Ethnographies of Change in the Postsocialist World,* ed. Michael Burawoy and Katherine Verdery, 19–52. Lanham, MD: Rowman & Littlefield, 1999.

Huỳnh Bửu Sơn. "Đồng bạc Việt Nam qua một chặng đường dài" [Vietnamese currency down a long road]. *Thời Báo Kinh Tế Sài Gòn* [Saigon Economic Times], April 27, 1995, 8.

Jackson, Peter. "The Enchanting Spirit of Thai Capitalism: The Cult of Luang Phor Khoon and the Post-Modernization of Thai Buddhism." *SouthEast Asia Research* 7, no. 1 (1999): 7–60.

———. "Royal Spirits, Chinese Gods, and Magic Monks: Thailand's Boom-Time Religions of Prosperity." *SouthEast Asia Research* 7, no. 3 (1999): 245–320.

Jellema, Kate. "Returning Home: Ancestor Veneration and the Nationalism of Doi Moi

Vietnam." In *Modernity and Re-Enchantment: Religion in Post-Revolutionary Vietnam*, ed. Philip Taylor, 57–89. Singapore: Institute of Southeast Asian Studies, 2007.

Kahin, George McT. *Intervention: How America Became Involved in Vietnam*. New York: Alfred A. Knopf, 1986.

Kamin, Craig. *Biography of the Dollar: How the Mighty Buck Conquered the World and Why It's Under Siege*. New York: Crown Business, 2008.

Keane, Webb. "Market, Materiality, and Moral Metalanguage." *Anthropological Theory* 8, no. 1 (2008): 27–42.

Keyes, Charles. "'The Peoples of Asia': Science and Politics in the Classification of Ethnic Groups in Thailand, China, and Vietnam." *Journal of Asian Studies* 61, no. 4 (2002): 1162–203.

Keyes, Charles F., Helen Hardacre, and Laurel Kendall. "Contested Visions of Community in East and Southeast Asia." In *Asian Visions of Authority*, ed. Charles F. Keyes, Laurel Kendall, and Helen Hardacre. Honolulu: University of Hawai'i Press, 1994.

Keynes, John Maynard. *Essays in Persuasion*. New York: Harcourt, Brace, & Company, 1932.

Kim, Annette M. "North versus South: The Impact of Social Norms in the Market Pricing of Private Property Rights in Vietnam." *World Development* 35, no. 12 (2007): 2079–95.

Klima, Alan. "Spirits of 'Dark Finance' in Thailand: A Local Hazard for the International Moral Fund." *Cultural Dynamics* 18, no. 1 (2006): 33–60.

Klinenberg, Eric. *Heat Wave: A Social Disaster in Chicago*. Chicago: University of Chicago Press, 2002.

Kopytoff, Igor. "The Cultural Biography of Things: Commoditization as Process." In *The Social Life of Things: Commodities in Cultural Perspective*, ed. Arjun Appadurai, 64–91. New York: Cambridge University Press, 1986.

Kwon, Heonik. *After the Massacre: Commemoration and Consolation in Ha My and My Lai*. Berkeley: University of California Press, 2006.

———. "The Dollarization of Vietnamese Spirit Money." *Journal of the Royal Anthropological Institute* 13 (2007): 73–90.

Lam, Andrew. *Perfume Dreams: Reflections on the Vietnamese Diaspora*. Berkeley, CA: Heyday Books, 2005.

Lê Đình Hanh. "Vài nét về ủy ban tổng phát hành giấy bạc Việt Nam Trung Bộ" [Several features of the committee for issuing money in Central Vietnam]. In *Một Thời Không Quên* [An unforgettable time], vol. 2. Hue: Nhà Xuất Bản Thuận Hoá, 2000.

Lemon, Alaina. "'Your Eyes Are Green Like Dollars': Counterfeit Cash, National Substance, and Currency Apartheid in 1990s Russia." *Cultural Anthropology* 13, no. 1 (1998): 22–55.

Lê Thị Hồng Phúc. "Cần có giải pháp đồng bộ đối với vấn đề vàng mã đồ mã" [Is an integrated policy necessary for votive offerings?]. In *Tín Ngưỡng Mê Tín* [Spiritual beliefs], ed. Văn Tăng Hà and Thìn Trương. Hanoi: Nhà Xuất Bản Thanh Niên, 1987.

Li, Tana. "The Water Frontier: An Introduction." In *Water Frontier: Commerce and the Chinese in the Lower Mekong Region, 1750–1880*, ed. Nola Cooke and Li Tana, 1–17. Lanham, MD: Rowman & Littlefield, 2004.

Lin, Man-houng. *China Upside Down: Currency, Society, and Ideologies, 1808–1856.* Cambridge, MA: Harvard University Press, 2006.

Lomnitz, Claudio. "The Depreciation of Life during Mexico City's Transition into 'The Crisis.'" In *Wounded Cities: Destruction and Reconstruction in a Globalized World,* ed. Jane Schneider and Ida Susser, 47–69. Oxford: Berg Press, 2003.

Luhmann, Niklas. *Trust and Power.* Chichester: John Wiley & Sons, 1979.

Luong, Hy V. "Gender Relations: Ideologies, Kinship Practices, and Political Economy." In *Postwar Vietnam: Dynamics of a Transforming Society,* ed. Hy V. Luong, 201–24. Lanham, MD: Rowman & Littlefield, 2003.

———. *Tradition, Revolution, and Market Economy in a North Vietnamese Village, 1925–2006.* Honolulu: University of Hawai'i Press, 2010.

———. "Urbanization, Migration, and Poverty: Ho Chi Minh City in Comparative Perspectives." In *Urbanization, Migration, and Poverty in a Vietnamese Metropolis: Hồ Chí Minh City in Comparative Perspectives,* ed. Hy V. Luong, 1–28. Singapore: NUS Press, 2009.

———. "Wealth, Power, and Inequality: Global Market, the State, and Local Sociocultural Dynamics." In *Postwar Vietnam: Dynamics of a Transforming Society,* ed. Hy V. Luong, 81–106. Lanham, MD: Rowman & Littlefield, 2003.

MacGaffey, Janet, and Remy Bazenguissa-Ganga. *Congo-Paris: Transnational Traders on the Margins of the Law.* Oxford: James Currey, 2000.

Malaby, Thomas. "Making Change in the New Europe: Euro Competence in Greece." *Anthropological Quarterly* 75, no. 3 (2002): 591–97.

Malarney, Shaun Kingsley. *Culture, Ritual, and Revolution in Vietnam.* London: RoutledgeCurzon, 2002.

———. "Festivals and the Dynamics of the Exceptional Dead in Northern Vietnam." *Journal of Southeast Asian Studies* 38, no. 3 (2007): 515–40.

Malinowski, Bronislaw. *Argonauts of the Western Pacific.* New York: E. P. Dutton & Co., 1922.

Marr, David. "Concepts of 'Individual' and 'Self' in Twentieth-Century Vietnam." *Modern Asian Studies* 34, no. 4 (2000): 769–96.

Marx, Karl. *Capital.* Vol. 1. New York: Vintage Books, 1977.

———. *Grundrisse.* New York: Penguin, 1973.

Maurer, Bill. *Mutual Life, Limited: Islamic Banking, Alternative Currencies, Lateral Reason.* Princeton, NJ: Princeton University Press, 2005.

Mauss, Marcel. *The Gift: Forms and Functions of Exchange in Archaic Societies.* New York: Norton, 1967.

Michaels, Walter Benn. *The Gold Standard and the Logic of Naturalism: American Literature at the Turn of the Century.* Berkeley: University of California Press, 1988.

Mihm, Stephen. *A Nation of Counterfeiters: Capitalists, Con Men, and the Making of the United States.* Cambridge, MA: Harvard University Press, 2009.

Miller, Daniel. *A Theory of Shopping.* Ithaca, NY: Cornell University Press, 1998.

Mills, Mary Beth. *Thai Women in the Global Labor Force: Consuming Desires, Contested Selves.* New Brunswick, NJ: Rutgers University Press, 2006.

Mitchell, Timothy. "Fixing the Economy." *Cultural Studies* 12, no. 1 (1998): 82–101.

Moors, Annelies. "Wearing Gold." In *Border Fetishisms: Material Objects in Unstable Places*, ed. Patricia Spyer, 208-23. New York: Routledge, 1998.

Murray, Martin J. *The Development of Capitalism in Colonial Indochina, 1870-1940*. Berkeley: University of California Press, 1980.

Neary, Michael, and Graham Taylor. *Money and the Human Condition*. New York: St. Martin's Press, 1998.

Nguyễn Bích Huệ. *Đồng bạc Việt-Nam và các Vấn-để Liên-hệ* [Vietnamese currency and related issues]. Saigon: Phạm Quang Khai, 1968.

Nguyen Duong. "Officials Vow to Get Tough on Illegal Land Dealings." *Vietnam Investment Review*, October 28, 2002.

Nguyễn Hữu Định. *Kinh Doanh Vàng tại Thành Phố Hồ Chí Minh: Chính Sách & Giải Pháp* [The gold trade in Ho Chi Minh City: Policies and issues]. Ho Chi Minh City: Nhà Xuât Bản Thành Phố Hồ Chí Minh, 1996.

Nguyen-Marshall, Van. *In Search of Moral Authority: The Discourse on Poverty, Poor Relief, and Charity in French Colonial Vietnam*. New York: Peter Lang, 2008.

Nguyêñ Minh San. *Tiếp Vận Tín Ngưỡng Dân Dã Việt Nam* [Approaching popular religion]. Hanoi: Nhà Xuất Bản Văn Hoá Dân Tộc, 1998.

Nguyen Ngoc Minh. "The Birth of an Independent Currency." *Vietnamese Studies* 7 (1965): 198-219.

Nguyễn Thị Hạnh. "Giấy bạc cụ Hồ ở Nam bộ trong kháng chiến chống Pháp" [Venerable Ho's notes in the South during the war against the French]. *SàiGòn—Thành Phố Hồ Chí Minh Thế kỷ XX: Những vấn đề lịch sử—văn hóa* [Saigon—Ho Chi Minh City in the twentieth century: Historical and cultural issues], ed. Nguyễn Thế Nghĩa and Lê Hông Liệm, 113-20. Ho Chi Minh City: Nhà Xuất Bản Trẻ 2000.

Nguyễn Thị Xuân Liêu. "Sài Gòn-Thành Phố Hồ Chí Minh trong bối cảnh chung của tiền tệ Ngân Hàng Việt Nam từ Cách Mạng 8-1945 đến nay" [Saigon-Ho Chi Minh City and the general circumstances of Vietnamese state-issue currency from the 1945 August Revolution until now]. Paper presented at the Conference on Three Hundred Years of Monetary History in Saigon, Ho Chi Minh City, September 1998.

Nguyen Van Quoc. *Socialist Republic of Viet Nam: Preparing the Ho Chi Minh City Urban Mass Rapid Transit Line 2 Project*. Hanoi: Asian Development Bank, 2010.

Nguyễn-võ Thu-hương. *The Ironies of Freedom: Sex, Culture, and Neoliberal Governance in Vietnam*. Seattle: University of Washington Press, 2008.

Nguyễn Xuân Óanh. *Đổi Mới Vài Nét Lớn Của Một Chính Sách Kinh Tế Việt Nam* [Renovation: Several important aspects of Vietnamese economic policies]. Ho Chi Minh City: Nhà Xuất Bản Thành Phố Hồ Chí Minh, 2000.

Ninh, erin Khuê. *Ingratitude: The Debt-Bound Daughter in Asian American Literature*. New York: New York University Press, 2011.

North, Peter. *Money and Liberation: The Micropolitics of Alternative Currency Movements*. Minneapolis: University of Minnesota Press, 2007.

O'Brien, Tim. *The Things They Carried*. Boston: Houghton Mifflin, 1990.

O'Doughterty, Maureen. *Consumption Intensified: The Politics of Middle-Class Daily Life in Brazil*. Durham, NC: Duke University Press, 2002.

Ong, Aihwa. *Flexible Citizenship: The Cultural Logic of Transnationalism.* Durham, NC: Duke University Press, 1999.

———. *Neoliberalism as Exception: Mutations in Citizenship and Sovereignty.* Durham, NC: Duke University Press, 2006.

Ong, Aihwa, and Stephen Collier. *Global Assemblages: Technology, Politics, and Ethics as Anthropological Problems.* Malden, MA: Blackwell, 2005.

Peck, Jamie, Nik Theodore, and Neil Brenner. "Postneoliberalism and Its Malcontents." *Antipode* 41, no. 1 (2009): 94–116.

Peebles, Gavin. *A Short History of Socialist Money.* Sydney: Allen & Unwin, 1991.

Peletz, Michael G. "Transgenderism and Gender Pluralism in Southeast Asia since Early Modern Times." *Current Anthropology* 47, no. 2 (2006): 309–25.

Polanyi, Karl. *The Great Transformation.* Boston: Beacon Press, 1957.

Poovey, Mary. *Genres of the Credit Economy: Mediating Value in Eighteenth- and Nineteenth-Century Britain.* Chicago: University of Chicago Press, 2008.

Rafael, Vicente L. *The Promise of the Foreign: Nationalism and the Technics of Translation in the Spanish Philippines.* Durham, NC: Duke University Press, 2005.

Robequain, Charles. *The Economic Development of French Indo-China.* London: Oxford University Press, 1944.

Robertson, Frances. "The Aesthetics of Authenticity: Printed Banknotes as Industrial Currency." *Technology and Culture* 46, no. 1 (2005): 31–50.

Rogers, Douglas. "Moonshine, Money, and the Politics of Liquidity in Rural Russia." *American Ethnologist* 32, no. 1 (2005): 63–81.

Roitman, Janet. *Fiscal Disobedience: An Anthropology of Economic Regulation in Central Africa.* Princeton, NJ: Princeton University Press, 2005.

Ruggie, John. "International Regimes, Transactions, and Change: Embedded Liberalism in the Postwar Economic Order." *International Organization* 36 (1982): 379–415.

Rupp, Katherine. *Gift-Giving in Japan: Cash, Connections, Cosmologies.* Stanford, CA: Stanford University Press, 2003.

Said, Edward W. *Culture and Imperialism.* New York: Alfred A. Knopf, 1993. Distributed by Random House.

Salemink, Oscar. "One Country, Many Journeys." In *Vietnam: Journeys of Body, Mind, and Spirit,* ed. Nguyen Van Hy and Laurel Kendall, 20–51. Berkeley: University of California, 2003.

Sangren, P. Steven. "Power and Transcendence in the Ma Tsu Pilgrimages of Taiwan." *American Ethnologist* 20, no. 3 (1993): 564–82.

Sassen, Saskia. *Territory, Authority, Rights: From Medieval to Global Assemblages.* Princeton, NJ: Princeton University Press, 2006.

Scott, James C. *The Moral Economy of the Peasant: Rebellion and Subsistence in Southeast Asia.* New Haven, CT: Yale University Press, 1976.

———. *Seeing Like a State: How Certain Schemes to Improve the Human Condition Have Failed.* New Haven, CT: Yale University Press, 1998.

Scott, Janet Lee. *For Gods, Ghosts, and Ancestors: The Chinese Tradition of Paper Offerings.* Seattle: University of Washington Press, 2007.

Senders, Stefan. "What Do You Want Me to Do, Bang My Head against the Wall?

Reflections on Having and Not Having in the Field." In *Money: Ethnographic Encounters,* ed. Stefan Senders and Allison Truitt, 83–92. Oxford: Berg Press, 2007.

Sennett, Richard. *The Fall of Public Man.* New York: Alfred A. Knopf, 1977.

Shenon, Philip. "Reaching for the Good Life in Vietnam." *New York Times,* January 5, 1992.

Sidel, Mark. *Law and Society in Vietnam: The Transition from Socialism in Comparative Perspective.* Cambridge: Cambridge University Press, 2010.

Siegel, James T. *A New Criminal Type in Jakarta: Counter-Revolution Today.* Durham, NC: Duke University Press, 1998.

———. *Solo in the New Order.* Princeton, NJ: Princeton University Press, 1993.

Simmel, Georg. *The Philosophy of Money.* London: Routledge Press, 1978.

Siu, Helen F. "Grounding Displacement: Uncivil Urban Spaces in Postreform South China." *American Ethnologist* 34, no. 2 (2007): 329–50.

Somers, Margaret, and Fred Block. "From Poverty to Perversity: Ideas, Markets, and Institutions over Two Hundred Years of Welfare Debate." *American Sociological Review* 70, no. 2 (2005): 260–87.

Stevenson, Jed. "Coins." *New York Times,* March 3, 1991, section 1, part 2, 65.

Stewart, Susan. *On Longing: Narratives of the Miniature, the Gigantic, the Souvenir, the Collection.* Durham, NC: Duke University Press, 1993.

Stoler, Ann L. "Imperial Debris: Reflections on Ruins and Ruination." *Cultural Anthropology* 23, no. 2 (2008): 191–219.

———. "Making Empire Respectable: The Politics of Race and Sexual Morality in Twentieth-Century Colonial Cultures." *American Ethnologist* 16, no. 4 (1989): 634–60.

———. "Rethinking Colonial Categories: European Communities and the Boundaries of Rule." *Comparative Studies in Society and History* 31, no. 1 (1989): 134–61.

Strange, Susan. *Casino Capitalism.* New York: Blackwell, 1986.

———. "The Persistent Myth of Lost Hegemony." *International Organization* 41 (1987): 551–74.

———. "The Politics of International Currencies." *World Politics* 23, no. 2 (1971): 215–31.

Strassler, Karen. "The Face of Money: Currency, Crisis, and Remediation in Post-Suharto Indonesia." *Cultural Anthropology* 24, no. 1 (2009): 68–103.

Tai, Hue-Tam Ho. "Monumental Ambiguity: The State Commemoration of Hồ Chí Minh." In *Essays in Vietnamese Pasts,* ed. K. W. Taylor and John K. Whitmore, 272–88. Ithaca, NY: Southeast Asian Program, Cornell University, 1995.

Taussig, Michael. *Defacement: Public Secrecy and the Labor of the Negative.* Stanford, CA: Stanford University Press, 1999.

———. "The Genesis of Capitalism amongst a South American Peasantry: Devil's Labor and the Baptism of Money." *Comparative Studies in Society and History* 19, no. 2 (1977): 130–55.

———. "Viscerality, Faith, and Skepticism: Another Theory of Magic." In *Near Ruins: Cultural Theory at the End of the Century,* ed. Nicholas Dirks, 221–56. Minneapolis: University of Minnesota Press, 1998.

Taylor, Charles. *Modern Social Imaginaries.* Durham, NC: Duke University Press, 2003.

Taylor, Philip. *Fragments of the Present: Searching for Modernity in Vietnam's South.* Honolulu: University of Hawai'i Press, 2000.

———. *Goddess on the Rise: Pilgrimage and Popular Religion in Vietnam.* Honolulu: University of Hawai'i Press, 2004.

———. "Modernity and Re-Enchantment in Post-Revolutionary Vietnam." In *Modernity and Re-Enchantment: Religion in Post-Revolutionary Vietnam,* ed. Philip Taylor, 1–56. Singapore: Institute of Southeast Asian Studies, 2007.

Teiser, Stephen F. *The Ghost Festival in Medieval China.* Princeton, NJ: Princeton University Press, 1998.

Thomas, Mandy, and Lisa B. W. Drummond. "Introduction." In *Consuming Urban Culture in Contemporary Vietnam,* ed. Lisa Drummond and Mandy Thomas, 1–17. London: RoutledgeCurzon, 2003.

Thomas, Martin. "Albert Sarraut, French Colonial Development, and the Communist Threat, 1919–1930." *Journal of Modern History* 77, no. 4 (2005): 917–55.

Toan Ành. *Phong Tục Việt Nam* [Vietnamese customs]. Ho Chi Minh City: Nhà Xuất Bản Đồng Tháp, 1998.

Trần Bạch Đằng. "Tính năng động, sáng tạo của người Việt sống trên đất phương nam" [The dynamic and creative character of Vietnamese in the southern region]. *Nam Bộ Đất & Người* [Southern land and people], ed. Lửa Huỳnh, 5–15. Ho Chi Minh City: Nhà Xuất Bản Trẻ, 2002.

Trần Dương and Phạm Thọ. *Lưu Thông Tiền Tệ ở Nước Việt-Nam Dân Chủ Cộng Hòa* [Circulation of money in the Democratic Republic of Vietnam]. Hanoi: Sự thật, 1960.

Trần Quốc Dụ, Nguyễn Hữu Thuận, and Nguyễn Bá. *Đồng Bạc Tài Chính, Đồng Bạc Cụ Hồ, 1945–1954* [Financial notes, Venerable Ho's notes, 1945–1954]. Hanoi: Nhà Xuât Bản Tài Chính, 2000.

Trần Văn Luyện, Trần Sơn, and Nguyễn Văn Chính. *Trật Tự An Toàn Giao Thông Đường Bộ: Thực Trạng và Giải Pháp* [Traffic order and safety: Realities and solutions]. Hanoi: Nhà Xuất Bản Chính Trị Quốc Gia, 2003.

Trinh Quang Do. *Saigon to San Diego: Memoir of a Boy Who Escaped from Communist Vietnam.* New York: MacFarland & Company, 2004.

Truitt, Allison. "Hot Loans and Cold Cash in Saigon." In *Money: Ethnographic Encounters,* ed. Stefan Senders and Allison Truitt, 57–68. Oxford: Berg Press, 2007.

Tsing, Anna. *Friction: An Ethnography of Global Connection.* Princeton, NJ: Princeton University Press, 2005.

Tuổi Trẻ. "Bạn gái sử dụng tiền lương như thế nào?" [How do young women use money?] August 22, 1985, 5.

Tuổi Trẻ. "Bắt đầu dùng chung thẻ ATM tại 25 ngân hàng" [A single ATM card at twenty-five banks], May 10, 2010. Available at http://tuoitre.vn/PrintView .aspx?ArticleID=379679. Accessed February 15, 2011.

Tuổi Trẻ. "Xe buýt TP.HCM: Trợ giá không đúng chỗ" [Buses in Ho Chi Minh City: Subsidies are not in the right place], March 27, 2007. Available at http://www.tuoitre .com.vn/Tianyon/Index.aspx?ArticleID=193354&ChannelID=3. Accessed August 17, 2012.

Turley, William S., and Brantly Womack. "Asian Socialism's Open Doors: Guangzhou and Ho Chi Minh City." In *Transforming Asian Socialism: China and Vietnam Compared*, ed. Anita Chan, Benedict J. Tria Kerkvliet, and Jonathan Unger, 95–119. Lanham, MA: Rowman & Littlefield, 1999.

Turner, Karen Gottschang. *Even the Women Must Fight: Memories of War from North Vietnam*. New York: Wiley, 1999.

Vann, Elizabeth. "The Limits of Authenticity in Vietnamese Consumer Markets." *American Anthropologist* 108, no. 2 (2006): 286–96.

Verdery, Katherine. "Faith, Hope, and Caritas in the Land of the Pyramids: Romania, 1990–1994." *Comparative Studies in Society and History* 34, no. 4 (1995): 625–69.

Viswanathan, Gauri. *Outside the Fold: Conversion, Modernity, and Belief*. Princeton, NJ: Princeton University Press, 1998.

Vo Dai Luoc. "The Right against Inflation: Achievements and Problems." In *Reinventing Vietnamese Socialism: Doi Moi in Comparative Perspective*, ed. William S. Turley and Mark Selden, 107–18. Boulder, CO: Westview Press, 1993.

Von Glahn, Richard. *Fountain of Fortune: Money and Monetary Policy in China, 1000–1700*. Berkeley: University of California Press, 1996.

———. "The Origins of Paper Money in China." In *Origins of Value: The Financial Innovations That Created World Capitalist Markets*, ed. William N. Goetzmann and K. Geert Rouwenhorst, 65–90. Oxford: Oxford University Press, 2005.

Vũ Văn Hiền. *Tiền Vàng và Tiền Giấy: Đồng Tiền Trong Nước Việt Nam và ở Ngoài, Trước và Sau Chiến Tranh* [Gold and Paper currency: Money in Vietnam and Beyond Before and After the War]. Saigon: Nhà Sách Vĩnh Bảo, 1949.

Wanner, Catherine. "Money, Morality, and New Forms of Exchange in Postsocialist Ukraine." *Ethnos* 70, no. 4 (2005): 515–37.

Weiner, Annette. *Inalienable Possessions: The Paradox of Keeping-while-Giving*. Berkeley: University of California Press, 1992.

Weller, Robert P. "Bandits, Beggars, and Ghosts: The Failure of State Control over Religious Interpretation in Taiwan." *American Ethnologist* 12, no. 1 (1987): 46–61.

Werner, Jane, and Daniele Belanger. *Gender, Household, and State: Renovation (Doi Moi) as Social Process*. Ithaca, NY: Cornell University Southeast Asia Program Publications, 2002.

Whitfield, Esther. *Cuban Currency: The Dollar and "Special Period" Fiction*. Minneapolis: University of Minnesota Press, 2008.

Wiegele, Katharine L. *Investing in Miracles: El Shaddai and the Transformation of Popular Catholicism in the Philippines*. Honolulu: University of Hawai'i Press, 2005.

Wilson, Ara. *The Intimate Economies of Bangkok: Tomboys, Tycoons, and Avon Ladies in the Global City*. Berkeley: University of California Press, 2004.

Wolters, W. G. "The Euro: Old and New Boundaries in the Use of Money." *Anthropology Today* 17, no. 6 (2001): 8–12.

Woodside, Alexander. *Community and Revolution in Modern Vietnam*. Boston: Houghton Mifflin, 1976.

———. "Territorial Order and Collective-Identity Tensions in Confucian Asia: China, Vietnam, Korea." *Daedalus* 127, no. 3 (1998): 191–220.

Yang, Mayfair. "Putting Global Capitalism in Its Place: Economic Hybridity, Bataille, and Ritual Expenditure." *Current Anthropology* 41, no. 4 (2000): 477–510.

Young, Iris M. *Justice and the Politics of Difference.* Princeton, NJ: Princeton University Press, 1992.

Zaloom, Caitlin. "Ambiguous Numbers: Trading Technologies and Interpretation in Financial Markets." *American Ethnologist* 30, no. 2 (2003): 258–72.

Zamaroczy, Mario de, and Sopanha Sa. *Economic Policy in a Highly Dollarized Economy: The Case of Cambodia.* Washington, DC: International Monetary Fund, 2003.

Zatlin, Jonathan R. *The Currency of Socialism: Money and Political Culture in East Germany.* Oxford: Oxford University Press, 2008.

Zelizer, Viviana A. *The Social Meaning of Money: Pin Money, Paychecks, Poor Relief, and Other Currencies.* Princeton, NJ: Princeton University Press, 1997.

Zhang, Li. "Spatiality and Urban Citizenship in Late Socialist China." *Public Culture* 14, no. 2 (2002): 311–34.

Žižek, Slavoj. *The Sublime Object of Ideology.* London: Verso, 1989.

INDEX

capitalist money, currency purposes, 32–33, 36

Caritas scheme, 135

car ownership, 169n3

cash: from ATMs, 120–25; as credit money, 113; for emigration, 56–57; household-based commerce, 51; lottery ticket mingling, 130; methodological importance, 6–8; with New Year's greetings, 94–95; quality factors, 107–9, 114–18; risk factors, 7, 118–19, 124; wedding gifts, 53–55, 70

casino capitalism, 135–36, 170n13

central marketplace, and household commerce, 50–52

Chín, Mrs., 50–52, 114

China: dollarization estimates, 165n34; money philosophy, 21; stock market study, 123, 143; and 2008 financial crisis, 148–49

Chợ Lớn, 150

chui, 168n1

citizenship classification, 36–37, 41–49

clipped coins, 108

cô hồn, 100

coins, 21–23, 91, 101, 108, 117–18

commerce, public spaces, 49–50

commerce backgrounds, postwar penalties, 42–43, 44, 136

Commercial Import Program (CIP), 67–68

commodity money, multidimensionality of, 3–8, 10–16, 149–53. See also specific topics, e.g., cash entries; imagery; spirit money

concealing strategies, money gifts, 112–13, 167n11. See also dollarization and dollars

"Con Ó" symbol, 21–22

construction projects, 126–29

contraband shipments, embargo period, 73–74

contractual debt, 85–87

conversion process, red dollars, 66–67

copper coins, 22

counterfeits: as ATM distrust factor, 123–24; big money, 116; lottery tickets, 131–32; monitoring for, 109–11; with propaganda notes, 34; serial number strategy, 65–66; spirit offerings, 92–93

credit cards, 104–5

credit money, non-institution networks, 113–14

Cứu Quốc, 25

Cuba, 73

currency consciousness, 3

currency exchange booths, 38, 106–7

currency issuances: Democratic Vietnam, 31–32, 33; Institut d'Emission, 20, 30; postwar Vietnam, 35–36, 37, 38, 49. See also inflation; State Bank of Vietnam

currency problem: piastre-franc, 22–23; during revolution, 26–31

currency substitution. See dollarization and dollars

currency swaps, 33–34, 67–68

đồng notes: denomination quality, 114–16; devaluations of, 4–5, 115, 165n33; issuance of, 20; motorbike purchase, 105–6; in remittance economy, 74, 75. See also cash entries; exchange rates, đồng; specific denominations

Đài's wedding, 54–55

Đổi Mới reforms, 16, 41, 43, 49

Daniel, Howard, 32

death anniversaries, 53. See also spirit money

Debt (Graeber), 158n1

debts, 85–87, 93, 95–99

Democratic Republic of Vietnam. See specific topics, e.g., cash entries; currency entries; imagery; spirit money

denationalizing money, Hayek's proposal, 79

denomination as quality factor, 114–16, 117

devaluation, 13, 64, 68, 82, 115, 149, 152.

See also currency *entries;* dollarization
and dollars; inflation
Dien Bien Phu, 30
District Two, real estate speculation,
136–42
dodging strategies: defined, 126, 168*n*1;
with lottery tactics, 132–36; motorbike
use, 129; for prosperity, 146–47; in real
estate speculation, 136–42; securities
exchange, 142–46
dollarization and dollars: ATM restrictions,
120; battlefield story, 65; as currency
substitution, 63–64; currency swaps,
33–34; domestic economy function,
76–79, 81–82; estimates of, 165*n*34;
gold exchange trade, 71–72; and gold
standard, 13, 25, 63–64, 68; identity
significance, 62–63, 64–65, 78–79, 81;
and offshore credit markets, 163*n*16;
with pegged exchange policy, 79–82;
remittance money, 13–14, 72–75, 87–
89, 92–95; for trade routes, 65–66;
and 2008 financial crisis, 149; during
Vietnam War, 13, 65, 66–68
dollarization of knowledge, 14
Dominguez, Virginia, 38
dual-price policy, effects, 36–37
dynastic coins, 20–21, 23

*Economic Policy in a Highly Dollarized
Economy* (Zamaroczy and Sa), 165*n*34
economic reform, as reordering of past,
8–9
embargo period, contraband, 73–74
emigration, 56–57, 60
envelope tradition, money gifts, 60, 70,
94, 111, 112–13
euro, 12, 149
Europe, money philosophy, 21, 22
exchange rates, đồng: black market, 67–
68; with dollar, 5, 67, 164*n*30; new
issuances, 31, 38; sovereignty problem,
32; visibility of, 71–72, 79, 106. *See also*
dollarization and dollars

feelings as valuation, 76–77, 145
fetishization of money, 155*n*9, 171*n*10
Fforde, Adam, 168*n*1
fieldwork, methodology overview, 6–8,
15–16
fifty-đồng notes, 35
fifty-thousand-đồng notes: and ATM
machines, 168*n*19; counterfeit problem, 109, 110; at gravesite offering,
84; polymer version, 116, 118; value
perception, 115
filial piety, as debt bond, 85–87
financial crisis (2008), 147, 148–49
five-hundred đồng notes, 34*f*, 115
five-hundred piastre notes, 25–26
five-hundred thousand đồng notes, 116–
17, 118
flag images, 35, 36*f*
folding technique, money stacks, 107, 114
foreign currency controls, restructuring
effects, 80, 165*n*33
For Gods, Ghosts, and Ancestors (Scott),
166*n*5
forsaken spirits, offerings, 99–103
France, 20, 22–26, 30–31
francs, 25, 27
From Plan to Market (Fforde and Vylder),
168*n*1

Geertz, Clifford, 142
gender-related patterns, 50–51, 58, 100
Geneva Convention, 30–31
German Democratic Republic, 31
ghosts, 91–93, 99–103. *See also* spirit
money
gifts: lottery tickets, 131; Lunar New Year,
94–95, 111–12; with new money, 111–13,
118; weddings, 53–55, 70
global capitalism, 3, 6, 9–10, 12–13, 15–16,
148–49
Goddess money, 91
gold: in contraband packages, 73–74;
Japanese transfer of, 25; motorbike
purchase, 105–6; for revolution, 26–27,

redemption possibilities, family backgrounds, 44–45

red envelope tradition, 94, 111, 112–13

red note. *See* hundred-đồng notes

reeducation camps, 45, 56

registration system, household, 43–44, 46, 47, 49, 60

reil, issuance of, 20

relocation zones, 42, 44

remittance money, 13–14, 72–75, 87–89, 92–95

renmibi, 149

renovation reforms, 16, 41, 43, 49

representational currency, 108

Republic of Vietnam. *See specific topics, e.g.,* cash *entries;* currency *entries;* imagery; spirit money

retail banks, 119–25, 168n17

returning home ritual, 93–95

reunification policies, 9, 35–39

revolution, currency for, 26–31

rice, 34

rituals, kin-based networks, 53–54. *See also* gifts; spirit money; spiritualization of money

Romania, 12, 135

Russia, 12

Sa, Sophanha, 165n34

sacrifice request, Hồ Chí Minh's, 26–27

Saigon, fall of, 9, 34. *See also specific topics, e.g.,* currency issuances; spirit money

Sài Gòn Giải Phóng, 37, 38

Saigon Jewelry Company, 71, 89, 105

salaries, in subsidized economy, 36–39, 47–49

Scott, Janet Lee, 166n5

securities exchange, 15–16, 142–46

self-referential terms, 24

Shanghai stock market study, 123, 143

silver coins, 21–23, 91

Simmel, Georg, 24, 109, 167n1, 171n10

socialist money, currency purposes, 31–32, 36–37

Socialist Republic of Vietnam. *See specific topics, e.g.,* cash *entries;* currency *entries;* imagery; spirit money

soft currencies, 68

Song dynasty, 21

songs, 4, 21–22, 28, 155n4

Southern Liberation Front, flag image, 35, 36f

sovereignty-based currrencies, significance, 19, 31, 35–39, 158n1, n4

spirit money: and debt bonds, 85–87, 95–99; gravesite offerings, 83–85; Hungry Ghost Festival, 99–103; and Lunar New Year's offerings, 93–95; politicization/rehabilitation of, 14, 88–89, 99; remittance money comparisons, 83, 87–88, 89; ritual blurring problem, 89–93

spiritualization of money, 5, 14, 151–52, 171n10

state allocation system, postwar, 9–10, 36–37, 43, 47–48

State Bank of Vietnam: ATM currency, 120; currency quality control, 108–9; dollar requirements, 76; foreign currency controls, 165n33; gold exchange regulation, 71–72; inflation responses, 37, 38, 114, 115; new money issuances, 111–12; peg exchange policy, 79; polymer money issuance, 116–18; transitional series, 35–36

state cemeteries, 92

state-issued currrencies, significance, 11–12, 19, 31, 35–39, 158n1, n4

street-front property, visibility effects, 50–52

subjective debt, 85

swap requirements/requests, 20, 27, 35. *See also* exchange rates, đồng

taels, 7, 70

Tai, Hue-Tam Ho, 39

CPSIA information can be obtained at www.ICGtesting.com
Printed in the USA
BVOW07s2157051014

369579BV00003B/271/P